To Gwen,

with best w~

Mwie.

Nov. 94.

FOOTBALL AND THE COMMONS PEOPLE

FOOTBALL AND THE COMMONS PEOPLE
edited by
David Bull and Alastair Campbell

Juma

Your purchase of this book has contributed substantially to the
Child Poverty Action Group.
Thank you.

First published in 1994 by
Juma
Trafalgar Works
44 Wellington Street
Sheffield S1 4HD
Tel. 0114 272 0915
Fax. 0114 278 6550

© 1994 by the Child Poverty Action Group

ISBN 1 872204 05 8

Cover credits:

Armchair viewers of test-match cricket, who have spotted Big Ben from
the Oval, might surmise that the front cover is a shot (colour-added?) of
the FA Cup Final (between 1874 and 1892, of course).

Nice try! It is formed, however, from two photographs kindly taken
especially for this book:

Big Ben (time intentional) by David Cairns of *Today* newspaper.

The Dell, Southampton (Saints v. Villa, 30 April 1994), by Mike
Atkelski, standing - during its final hours - on the Milton Road terrace.

There should, I think, be a certain mutual sympathy between Members of Parliament and professional football players. We both suffer from acute insecurity of employment. Both are too likely to suffer from premature retirement. We both do our work for the most part in public, and our mistakes are subject to the harshest criticism.

Philip Goodhart, MP
(House of Commons Debates, 21 November 1960)

A note on the Editors:

DAVID BULL is a longstanding member, and former Chair, of the Child Poverty Action Group. A Social Policy teacher at the University of Bristol, he was previously at the Universities of Exeter and Manchester, the latter when it meant foresaking the likes of Best, Law and Charlton to follow Southampton at the likes of Bury, Carlisle and Rotherham. A regular columnist in the Southampton FC programme and the *Redstripe* fanzine, he edited *We'll Support You Evermore*, a 1992 collection written by fans for fans.

ALASTAIR CAMPBELL is Press Secretary to the Labour Leader, Tony Blair. A former political editor of the *Daily Mirror*, he was more recently a columnist, leader writer and assistant editor at *Today* newspaper, when he also had his own Radio Five show, presented Radio 4's *The Week in Westminster* and appeared regularly on TV. Although he was usually talking about politics, he unashamedly plugged Burnley FC in whatever context he could. Has followed Burnley from the top of the Football League in 1960 to the bottom in 1987, and now a bit of the way up again. Contributed a chapter on Burnley to *We'll Support You Evermore*, but has left Alex Carlile, this time, to fly the Claret and Blue flag.

A note on the editing:

Alastair Campbell was effectively the commissioning editor for this book, analysing MPs' claims of footballing allegiance before lurking in the lobbies to recruit contributors and then, hardest of all in some cases, getting them to deliver on their promises. He also helped two of the more modest contributors to put their thoughts and experiences down on paper.

David Bull then took over, as the sub-editor who, having wrestled to make some of the contributors stick to the point, became an even greater fan of Betty Boothroyd. It followed that he should take responsibility for the Introduction to the book, with several penetrative 'assists' from his co-editor.

CONTENTS

Acknowledgments ....(v)

Introduction - Politicians As Football Fans - Incredible! 1
   David Bull

FANS OF FOOTBALL (chapters 1 - 26)

1. All Leeds Road To Wembley 15
    William Mallalieu
2. On The Left For Argyle...29
    Michael Foot
3. Wedded To Wednesday: The First Fifty Years 33
    Roy Hattersley
4. Ulster Unity..45
    Clifford Forsythe
5. Glory, Glory - We're United 57
    Stan Orme
6. Forest First And Foremost 65
    Kenneth Clarke
7. Plenty To Sing About With The Canaries 73
    Michael Carttiss
8. On Edgeley 87
    Peter Snape
9. Three Into One Can Go 97
    Michael Howard
10. On The Spot With York City And Arsenal............................103
    John Greenway
11. Well Of Memories For A Happy Wanderer...........................119
    Ann Taylor
12. Life With The Lions 131
    Brian Wilson
13. Why Scotland Means The World To Me..............................141
    Gordon Brown
14. Vintage Claret And Welsh Rarebit 149
    Alex Carlile
15. Fan Across The Mersey...157
    David Hunt

16. Bouncing Back With The Bairns 167
Doug Henderson
17. Supporting The Arab Cause 177
Mike Watson
18. True Blue Heaven 189
Alistair Burt
19. Fortune's Always Hiding 201
Mike Gapes
20. Wear By Far The Greatest Team... 215
Hilary Armstrong
21. Pigeons And Pipedreams Over Goodison 223
Alan Simpson
22. Memories Of Stoke... And Member For Port Vale 231
Joan Walley
23. Heart Of My Hearts 245
George Foulkes
24. Bobbing Along With The Robins 255
Nigel Jones
25. My Twin Towers - Blackpool To Wembley 269
Nick Hawkins
26. Marching Altogether - Leeds, Leeds, Leeds! 275
James Clappison

CHAMPIONS OF FOOTBALL (chapters 27 - 30)

27. The Golden Strike 283
Philip Goodhart
28. The First Minister 293
Denis Howell
29. Luton Town 2 Establishment United 3 303
David Evans
30. Football Champions At Westminster 311
Tom Pendry

Read More About It 316

ACKNOWLEDGMENTS

If the end of this fund-raising exercise is to attract a few thousand *paying* contributors, we always expected that the production of this book would depend upon plenty of *volunteers*.

Our gratitude is most fundamentally owed to those MPs who made time, in busy schedules, to write for the book and to others who permitted reproductions in ways acknowledged below. And we are indebted to all of them for waiving royalties in favour of the Child Poverty Action Group.

Several contributors also dug into their collections of programmes, photos and other memorabilia and/or arranged for the local newspaper or the club to send us material direct. An itemised appreciation follows overleaf. We cannot do justice there, though, to the resourcefulness of three special kinds of historian. First, all those photo librarians, who went to so much trouble to check files and to organise reproduction rights. Secondly, we were able to tap the resident record-keepers at clubs, where we needed help with line-ups, and a resourceful switchboard operator who could recite the club's recent records more fluently than her local MP. Finally, Dave Adlem and Mike Swain gave of their research time in so many ways, the latter as the book's chief historian, checking facts that contributors couldn't remember - or wrongly imagined they could.

We are indebted to Martin Lacey at Juma for taking on the project and coping so patiently when his schedules were thrown out by the half-dozen contributors whose typescripts arrived later than Martin Peters. That the majority of scripts arrived on time owed much, we know, to the secretaries, advisors and others - in Westminster, Whitehall or constituency offices - whose efforts guaranteed delivery (by 'ghosting' the chapter in at least two cases). We should like to record our gratitude to them - perhaps especially to the constituency secretary who told us she hated football and that the chapter she had just typed was the 'most boring' thing she had ever had to do for her boss.

We very much hope that she's alone with her heresy.

Illustrations

Thanks to the charity of those acknowledged below, we have been involved in only one commercial arrangement - with the Press Association for permission to reproduce the photo on p.61.

We are immensely grateful to the following for allowing us the free use of the material indicated:

Contributors who have delved into personal collections for illustrations: Alistair Burt (pp.197, 273); James Clappison (p.279); Mike Gapes (pp.203, 206); John Greenway (pp. 110, 113); Ben Mallalieu (p.27); Joan Walley (p.241B); Mike Watson (pp. 179B, 185 - both) and others whose memorabilia did not fit the spaces available.

Friends and acquaintances who have likewise raided their collections: Dave Adlem, Harry Fletcher and Mike Swain, for cards and programmes; Dave Espley(p.93) and Craig Young (p.251), fanzines; Maurice Cooper for his first-day cover (p.265T); and Tony Matthews for most of the club badges and many photos (pp. 21, 67, 99, 151 (both), 164 (both), 212, 273 inset).

Organisations like the Professional Footballers' Association (photo, p.289T) and the Football Trust (ad', p.301).

Clubs for a variety of material: Everton (p.225); Falkirk (p.166); Hearts (p.247B); Llanelli (p.96); Motherwell (pp.118, 123, 129); Norwich City (pp.75, 81 (both), 84); Swindon Town (pp.259 (both), 262 (both), 265B); Stockport County (p.89); West Ham United (p.213) and others whose materials exceeded our needs.

Cigarette cards, courtesy of Trebor-Bassett (for Barratt cards); Ritmark (Turf); and Imperial Publishing (Player's and Wills's).

Newspapers and related copyright owners: Dave Brown (p.313); *County Times* (two on p.154); *Crumnock Chronicle* (p.247T); *Daily Telegraph* (pp.143BL, 146T, 289B); *Glasgow Herald* (p.133); Little Brown (pp.143BR, 146B); Mercury Press Agency (pp.158, 161); News International (two on p.307); *The Sentinel*, Stoke (p.233 (both), 241T); Sport & General (p.276); *Sunderland Echo* (three on p.218); D.C. Thomson (pp.137, 179T); *When Saturday Comes* (p.3); *Yorkshire Evening Press* (two on p.113).

Our assiduous efforts to trace copyright ownership were occasionally foiled by inadequate information. If that has resulted in our unwittingly using copyright material, the editors and publisher would be pleased to hear from the copyright holders.

Reproductions

Four chapters have entailed reproduction, to varying degrees, of previously published material:

Chapter 1 has been derived, with the kind permission and warm encouragement of his family, from the writings of the late Sir William Mallalieu - notably from several chapters of his classic collection, *Sporting Days*, plus a few paragraphs from his introduction to the autobiography of Jimmy Guthrie.

Chapter 2 has been reproduced, with kind permission and slightly revised, from Stephen F. Kelly's *Kingswood Book of Football*.

Chapter 3 has been compiled, with kind permission, from three previously published works by Roy Hattersley: his memoirs, *A Yorkshire Boyhood* and *Goodbye to Yorkshire*; and an 'Endpiece' in *The Guardian*, 27 September 1993.

Chapter 30 is an expanded and updated version of a piece originally written as an introduction to *It's Twelve Inches High*, a 1991 collection of fanzine writing compiled by the Football Supporters Association in aid of Action and Research for Multiple Sclerosis.

Full references to the six books cited are given at the end of this book.

Introduction

POLITICIANS AS FOOTBALL FANS - INCREDIBLE!

David Bull

So you think you'd like to read what 30 Members of Parliament have to say about watching football?

Good! That ought logically to spare us all a long introduction, pondering the relationship between our national politicians and our national game.

Convention seemingly demands, however, that editors go onto the defensive to explain why they and their publishers have produced a book or - very often - *another* book on this or that subject. In the present case, the question to be addressed comes in two parts: why another collection by fans; and why MPs? Each part can be answered positively. But, in the nature of these things, it is necessary to respond to a negative or two.

By fans, for fans

First, there's a possibility that the recent growth of football writing by fans - reacting to a realisation that 'what the fans were doing was more interesting than what they were watching' - is already 'in danger of burning itself out'. That's the view put to *The Big Issue*, in its February 1994 focus on the 'soccerati', by Nick Hornby, whose *Fever Pitch* did so much to establish this *genre*. Who'd have thought it - a football book on the list of bestselling paperbacks throughout the 1993-94 season, followed by a dramatic entry at the Edinburgh Festival? Yet I must admit to a preference for collections over one-fan shows: I'm one of those deviants who enjoyed Hornby's subsequent compendium, *My Favourite Year*, more than his solo effort.

As an antidote to Hornby's concern about 'burn-out', the annual *When*

Saturday Comes poll (reported in the August and September 1994 issues) revealed that the 'types of football writing' its readers 'particularly enjoy' amount to '*anything* from the fans' perspective'.

But does 'anything' necessarily include writing by *anybody* - even MPs? The second negative is a concern that politicians are not to be trusted as commentators on football. A most sceptical version was put by Richard Turner, in 1990:

> '*Politicians of all shades have shown absolutely no interest in football, unless there are votes to be won in condemning hooliganism or turning up at the Cup Final for a press photo-call*'

I might have been inclined to dismiss this verdict as just another piece of opinionated football-writing - *is* there any other kind? - worthy of a smile and no more. But I am quoting from a carefully researched pamphlet which cites more parliamentary debates than you'd normally expect in a shelf-full of football books. So it's rather chastening that this young Stockport County fan should be so bitter about MPs. Moreover, his view has been echoed in the 'Whistle Blower' column of the *Sunday Times*, where Dave Thomas recently concluded (23 January 1994) that MPs' support is

> '*usually token ... A couple of appearances a season at a ground satisfies the politicians' love for the people's game. And the football bandwagon offers ample opportunity for self-promotion because football-loving voters are more likely to identify with somebody who seemingly shares an interest in their sport*'.

That all sounds simple enough and it works well at the level of a joke - like the one opposite. But are such assertions representative and can they be substantiated? And, as Fantasy Leagues offer MPs new opportunities for exposure, will the scepticism get worse? Or will this help them to demonstrate their genuineness?

It has to be said that suspicion of politicians' motives is not especially new. Alan Tomlinson has recently reminded us of the public rebuke - by Sir Stanley Rous, no less - of the then Prime Minister, Harold Wilson, when he contrived to be photographed with the 1966 World Cup winners. Sir Stanley reasoned, in his memoirs, that if any politi-

cian had earned the right to pose with the triumphant England team, it was Denis Howell - by virtue of his hard work for the World Cup, as outlined in his chapter below.

Nor is this phenomenon especially British. Take Diego Maradona's reactions, during his brief visit to the 1994 World Cup, to the pretences of Argentina's president, Carlos Menem:

> *'Instead of swanning around and boasting ... we are going to win the World Cup, he should think of the poor people at home, on the street and without jobs'* (Boston press conference, reported in the *Sunday Times,* 26 June 1994*).*

And, if we are going to use international yardsticks, I take it that British sceptics do not envisage ownership of a football club being exploited for anything more than financial power - Maxwell-style - rather than political enhancement in the manner of Bernard Tapie in Marseille or Silvio Berlusconi in Milan. Jack Walker for PM? Really?

So why MPs?

The questions posed above can remain rhetorical, while I try to answer a more basic one: why, against such a background of scepticism, have we assembled the thoughts on football of 30 MPs? The simple answer is 'because I was asked'. Two MPs wondered why they had not been invited to contribute to *We'll Support You Evermore,* a 1992 collection of pieces by fans, including John Major, which I had edited. One of them advised me that his memories would, and should, grace *We'll Support You Ever, Ever More.*

The idea of some such follow-up grew. Why not invite some of their Westminster colleagues to join these two complainants in a book written entirely by MPs (give or take a former Member or two)? Alastair Campbell approved and came aboard. As a contributor to *We'll Support You Evermore* - with a well-received chapter on Burnley - he knew what we were after. And, as a journalist then working in the House of Commons, he had a good idea whom we should be after - not to mention the skills of getting those who promised a contribution to deliver it.

One or two, whose shame we shall keep to ourselves, defied those skills. It was nonetheless apparent that we would have no difficulty in locating at least 80 - and perhaps nearer 100 - MPs who claimed to follow football and, in most cases, a particular team. In narrowing down to 30, we have had to omit several keen followers and their teams, great and small - although the shortfall of non-league clubs can be explained by the late withdrawal of two promised contributors.

The final squad is, we hope, a balanced one - not easily achieved when you consider the lopsided membership of the House of Commons. Thus, we have three women - one in ten - a better ratio than that of the House, if inferior to that of the terraces. We were determined to get out of England - to Wales and Northern Ireland and to half a dozen Scottish clubs. And, by overlooking a considerable number of eligible Labour MPs, we have achieved a cross-party mix.

It must be for readers to judge whether that mix is rich enough to avert the risk - the downside of any compendium - of sameness. We feel it is. Moreover, the ordering of the chapters should help in this regard. The sequence is more or less chronological - from those who grew up on the inter-war terraces to those whose loyalties were formed, in the 1960s and 1970s, by watching TV (when the risk was falling for Liverpool). This should enable the reader to identify changing expectations amid a certain uniformity of passion.

Uniformity? Obviously, the degree of commitment varies: a certificate of obsessiveness was not required of contributors. Contrary to the cynicism of those quoted above, though, we feel that we have recruited plenty of *true* fans. Moreover, we have been reinforced in our belief that MPs make an especially interesting bunch of football followers - for reasons that can be summed up as the four C's: 'corners', credibility, constituency and clout.

Corners

I borrow this metaphor from Susan Crosland's biography of her late husband and former Foreign Secretary, Anthony Crosland - who, she reveals, once had Henry Kissinger's 707 diverted from Heathrow to Lincolnshire, so that he need not miss Grimsby Town, at home to

Gillingham. Although she looked upon football - and, specifically, *Match of the Day* - as her 'rival', she indulged her husband in his 'passionate love affair' with the game and with Grimsby Town in particular. This was a 'corner' of his life which, having 'nothing to do with his own work and talents', offered him 'total relaxation'.

That claim for football is repeated often in this book. Thus it is an 'important relaxation' for Michael Carttiss and 'a welcome retreat' for George Foulkes. And it has a 'therapeutic' effect on Mike Watson. But so what? Lots of busy people have 'corners' into which they can retreat: why are politicians any different?

If we address that question in terms of the 1990s rather than the 1960s of which Susan Crosland was writing, let us suppose that we have just seen Nigel Kennedy interviewed about the fortunes of his favourites. Would it surprise us to learn that he did not play the violin, day and night, 52 weeks of the year, and expected to have time to watch Aston Villa? And would not the same go for, say, composer, Michael Nyman, and QPR? Or for actor, Tom Watt, and Arsenal? This could be a long showbiz list.

But when John Major began to pop up, on Radio 5, with his half-time thoughts from Stamford Bridge, he was surely having to counter the impression his predecessor had consistently given: that working *nearly* all hours, day and night, *almost* 52 weeks of the year was required of any politicians worthy of their constituents' trust. It was in the Thatcher era, after all, that needing to 'spend more time with one's family' became a resignation catchphrase.

And even if one's family provided a legitimate excuse for relaxation, sport didn't. If I heard him correctly, as he explained the struggle to promote the return of the Olympic Games to England, Bob Scott (subsequently *Sir* Bob for his frustrated efforts) felt that sport had been, for Mrs Thatcher, 'what the great unwashed do on Saturday afternoon'. Kenneth Clarke makes a similar point, about his former Leader's attitude to MPs who dared to watch football, in his chapter of this book - although John Greenway suggests, in his chapter, that such Thatcherite disdain might be reserved for *Conservative* MPs, who were expected, he had found, to follow sports other than football - like cricket and rugby.

6

But there is, perhaps, a more fundamental distinction to be made - between sport in the sense of human beings competing with each other and sport in the sense of human beings maiming or killing animals. Attempting, in 1947, to identify a 'Philosophy of Conservatism', Quintin Hogg derided Labour MPs who took their politics too seriously to allow space for corners. In this, they differed from Conservatives, who

> *'do not believe that the political struggle is the most important thing in life ... The simplest of them prefer foxhunting, the wisest religion.'*

If that were true 50 years ago, then things appear to have changed for both parties. The Conservatives have been selecting fewer candidates from a rural background. By 1987, Jeremy Paxman has noted, so few - a mere 24 - of the new intake of MPs were listing field-sports as a 'recreation' that *The Field* was moved to complain: a new breed of politician had been 'nurtured ... in towns and suburbs' and did not 'know (or care) about ... field sports'.

And, even if Quintin Hogg's characterization of Labour MPs were true of those elected pre-war, it has certainly not been true of the post-war generation. Thus, the 1945 intake included not only William Mallalieu and Michael Foot - the opening contributors to this collection - but also, of course, Harold Wilson. Prime Minister Wilson was capable of irritating not only Sir Stanley Rous but also Richard Crossman, a Cabinet colleague who makes no secret, in his diaries, of his disdain for football. Take his entry for the evening of 29 May 1968, when Manchester United beat Benfica at Wembley to win the European Cup. For Harold Wilson, the occasion demanded that he be at Wembley. For 'everyone' who remained in the House of Commons that evening, it meant watching the game on television. Mr Crossman not only abstained, but told the Prime Minister that he thought it 'a waste of time' - a challenging remark to someone who considered 'the mark of a leader ... to be a man who sees football or at least watches it on television'.

Harold Wilson stands accused, it seems, within both FIFA and his Cabinet, of using football not so much as a 'corner', a private retreat, as something to shout about - something to add to his political credibility.

Credibility

Having read more than my share of political diaries and biographies - vital sources when my job requires me to measure the gap between politicians' promises and product - I've enjoyed the occasional bonus of coming across references, in them, to a sneaking interest in football.

These are rare. And yet there are surprises - like the intriguing diary entry by Tony Benn. On 7 April 1973, his son, having barely recovered from a serious football injury in time for his wedding, spent the first night of his honeymoon at his parents' home, watching *Match of the Day*. Tantalisingly, the diary makes no mention of the game selected by the BBC. John Motson's records show that it was semi-final day, when Leeds beat Wolves 1-0 to secure a Wembley appointment with Sunderland that Hilary Armstrong rather lovingly recalls in Chapter 20.

These have been amusing diversions, though, from the professional obligation to study these sources - an experience that has made me wary of attaching credence to what MPs say. Many voters need, of course, no occupational excuse for such scepticism. This is not the place, however, to delve into opinion poll data on the low credibility of politicians - not that we'd expect the pollsters, anyhow, to assess responses to MPs' statements, whether by word or deed, about *football*.

Never mind! The topic lends itself to gut feelings and impressions. But suppose that we were to pretend to a rational assessment: on what criteria might we distinguish between the genuine follower and the *poseur*? Two yardsticks - both of them 'F' words - spring to mind: frequency and fidelity.

Frequency is probably less important. Exchanges with fanzine folk suggest that genuineness does *not* depend, in their eyes, on getting to 40-odd, or even 30, games a season: it is recognised that lots of busy people will have often to work on Saturdays and will hardly ever see an evening match. Thus, when Kenneth Clarke complains, in his chapter, that being Chancellor of the Exchequer proved to be such a demanding job that it reduced his 1993-94 attendances to a personal low of 10 matches, that in no way diminishes, surely, his credibility as a fan.

After all, it is five times the norm asserted by Dave Thomas.

How does Kenneth Clarke fare, though, on the second test: can a *real* fan follow more than one team? For him, the answer is simple: he's a Forest fan, but likes watching football anywhere - even if it's a matter of taking in Stockport v. Hartlepool on the way to a political engagement. His Conservative colleague, Alistair Burt, tells a similar story. The possibility of supporting two teams is seriously addressed by another Conservative: David Evans. I mention the party affiliation as, among our contributors, two-timing (to say nothing of Michael Howard's promiscuous pursuit of *three* teams) is an especially Conservative tendency.

It is my distinct impression that divided loyalties - or readily displaced loyalties - tend not to please the fanzine faithful. Two famous examples of MPs spring to mind: Jack Dunnett, a Labour exception to the above rule - how could anyone who had claimed to be a Notts County loyalist become a director at Fratton Park? - and David Mellor: how *could* he defect from Fulham to follow their nearest neighbours?

David Mellor has had an opportunity, on *Six-o-Six*, to restore his credibility. It would appear that he still has some way to go: he was voted, in 1994 just as in 1993, the most unpopular radio pundit among *WSC* readers, only 4 per cent of whom consider him the 'ideal' presenter of *Six-o-Six*. Was that a reflection, though, of his past record or of his reluctance, as one *WSC* correspondent has put it (April 1994), to use 'his two ears and one mouth in the right proportion'?

As one who found the Mellor style such a welcome relief from that of Bob 'The Cat' Bevan, I further warmed to his use of the programme as a kind of ombudsman for aggrieved fans, especially - as Tom Pendry reminds us in his chapter - for Manchester United fans returning (some of them later than they had intended) from Istanbul. That raises the question of how much MPs are in a position to do - often unheralded behind-the-scenes - for football and its fans. We can ponder that potential when we come to 'clout' First, though, there is the matter of 'constituency'.

Constituency

We all have our stories of how the football 'card' can be played in all manner of social situations. But be honest, now: would you expect football loyalties to be at issue when a selection committee assembles to find a parliamentary candidate? We have tongue-in-cheek accounts of this happening in the chapters by Michael Howard and Joan Walley, each of whom was selected despite supporting the 'wrong' local team.

Joan Walley goes on to explain something of the MP's obligation to represent his or her constituents' interests when it comes to matters affecting their local football club. Reading her chapter, I found myself feeling sorry for those representatives of the people who have to speak for such interests while having no interest in - perhaps even a Crossman-like loathing of - the 'People's Game'. How wretched Mr Crossman must have felt on 23 May 1966. To fulfil a promise by Harold Wilson, he was obliged, as the Member for Coventry East, to lunch at Highfield Road with Jimmy Hill. The pain recorded in his diary is palpable:

> *'I had never visited the ground before or seen a football match there but I found Jimmy Hill a nice person'.*

It makes you wonder, as Kenneth Clarke does, why any MP would think there are votes in being seen at the local ground in the way that Dave Thomas alleges. When it stops being an obligation of 'constituency', backing the local team is surely not a good bet for improving your credibility.

Clout

Members of Parliament may not always be able to do much about the interests of those they represent, but they have, of course, more power to do so than most of us.

While we were always clear that this book should be about fandom rather than power, we nevertheless decided, from the outset, that a few chapters would be devoted explicitly to uses of political power in the cause of football. Given the emphasis, in recent years, on the legislative control of football's *fans*, I have been interested to discover examples of parliamentary activity, in the 1950s and 1960s, on behalf of *players*. Thus we learn, from the autobiography of Jimmy Guthrie, the players' leader (1945-57), that he was 'in constant contact with MPs'. Prominent among them was William Mallalieu, whose foreword to Guthrie's book forms part of Chapter 1 below. The PFA's official history elaborates on Guthrie's aims in cultivating 'radical' MPs. These included a levy on the pools for the benefit of the game - anticipating what was to be achieved by Denis Howell, as he explains in the piece he has written for us on his years as Minister for Sport.

Guthrie's successor, Jimmy Hill, pays tribute, in his memoirs, not just to the efforts of William Mallalieu and Labour colleagues who championed football's 'slaves' but to the novelty of Conservative support in the form of Philip Goodhart. Sir Philip recalls, in his chapter, what he did, in 1960, to merit that accolade from Jimmy Hill. Thus chapters 27 and 28 highlight some of Westminster's contributions to football from 1960 to 1979. Tom Pendry takes up the story from thereabouts, with illustrations of more recent negotiations and lobbying activities on behalf of the game - with the emphasis, as I say, on the fan.

Over and above those special chapters on power, we generally encouraged contributors to digress from their memories as fans so as to note any interventions on behalf of football. Cynics would expect opportunist MPs to respond eagerly to such an invitation to brag. In fact, the first chapters received indicated such a reluctance to mention this role that a reminder had to be sent out.

This flushed out a few examples. John Greenway illustrates what can be done at the centre of things if you are a member of the Home Affairs Committee. Other interventions have been at club level, whether by Joan Walley challenging the Football Trust, on behalf of Port Vale, or by Peter Snape taking on the Treasury on behalf of Stockport County.

The Greenway and Snape accounts illustrate another kind of power - that of the boardroom. But we asked David Evans to do this more explicitly. Chapter 29 is a most explicit response. It takes an interesting stance for a Conservative in that he would have liked further Government intervention - notably in the form of identity cards. Other Conservatives disagree, with some of them dissenting, even, from the call for all-seater stadia.

11

That raises, for me, a fundamental question, which I put, in fact, to contributors: if football has so many friends in the House, why has it not been better served? The most withering answer to that question is provided by Kenneth Clarke, when he complains, in his chapter, that he 'was never involved in any discussions within Government about what to do about violence in the game'. He explains, more generally - in a passage to which I have already alluded and which is echoed, albeit in a gentler tone, by Michael Carttiss - that

> *'Mrs Thatcher ensured that Ministers who actually went to football had no say at all in developing the policies. I think she found it difficult to understand why anyone would want to go to a football match at all'.*

So now are you going to believe them?

I rest my case. Whether or not you accept the depictions of football's friends at Westminster being helpless against raw prime ministerial power, there is surely no disputing that MPs *do* have something different to say about the game. A large part of the fun for me - and, I hope, for you, too - of reading their accounts has been to ponder those differences while confirming that, in most respects, they are just like other fans.

That's to say that - regardless of whom they support - so many of those MPs whose confessions follow have obsessions and idiosyncracies, and a long-suffering irrationality, with which I can readily identify.

For Alastair Campbell and me, that prospect of identification is *the* essential feature of any football book written by fans for fans. And when it comes to a collection, different readers are able to identify with different chapters. This collection works at that level for us. We hope it does for you.

Full references to the books cited above are given in the further reading at the end of this book.

FANS of FOOTBALL

*Twenty-six chapters on
loves and loyalties*

HUDDERSFIELD TOWN

J.P.W MALLALIEU (Labour, Huddersfield, 1945-50; Huddersfield East, 1950-79)

The late William Mallalieu (1908-80) held ministerial posts (Defence, Trade and Technology) in Wilson's 1964 Government. Knighted 1979.

An author and journalist, he wrote a sports column for the *Spectator*. Some 48 pieces from that column - reports on football, cricket, hurling, billiards and 'any other sport which fills in gaps between Huddersfield Town's home matches' - were reproduced in *Sporting Days*.

1

ALL LEEDS ROAD TO WEMBLEY

J.P.W Mallalieu

Every year, round about the time of the third round, I dream that Huddersfield Town will win the Cup.

I think that is a perfect opening sentence. Those readers who want the class war, or an analysis of *Labour Believes in Britain*, or the inside story of What Really Happened About Insurance, or a forecast of which election the Tories will finally be compelled to fight on policy, turn elsewhere at once on reading it.

Those readers who, without deep roots, happen to follow Bolton Wanderers, Accrington Stanley, or worse, will do the same. So, too, will those who play games but think that watching them is effete. Which leaves me with those who like sentiment, prejudice, bias, instinct and, here and there, a touch of malice - in other words, who value loyalty.

What follows is about loyalty, about partisanship, about bias. The FA Cup - most notably the Third Round and the Final - offers especially rich examples of the joys of partisanship. It must be acknowledged, though, that partisanship also makes its demands.

Partisanship can be tiring

I am a spectator. It is no passive occupation. If you go to watch regularly, you take an active and exhausting part. You are almost as much in the game as the players themselves; and though you may not have a player's skill you must have a player's knowledge if you are to be a true spectator.

I am a vigorous partisan, full of wholehearted bias. I do not fully enjoy a game unless I really want one side to win. When I am watching

Huddersfield this presents no difficulty, but with other sides I am usually reduced to backing the more northerly of the two; and when even this distinction becomes meaningless, as in Brentford v. Fulham, I decide my allegiance by choosing the team whose victory will do less harm in the League table to my own club. So, far from being passive, this natural urge for partisanship has sometimes proved more exhausting than playing used to be.

But there is something more about watching than the excitement of partisanship. There is a sense of unity which is not often found elsewhere. Every individual is at one with himself and at one with the great crowd. Maybe there is something wrong with a society which allows so many of us to feel fulfilment only in sport. But there is fulfilment there; and those who have never experienced it have missed great delight.

Partisanship and Sporting Manners

Even the majority of pleasantly tempered players do not think that courtesy should come into soccer. If a wing half is about to throw in and is told that it is his opponent's ball, he does not hand the ball over. He throws it on the ground, preferably well out of reach. To most players that is not rude. It is just common sense. If a player handed the ball over courteously on the touch-line, his team might be a man short for vital seconds, since his opponent would certainly not repay the courtesy by waiting until he had got back into play.

I personally have never been able to make up my mind about courtesy, or about the somewhat wider question of 'being sporting' in games. In mid-week, sitting at home, I like to think that all Huddersfield players behave like perfect gentlemen on the field. But if, on the following Saturday, one of them gave a goal away by being 'gentlemanly', I should be very angry.

I have read of a Corinthian back who gave away a penalty by stopping an otherwise certain goal with his hand. Thereat the Corinthian captain ordered his goalkeeper to stand aside while the kick was taken so that his team should not have even the chance of profiting by a deliberate breach of the rules. I think that captain's action was magnificent.

But if at a critical moment some Huddersfield captain had done the same, I do not think I should have been pleased.

My attitude, clearly, is not edifying. But whose attitude is? The conventions about what is sporting and what is not have always, to me, seemed arbitrary and illogical. If someone will tell me where to place the dividing line between what is unsporting and what is sporting, I'll try to apply the line to my own spectating morals. But in the meantime, I'm afraid, I shall continue to demand absolute and pure sportsmanship from all teams and players in whom I have no partisan interest. But I shall expect Yorkshire and Huddersfield to look on absolute and pure sportsmanship as a luxury to be enjoyed only when they can afford it - when they are winning by 200 runs or three clear goals.

FA Cup Third Round 1951: Huddersfield T. v. Tottenham H.

I explain at once that emotion will be excluded from what follows. I offer you a report which is to be coldly, almost analytically, factual. There is to be no bias, no exaltation. Just the facts.

The first fact is rain. On Saturday, 6 January 1951, it rained in Huddersfield. It rained like anything. It rained all morning. When I looked from my bedroom window I could hardly see across the road for the rain.

The second fact is mist. If there had been no rain I'd still have had some difficulty in seeing across the road. For the mist, which hung thickly on the high surrounding, moors, trailed dark wisps down the hillside into the main streets of the town itself.

On normal days the walk from town to Leeds Road is one of the greatest pleasures of my football Saturday. I leave the main street where people are sauntering purposelessly, and, in a side street, I join a trickle of men and women who are walking intently. In this trickle I emerge on the old Beast Market and that great slum-cleared waste below Southgate. Other trickles emerge from other side streets and converge on the far corner by the gas-works. If the wind is right, you get the smell from the gas-works, and maybe from the sewerage works as well; but it's not the smell that makes you hurry. You hurry for excitement,

17

excitement which feeds on itself as the trickles converge into a stream and the stream converges into a flood, a flood of blue and white scarves, of clattering feet and, even on the brightest day, of precautionary mackintoshes (for in Huddersfield, during the football season, you never know).

On this walk I have no care. The world is young, and when the match is the third round of the Cup and the favours and rattles are out for the first time, the world is not only young but gay as well.

But there was no walk for me this third round. I was kept so late at the office that I took a taxi. And there were no floods, nor streams, nor even trickles of men and women. Those who were eager enough to brave the day at all had long since reached the ground. From the streaming windows of the taxi I could see only a few stragglers swirling through the mist.

The ground itself was appalling. Water trickled off the crown to the surrounding running-track or lay in wide pools. How could anyone play football on such a quagmire? And if they did play, how would anyone see? The terraces on the far side loomed faintly through the mist; and, outside the ground behind one of the goals, a ghostly mill peered for a moment warily and then withdrew. The world, it seemed, had closed in around this watery, silent space. The water, the mist and the space remained throughout the afternoon, but not the silence.

As soon as the game began the pitch tried to assert itself. Yet it was clear that the Spurs would beat the pitch and play brilliant football. It also seemed likely that they would beat Huddersfield. They gave their attacking passes a split second before a defender tackled, and almost always found their man, so that by thrusting interchanges Baily and Medley, for example, would take the ball from one end of the field to the other while one after another of Huddersfield's defenders challenged just too late. The Spurs supporters roared their encouragement.

But while throughout the first half the Spurs played football that, in the conditions, was miraculous, I did not feel at any time that they were likely to score - and I am a spectator who always assumes that opponents are likely to score the moment they get the ball clear of their own penalty area. Beautiful, artistic, patternweaving football, yes. But goals, no. Not in the first half.

Yet the second half might be a different story. The Spurs, true to the textbooks, were making the ball do the work, whereas Huddersfield, pitting enthusiasm against science, were hurling themselves energetically through the mud. At that rate they must soon wilt and the Spurs stride through them at will. So at half-time, though the score was 0-0, the signs were out for a Spurs victory.

'... Baily and Medley would take the ball from one end of the field to the other...'

During the interval I tried to calculate what chance there was that the game would be abandoned before the finish because of bad visibility. My calculations continued with increasing urgency after the interval, because Spurs continued to flash the ball over the ground just that second ahead of the defenders, whereas when a Huddersfield forward got the ball he held on to it until both he and it drilled themselves into the mud. The Spurs roar continued. But after about 10 minutes of the second half there came a perceptible change. Either the Spurs became a fraction slower or Huddersfield became a fraction faster. Anyway, those swift, thrusting passes suddenly were no more.

More than that, Huddersfield forwards, instead of trying to beat five men in brilliant solo runs, began to combine; and, almost without warning, two Huddersfield forwards and the ball arrived in the Spurs penalty area with only Ditchburn to beat. Ditchburn flung himself and just got the ball, but it was a near thing. The greater roar was now coming from Huddersfield supporters, but two minutes later they gave out a sound of another kind. For the first time in the match the Spurs defence was sucked into the mud, and while they laboured with their feet a Huddersfield forward danced like a will-o'-the-wisp towards the empty Spurs goal and shot - just wide. At that I heard a wail, eerie and wolf-like. Turning round to see who had made it, I found I had.

Skipping all emotion and dealing only with the facts, I could have cried. Two easy chances, both missed, within two minutes. You can't do that against the best club football team in the world and survive.

But by now the Spurs were no longer playing like the best football team in the world. They were becoming short-tempered, if not short-winded - and after one incident the Huddersfield crowd treated them to the loudest booing I have heard outside the House of Commons. A moment later the Huddersfield team treated them to the sweetest goal I never saw. Who scored it and how, I did not know. All I did know was that there was a sudden, sectional yell from behind the Spurs goal and then, as the Huddersfield players ran back to the centre shaking each other's hand, the yell exploded over the whole ground.

We had barely settled in our seats when Huddersfield scored again. I saw Glazzard cut in from the wing. I saw him twist and fire. I saw Ditchburn crouched, dead in line, as it seemed, with the shot and when for a second or two he remained crouched I assumed that he had gathered the ball into his stomach. So, it seemed, did the rest of the crowd for there was a moment's silence. And then the silence burst. The shot had been oblique, had passed into the corner of the net, and for perhaps half a minute there was no one else on the ground but me. When I recovered to find myself still standing long after the game had restarted I looked round shamefacedly. But everyone else was standing too - except for the grey-faced line of Spurs directors immediately in front.

Oh, the agony of the last 10 minutes! Oh, that final whistle's blessed sound! Did I say facts only? In the third round of the English Cup, Huddersfield Town beat Tottenham Hotspur by two goals (Taylor, Glazzard) to none.

FA Cup Third Round 1952: Brentford v. Queen's Park Rangers

Yet it began so well ...

When I fed the rabbits, the sun was as high as it can go in January, and the frost on the lawn was melting. The whole morning seemed to glisten. So it should; for this was the shiniest morning in the football calendar, the third-round-of-the-Cup morning, when the big clubs come in for the first time and those little clubs which have insinuated themselves through earlier rounds think they are going to knock the Brylcreem off their betters.

What a morning this always is! The earlier rounds are important, no doubt, to those who habitually engage in them. But the third round is real. You get the clash of the great, like Newcastle and Aston Villa. You get the minor local 'Derbies' like Brentford and Queen's Park Rangers. Above all you get the babies against the giants, like Scunthorpe against the Spurs or Workington against Liverpool. How we all hope that these babies will repeat the fairy story - and well they may if they are playing on their own ground. These baby teams sometimes have baby grounds which cramp the giants; and on these baby grounds there are sometimes baby hillocks and baby valleys which upset billiard-table players from the First Division. How everyone

Glazzard
v.
Ditchburn

laughs when one of the giants comes a cropper, when Arsenal falls to Walsall or Sunderland gets stuck at Yeovil. That's all part of the Cup. Anything can happen. So the morning of the third round glistens, even when, as often happens, you can't see a yard in front of you for fog.

There was no fog for *this* third round. The warmth of the sun had made even rabbits lazy. At any rate, they had not bothered to burrow into my lawn. After feeding them, I sat in the sun and wondered idly which team I would back that afternoon. I have explained why I usually pick North v. South, but I couldn't decide which was which from Brentford v. Queen's Park Rangers. I plumped for the Rangers, only because their manager, Dave Magnall, used to play for Huddersfield, and because their inside-right, Conway Smith, not only played for Huddersfield himself, but is the son of the late Billy Smith who for 20 years almost was Huddersfield.

Leaving my rabbits to the sun, I set off by car for Griffin Park. Most English football grounds are so hidden by terraced, redbrick houses that you would think the game was some sort of sin, to be kept from the notice of the police and the churches. But on a Cup-tie day there's no disguising them. Those three mounted policemen trotting up the street - I'll bet they are not defending the Brentford gas-works; and those newspaper bills, tied round lamp-posts, advertising all the sport - they're not *always* showing in back streets. These are the pointers to a football ground which even Dr Watson could not have missed; and if you follow them, as I did, around midday, you will find the little queues, rubbing their noses against closed gates, which are the final proof without which Holmes never closed his mind.

Little queues? I was surprised myself. But the older I get, the more I become like Dr Watson. So I drew no sensible conclusion. After circling the ground and finding only little queues, I assumed that there would be no difficulty about seeing the match. So I left my car and went into *The Griffin* for a sandwich and a glass of beer. In the pub I discovered that this Cup-tie was 'ticket only'; and I had no ticket.

I appealed to the landlord. No go. The landlord appealed all round the bar. No go. The landlord's son, aged 10, announced that *he* had a ticket but made it clear that that was no go either. Then someone remembered that, 20 minutes ago, the local butcher had had a spare ticket.

The landlord rang him up; the ticket was still spare; the landlord's son trotted off to fetch it, and I was in. I was among strangers in *The Griffin;* but if you are a real football fan and meet other real football fans you are among strangers no more.

I was able to pick my place, on the rails, right behind one of the goals. The empty stands had all the hollowness of a main-line railway-station in the early morning, so that the rattles and the shouts of the men who, quite seriously on this January morning, were selling ice-cream echoed against the corrugated iron roofs. But, hollowness and ice-cream notwithstanding, I felt warm in expectation. I remembered the first time, 32 years ago, that I had stood directly behind a goal. Within two minutes of the kick-off my Huddersfield had fired a beautiful, new yellow ball into that goal and had almost blown the net away. I thought cosily of Huddersfield playing an easy match, 190 miles away, playing an easy match which might even at the eleventh hour provide the spark to light them home.

By the time the loudspeaker announced that 'the kick-off will be in, approximately, seven minutes. Will people standing on the gangways move away?', there was nowhere for the people on the gangways to move away to. I had been edged from the rails, politely but effectively, by four small boys, who unscrupulously used their lack of height to play on my better feelings. However, I could still see, and anyway was spellbound in those magic moments which immediately precede the launching of a Cup-tie.

Yes, the day had begun well.

The game itself cast no spells - except, perhaps, on the players. Brentford won 3-1, which pleased the boys who had stolen my place on the rails; but I was really waiting for the half-time scores on the board at the far end of the ground and for *Sports Report* with the final results on my wireless at home. In the meantime, I watched the Brentford goalkeeper, Gaskell, who kept his watch some five yards in front of me. He had a busy afternoon. Someone had left tiny bits of straw in his goal-mouth, all of which had to be picked up and placed carefully in the back of the net. Gaskell lumbered up and down, shoulders bent, eyes on the ground, picking up these bits. These salvage operations were seldom interrupted. Indeed, when Gaskell dived to a sudden shot from

Rangers, I believe he was really after another of those straws. I shall ask him to train at our house until the carpetsweeper is repaired.

Half-time came and went with the score satisfactory 190 miles away; and, by and by, I was home for tea and the time was half past five. I do like *Sports Report*, even though the man who reads the League results continuously tells people that Huddersfield Town have lost. But this evening I waited calmly, even tolerantly, for the inevitably satisfying end to a satisfying day. I was even unruffled by my children, who were in a teasing mood and kept shouting 'Vote Conservative!'

Then, quite suddenly, I was alone in the world. The wireless crackled with the uncontrollable laughter of millions, my children cheered and my rabbits began a large-scale excavation of my lawn, while I began to pick little pieces of straw from the carpet and put them in my hair. For the BBC (Psychological Warfare Department) had just made the following announcement:

Huddersfield Town 1   Tranmere Rovers 2.

Yet it began so well ...

On the art of being a passionate neutral at Wembley

When my own team is not playing in the Cup Final, I usually back the more northerly of the two teams. So, in 1947, I could favour Burnley against Charlton. Burnley are, after all, from Lancashire, which even prejudiced observers admit to be the second-best county. Moreover, was not Alan Brown, the Burnley captain, then fresh from playing with Huddersfield Town, where he learned his football? So up the claret and blue.

But I broke the rule in 1951, when Newcastle beat Blackpool 2-0. Newcastle were the more northerly. Further, Newcastle means miners, whereas Blackpool tends to mean landladies. But, in spite of that, I was backing Blackpool for the sake of Stanley Matthews, one of the greatest footballers of all time, the man who had won every football honour except a Cup winner's medal. Twice in four years he had played with the losing team in the Final. He was now 36 years-old and his chances of reaching the Final again must be slight. And so was everyone else backing Blackpool - outside the north-east coast. When Matthews did not win the prize we all grieved.

There were other disappointments, one of them personal. As I settled in my seat I found I had broken my spectacles. During the previous week I had been involved in political controversy around the question of charges for teeth and specs from the National Health. I can afford to pay for any specs I need. The Chancellor's new charges would mean no hardship to me, but I am against them on principle. The moment I realized I was going to have difficulty in seeing this game, all my opposition to charges flared up into irrational anger with the Chancellor, Hugh Gaitskell, as though he had climbed to the rafters of Wembley above my head and had personally broken my specs.

All the time another irritation was spoiling my pleasure. For some people - good luck to them - Cup Final day means a trip to London, sightseeing, a couple of beers, and home by the evening train. But for some others it is a social occasion. They don't watch football and are interested in Wembley only because Royalty will be there and it is fashionable to be seen there too. They somehow get themselves Cup Final tickets while real football fans are turned away. They ought to be prosecuted. So ought the people who let them have the precious tickets.

Because of them, real fans are kept outside. These fans have followed the team since August when the crowd sat in shirt-sleeves and the grass was green, through the wet and cold of December until the grass has turned to mud, followed them groaning, followed them protesting, followed them cheering, but always followed them hoping that, this year, the team will have a run in the Cup. Now the spring is here, their team *has* had a run in the Cup, their team is at Wembley, flashing over the velvet turf. But they are outside; and the ticket touts want £6 for a 3s 6d ticket. And all the time there are people inside who don't care which team wins, who don't know the rules and who chatter.

It is an agonizing tragedy. Right through the season the fan has given his advice, without charge, to countless referees; he has exhausted his nerves on those long-drawn-out 'ees' and 'oos' and 'ah's' that betoken a close shave, or thrown his whole being into that ecstatic shout that betokens sudden triumph. But now he is outside Wembley, outside the deep communal delight of unthinking, whole-hearted passionate bias.

And I was inside. Normally, I am inside Wembley only when Huddersfield are playing, as they did play five times between the wars -- five times and only once an honest referee.

Football and Politics

There might have been a sixth inter-war final for Huddersfield in 1939, had Jimmy Guthrie not taken control of the semi-final at Highbury.

I recall that Spring afternoon. The snow was driving straight into the Huddersfield goalmouth. And so was Jimmy Guthrie. Town had led Portsmouth 1-0 for most of the game; but, in 15 minutes of over-power, Guthrie imposed two goals which took his team to Wembley. I cursed him and hoped that I would never see him again.

In fact, I was to see a great deal of him. We met in Portsmouth during the last year of the War; and when the War was over and he had become chairman of the Players Union, he used to come frequently to the House of Commons to see Ellis Smith - my long-serving Labour colleague for Stoke-on-Trent - and myself.

At that time, professional football players were subjected to a maximum but had no minimum wage. They could be bound by contracts even when those contracts had expired. They could be bought and sold like chattels. The football industry was one of the last relics of feudalism. Under Jimmy's prompting, Ellis and I set about stirring political opinion. We helped get Arbitration machinery in motion, we got the Ministry of Labour to set up an enquiry and we roused interest in the TUC. But the real work was done by Jimmy, as single-minded and purposeful off the field as he had once been off it. He did more than any other individual to improve the working conditions of professional footballers.

That recollection of Jimmy Guthrie apart, most of the above accounts were originally written for the *Spectator*. Any inaccuracies have been retained. I can never be sure of a fact. So often, when a fact was being established before my eyes, when a batsman was being bowled or a goal scored, I would miss it because I was sneezing or arguing with a neighbour or wondering what would happen next week in the House of Commons; just as in the House of Commons I sometimes missed great moments of history because I was wondering how a batsman *did* get out, or who *did* score that goal, the previous day.

I could not, or at least I did not, concentrate at the right time, which may be one of the reasons why I never played for Yorkshire, nor captained Huddersfield Town nor became Prime Minister.

The author of the next chapter *(*Michael Foot, *right)* entertains the author of this chapter at Home Park in the 1952-53 season. William Mallalieu clearly has more to shout about: Huddersfield Town beat Plymouth Argyle 2-0, won the Second Division and went straight back to the First.

PLYMOUTH ARGYLE

MICHAEL FOOT (Labour, Plymouth Devonport, 1945-55; Ebbw Vale, 1960-83; Blaenau, 1983-92)

Born into Plymouth politics, he entered parliament in 1945, as Member for the Devonport division of that city.

A wartime editor of the *Evening Standard*, he was a political columnist for the *Daily Herald* (1944-1964) and managing director (with spells as editor) of *Tribune* (1945-74). Became the Member for Ebbw Vale (later renamed Blaenau Gwent) in 1960, following the death of that constituency's MP, Aneurin Bevan, whose two-volume biography he completed in 1973.

Secretary of State for Employment in Wilson's 1974 Government, he was Deputy Leader of the Labour Party, 1976-80, and Leader, 1980-83.

2

ON THE LEFT FOR ARGYLE

Michael Foot

His name was Sammy Black, and he played outside-left for Plymouth Argyle. Having been born in Scotland, he naturally qualified for what the sports writers of those days called 'international honours'. But once the Scottish selectors, after a few trials, failed to renew the appointment, I lost interest in such distant, diversionary rites. He was the greatest outside-left of his day, in an age of outside-lefts.

His style was his own; he was deadly and *insouciant*. I have never dared use the word before: I doubt whether I shall ever need to do so again. His method was mostly to saunter along the touchline, utterly impassive, unprovoked by events on or off the field, oblivious certainly of any catcalls or encouragement from the crowd. The arrangement whereby his black shorts, concealing his white knees, draped that diminutive body all added to the air of calculated unconcern. But when required he would leap into action with electric assurance.

He could hold the ball, beat his man, initiate movements of his own, but all these desirable faculties were quite subordinate to his special exploit, once the enemy penalty area came within range. The point of argument in all the Plymouth pubs was whether he was more lethal with his left foot or his right. The narrower the angle, the more he revelled in the test. Rarely did the cannonball rise more than a few inches above the ground.

He had a few partners in glory, most notably Jack Leslie, one of the first black footballers to make his mark in the English league, a truly cultured, constructive inside-left, and one who could recharge the Sammy Black cannon more smoothly than anyone else. Another was the Welsh left-back captain, Moses Russell, whose head was as bald as Yul Brynner's and who drew rapturous applause from the Feverell end on any wet Saturday when he acquired the first black patch upon that shining, white scalp. A third was another Scot, the goalkeeper Fred

Craig, who also, according to one of our favourite Argyle idiosyncrasies, took the penalties, and just occasionally, when Argyle were safely two up, we almost wanted him to miss, just to see him sprint back homewards. But he never did.

Argyle were good; no doubt about that. It was generally conceded that they played better football than any other team in the Third Division. But somehow they tended to lack the so-called 'killer' instinct, particularly during the critical Easter holiday engagements. Year after year, after excruciating lapses, they finished second (in those far off times only two teams were promoted, one from each section of Division III). So much so that ugly suggestions and suspicions spread throughout the city: one, that the unique but unlucky colours, green and black, should be abandoned; second, that the alien and inexplicable sobriquet 'Argyle'

S. BLACK (PLYMOUTH ARGYLE)

ASSOCIATION FOOTBALLERS

A SERIES OF 50

4

S. BLACK
(*Plymouth Argyle*)

As a junior with Kirkintilloch Rob Roy, Black was so small and frail that it was doubted whether he would ever have the physique for first-class football. Mr. Robert Jack, the Plymouth Argyle manager, however, signed him on in June 1924, and it was not long before he became one of the best outside-lefts in the game. To-day, Black is 5 ft. 6¼ in. in height, and weighs 11 st. He is very popular and when some time ago it was feared that he might have to leave Plymouth, a fund to "Save our Sammy" was raised. He is a tricky wing player and a great shot.

W. & H.O. WILLS

M. RUSSELL
PLYMOUTH ARGYLE

should be abandoned too; and third, and most sinister, that the directors just didn't want promotion. They preferred the big crowds and fat profits afforded by a sure place at the top of the lower league.

This last explanation gained added credibility one desolate winter afternoon when infallible Fred Craig appeared to let through on purpose a late equaliser for Swansea Town, the dirtiest of all our rivals by any reckoning: 'robust' was the euphemism preferred by the football reporters, of whose prose I made a deep, linguistic study. To add to the injury, Swansea went up instead. Nothing was spared us. Only Sammy Black was unperturbed. He reminded me of one of my father's Cromwellian generals, who would return from victory as if it were a defeat. What recoveries from desperate plights did we owe Sammy's poise.

Eventually, after no fewer than six consecutive years as runners-up, we did go up ourselves in 1930, to join Swansea and Southampton and a few others who had scrambled there before us, and, lo and behold, we were heading for our rightful place in the providential scheme of things. In our second season we finished fourth. First Division football was there within sight for all Home Park to see. Only the Second World War, it seems now in retrospect, intervened to rob us of our destiny. But even Armageddon and all its worst could not quite efface the imprint which Argyle left on the Second Division style of the 1930s.

One casual recollection should be enough to clinch the case. It was Christmas 1935, or 1936 maybe, and I found myself, not quite accidentally, working over the holiday in London alone, and unable to get home to the West Country. Argyle were playing Spurs at White Hart Lane on Christmas Day morning.

I was there on the terraces in good time, well placed to see any Argyle goals from the left and to engage in protective argument with any too-aggressive Tottenham supporters, who somehow still fancied their chances of a return to the First Division.

I had never been on a London ground before; I knew nothing of cockney chauvinism. I could not help imagining that Tottenham players must be Homeric figures, Olympian Gods; how could we prevail against the tricky footwork of Mercury, Jupiter's resourceful, defensive skills? Yet they were human after all. Argyle won, 2-1, both of ours scored by Sammy Black, one with each foot.

An hour or so later, I found a restaurant called *The Criterion* open in Piccadilly Circus. No Christmas turkey before or since ever tasted quite like that one. Never in the realms of human conflict had two away points been so spectacularly or insouciantly garnered by one man.

31

SHEFFIELD WEDNESDAY

ROY HATTERSLEY (Labour, Birmingham Sparkbrook)

Born in Sheffield, where he was a member of the local council, 1957-65.

Elected to parliament in 1964, he held several posts in the Labour Governments of 1964-70 and 1974-79, latterly that of Secretary of State for Prices and Consumer Protection, 1976-79. In opposition since 1979, he was on the front bench until 1992 and Deputy Leader of the Labour Party, 1983-92.

A journalist, essayist and novelist, he has announced his retirement from Westminster, to take effect from the next election and to release him for more writing.

3

WEDDED TO WEDNESDAY: THE FIRST FIFTY YEARS

Roy Hattersley

Football began for me on a sunlit autumn afternoon in 1944 when Sheffield Wednesday were at home to Nottingham Forest in the wartime Northern League. Nottingham was my father's town and Forest his team, so off we went to Hillsborough, me filled with hope and him full of nostalgia. Wednesday have been my team ever since.

Partisan Passions

When Wednesday played away from home, my father, my Uncle Syd and I would agonise between watching the reserves and making the journey across the city to Bramall Lane and Sheffield United.

Supporters of Wednesday and United eye each other warily lest by some freak of chance (merit being out of the question) the 'other side' is first amongst the honours. The rivalry between the city's teams is of the fratricidal not fraternal variety. As a boy, I genuinely believed in the man who never ate bacon because its red and white stripes reminded him of Sheffield United - indeed in my blue-and-white Wednesday heart I applauded and supported his loyalty.

So, I spent most of those afternoons at Bramall Lane, staring anxiously at the 'results board' that had been erected in front of the pavilion. The half-time scores of all the major matches were hung from its iron frame; and the latest score in the game that Sheffield Wednesday was playing away to some far-flung and exotic opponent like Luton Town or Cardiff City was exhibited at 15-minute intervals. I was really at Sheffield United's ground to chart the quarter-hourly progress of Sheffield Wednesday, to cheer in company with other Wednesdayites when we were ahead; to groan in unison with my desolate co-religionists when we were behind.

At Bramall Lane, then, we existed vicariously. But at Hillsborough, we lived life to the full, experiencing every emotion known to man, boy or beast. Standing on Wednesday's terraces, I roared my partisan passions. Sitting in the stands, I properly suppressed the baser expressions of joy in victory and the cruder manifestations of defiance in defeat. Huddled behind the goal, I waited for the crackling tannoy system to splutter into life with the announcement that every schoolboy expects, but knows will never come: 'Goodfellow' (or Morton or McIntosh - the fantasy survived several generations of goalkeepers) 'has been taken ill. Will Roy Hattersley come to the players' entrance at once and bring his boots and jersey with him?'

Even when the game started without me, I felt that I was down there on the pitch tackling the opposing forwards with Swift and Westlake, nodding crosses clear with Packard and Turton, and creating all manner of openings and opportunities for Jackie Robinson. When Robinson swung at the ball the man in front of me felt the kick on the back of his legs.

Jackie Robinson was the hero of the Wednesday song which, high up on Spion Kop, I learned and sang.

Roll along Sheffield Wednesday, roll along,
Put the ball in the net where it belongs,
When Jackie Robinson gets the ball,
Then it's sure to be a goal,
Roll along Sheffield Wednesday, roll along.

The lyric lacked both the literary invention and the tribal significance that scholars have discovered in the football songs of the 1970s. It did not even possess the graceful parody of Sheffield United's 'Wonderful, wonderful Jimmy Hagan ...' But it was my song, pure blue and white. I sang away the Saturday afternoons through mouthfuls of Nuttalls' Mintoes and listened to stories of great golden days between the wars.

Jackie Robinson was the last relic of Sheffield Wednesday's Cup-winning team of 1935. In fact, he had not played at Wembley. But Wednesday fans claimed for him the esoteric record of being 'the youngest man ever to play in a semi-final'. And starting from such juvenile distinction he had gone from personal strength to strength asthe team he served declined into the Second Division. He played a

'Jackie
Robinson
was my
hero'

few times for England - scoring twice in Berlin, in the famous Nazi Salute match, in 1938 - and, in the mid-1940s, was north Sheffield's answer to Jimmy Hagan.

Robinson was my hero. Even after he left Wednesday for Sunderland I looked anxiously at the *Green 'Un* each Saturday night in the hope that he had scored. But if Sunderland had ever played Wednesday there would have been no problem of divided allegiance. I always wanted Wednesday to win. Unfortunately, during the early years of my fervent enthusiasm, they rarely played such elevated opposition.

Football Association Cup associations

When Wednesday were in the Second Division the great clubs came to Hillsborough only for Cup ties. And then only for what, in those ancient days, was called the 'Third Round Proper'. For that was the round when Wednesday entered the competition and the round when they left it.

Our compensation was that one of the Cup semi-finals was almost invariably played at Hillsborough, a match which became the highlight of the Sheffield football purists' year. For the partisan, no game could compare with a confrontation in which one of the local favourites took part. What I wanted to see was Sheffield Wednesday winning. But once a year I looked forward to the more relaxed pleasure of Derby County versus Manchester United or Newcastle against Wolves. Indeed, like my father, I was so keen on enjoying an uncommitted ninety minutes that I rose at half-past six on the Sunday when the tickets were sold. By seven we were in the queue, waiting with anxious calm for noon and the moment when the sale actually started. By one o'clock we had reached a turnstile and were about to take possession of the two tickets which each frozen enthusiast was allowed. By half-past one, we were back home, having missed *Family Favourites* and the *Billy Cotton Band Show,* but the proud possessors of the ability to take our place on Spion Kop on the next Saturday.

I could of course have gone on my own to buy the two tickets that my father and I needed. The extra tickets which we always bought were less of a boon than a burden. We never even thought of selling them at a profit, and there was always much embarrassed confusion about who should buy them at face value. Indeed, there were times when - for all their scarcity - we were almost left with the valuable property on our hands. We bought them because the offer seemed too good to refuse, and the idea of queueing all those hours and then taking only half the number of tickets we were offered seemed self-evidently ridiculous. Of course, one of us could have stayed in bed while the other made the early morning expedition. But football was for my father and me a joint enterprise. We stood on Spion Kop, eating our Mintoes together. And together we queued for the tickets.

On the day of the big game we took our places on the red shale terraces two hours before the time of the kick-off. Queueing combined with waiting for the kick-off lasted four times as long as the match itself. But the game was always worth it and there were diversions to help us pass the time.

There was, of course, the local Steelworks Band, playing martial music in a wholly unmilitary way - which was entirely consistent with their wholly unmilitary appearance. And there was the crowd itself - Blackpool fans walking with an orange-ribboned duck along the touchline; wandering Wolverhamptonites passing a black-and-white coffin over their heads in preparation for the slaughter of Newcastle United, and the whole panoply and pageant of coloured hats and supporters' club songs. And that was all before the match began.

After the first whistle blew, there were Stan Mortensen of Blackpool and Billy Wright of Wolves, and for two marvellous consecutive years the magpies of Newcastle who won at Hillsborough and went on to win the Cup - Jackie Milburn, Bobby Mitchell, Joe Harvey and the Robledo brothers from South America. The triumph - and the glory road to Wembley - belonged elsewhere, to Lancashire and London, the Midlands and the north-east.

It had not always been like that. In the twenties and thirties, when Arsenal was making history by giving its ageing players monkey glands, Yorkshire was dominating Cup and League. Huddersfield won the Championship three seasons running and came a close second for the next two years. Then Sheffield Wednesday won the League (once by a margin of ten clear points) in successive seasons and came third four times in the next five seasons. Sheffield United brought the Cup home to Bramall Lane in 1925, the middle of a decade of absolute Yorkshire domination, when the names which schoolboys conjured with were Stevenson, Capstick, Gillespie, Needham, Blenkinsop, Leach, Marsden and Seed.

In a game which thrives on innovation, the supremacy of Sheffield and Huddersfield could not last. The final fling (putting aside the dying fall of Wembley defeats in 1936 and 1938) was Sheffield Wednesday's Cup in 1935. I was wheeled down to Middlewood Road to see the victorious team come home: eleven heroes on top of an open bus, not wearing the double-breasted blazers and sharp suits of postwar idols, but dressed in the thick shirts and heavy square-toed boots which they wore on every winter Saturday afternoon.

At least that is how I imagine it. I was two at the time. Strapped in my push-chair, I enjoyed a less than perfect view of the triumphant homecoming. But of one thing I am certain. The victorious captain, holding the Cup aloft for all but the smallest and most restricted spectator to see, was Ron Starling. I know because we talked about it in his paper shop during the dismal football days of the 1950s. We bought our papers there to ensure that, during an adolescence in which I was denied no advantage, I should handle a *Manchester Guardian* handed to me by a man who had held the FA Cup.

37

Yorkshire and higher galaxies

It was nearly 40 years before a Yorkshire club brought home the Cup again. Between the end of the war and Leeds United's great epoch, Yorkshire supporters had to be content with teams which won no honours, the occasional international who lost his place as soon as he won his cap, the potential star who shot into a new firmament the moment that news of his sparkle and shine penetrated the light years between Yorkshire and football's higher galaxies, and the faded glory of great names who added a touch of retrospective distinction to teams in the Third and Second Divisions.

For Doncaster Rovers to have the ageing Peter Doherty on their playing staff was probably the greatest achievement in the club's history. Horatio Carter's silver hair and long shorts never really suited the yellow and black 'tiger' image of Boothferry Road. But no one like him has played for Hull City before or since. Only in the far north-east, at Ayresome Park, were regular contemporary internationals on view in Yorkshire. Hardwick - immaculate in appearance as well as style - was permanent left back for Middlesbrough and England. Wilf Mannion, his club colleague, was left out of the national team only when injury or the inability of the selectors to recognise true genius denied him his rightful place. But for 10 years after Hardwick and Mannion had gone, Yorkshire internationals either faded and were dropped, or prospered and passed on to more successful clubs.

The Yorkshire schoolboys had no real cause for complaint. The loyalty of football supporters has to be to a name and a ground not to a team. The club players on whose success our Saturday evening happiness depends are the best that transfer fees and bonuses can buy. They are mercenaries, fighting for money and love of battle, with no permanent allegiance to any standard, who rally round today's flag because that is what they are paid to do. Although Wednesday was my local team, I never thought of it as part of my local heritage. There was nothing especially Yorkshire about the football they played - no special Yorkshire style, tradition, grace or virtue that distinguished it from football played across the Pennines or south of the Humber. It took 20 years of unswerving support to discover that a real Yorkshire pulse

FOOTBALL - SHEFFIELD WEDNESDAY

SPORTING EVENTS
AND
☆ STARS ☆
SERIES OF 96.
No. 5

SHEFFIELD WEDNESDAY
Yorkshire's pride who brought football's most coveted trophy, the F.A. Cup, to the North for the fourth year in succession, beating in the Final at Wembley, April 27th, 1935, West Bromwich Albion by 4 goals to 2. This was the Wednesday's first cup win since 1906-7, when they beat Everton 2—1, and their success was due in a large degree to the novel training methods employed by their Manager, Mr. Billy Walker. The team reading left to right are :— Back Row.—Geo. Irwin (Trainer), J. Nibloe (right back), J. Brown (goalkeeper), Mr. W. H. Walker (manager), A. Catlin (left back), W. Millership (centre half), H. Burrows (left half).
Front Row.—W. Sharp (right half), M. Hooper (outside right), J. Surtees (inside right), J. Palethorpe (centre forward), R. Starling, Captain (inside left) and E. Rimmer, goal scorer in every Round (outside left).

These interesting Photographs are issued with the following Cigarettes :—
SENIOR SERVICE .... *10 FOR 6ᵈ*
JUNIOR MEMBER .... *20 FOR 1/4*
ILLINGWORTH'S Nº 10 ... *25 FOR 1/-*

TURF CIGARETTES
WILF MANNION MIDDLESBROUGH & ENGLAND
50 FAMOUS FOOTBALLERS Nº 30

'...the supremacy of
Sheffield...'
FA Cup-Winners 1935

'...at Ayresome Park,
regular internationals
were on view'

"TURF" CIGARETTES
GEORGE HARDWICK
MIDDLESBROUGH & ENGLAND
50 FOOTBALLERS Nº 35

throbbed at least through the two Sheffield teams. The heartbeat could
- and still can - be recorded, in the directors' box.

Football Directors are nobody's friends except when there are Cup
Final tickets to give away, but they represent continuity whether the
club fails or flourishes in a way that transient players and insecure
managers cannot. They spring from the local soil, take root and often
become impossible to dislodge even when the sap no longer rises and
the leaves are brown and withered. They are the team's spirit, its tradition, its continuity.

For a man who spent his boyhood on Spion Kop, an invitation to sit in
the Wednesday Directors' Box was like a Royal Command. I already
knew the 'Royal Family'. Eric Taylor - 'football's longest serving manager' - was our neighbour. We admired his durability and canniness.
For years he painted his house in blue and white stripes. In bad years
after the war (and there were many), dissident fans would be told about
the loyalty of his decorations and would instantly accept that a man of
such obvious devotion was indispensable to the club. It was Mrs Taylor
who suggested that a young Scot - recently arrived from Edinburgh and
making ends meet as Sheffield Wednesday's doctor - might find the
cure for my bronchitis that had already eluded a succession of GPs.
Twenty years later he was introducing the Queen to Cup Finalists at
Wembley: Sir Andrew Stephen, Chairman of the Football Association.

But nodding to neighbours and coughing for doctors was one thing.
Meeting them in their glory as the men behind the team, behind almost
every other team in the Second Division, was quite another. We did not
come straight from the wet and weather-beaten terraces. On the day I
tried to put my umbrella up behind Manchester United's goal my father
and I agreed that he was too old and I was too decadent for the concrete
steps. Indeed, the Mancunians, whose view I obscured, made much the
same point, though in different language. So we bought tickets for the
extremity of the old stand and squinted from our seats over the corner
flag. But we were still unprepared for the padded seats and the heated
footrests of the first four rows at the centre line.

We gave up Nuttalls' Mintoes. We learned to stroll nonchalantly into
the ground at five to three rather than rush at the turnstile at quarter
past two. We sat prim and proper and boasted to each other that we

had watched Wednesday from every part of the ground. But I never felt confident in the exalted company until the late sixties. Then, with Yorkshire two hundred miles and five years behind me, I followed the Club and its Directors on their visit to London grounds and relaxed in all the friendly familiarity of exiles in an alien land.

In January 1974, I arrived at Stamford Bridge, a hanger-on with the Sheffield Wednesday visitors. I was late for my rendezvous. A minute before the kick-off I stood blinking at the back of the Directors' Box, adjusting my eyes to the light and deciding where to sit. On my left was carefully cut hair, brushing the back of corduroy suits and touching the velvet collars of cavalry coats. On the right were heads cropped as close as boil-scars would allow. I recognised the men with graces but with few airs, men of property, who had no intention of flaunting or wasting what they had earned. I had no doubt which side I was on.

At the end of the match we all went to drink together - not just the victorious and vanquished directors linked in a moment of mock modesty and bogus sportsmanship, but wives and daughters, joining men with serious business to discuss and serious results from other grounds to ponder. Chelsea beat Wednesday 3-2. But, as we say in Yorkshire (after we have lost),

'Some things are more important than winning.'

Premier Days for a Different Sort of Big Club

Twenty seasons later - and 50 years since I became a fan - football has got on in the world. And it may have left me behind.

There has never been a time when I have felt more detached - the proper word may even be alienated - from professional football. No doubt there will still be Saturday afternoons when I shall be sitting in the stand at Hillsborough and at five minutes to three all the old tingling joy will once again engulf me. But, early in the 1993-94 season, I realised that an essential element of the old passion was missing.

My problem can be summed up in a single synthetic noun. *Premiership.* That near-illiterate invention was clearly cobbled togeth-

41

er by marketing men who thought that a new brand name would help to sell the product. For all I know their commercial instinct may be impeccable. But I do not want football to be a product. I want it to be a game.

Disillusion set in towards the end of the first Premier season. On the evening when Manchester United knew that they had won the championship, Alex Ferguson and Bobby Charlton - two of the most respected and respectable figures in the game - appeared on television to comment on the triumph. United still had another game to play. The new and garish trophies were yet to be presented to the victorious team and the tide of celebration which was to sweep through Old Trafford was just building up from a ripple to a wave. Yet both men, manager and director, made the same promise. The club intended 'to strengthen the squad'. That is football speak for buy more players.

Roy Keane - a young man of immense talent with a 10-year potential - moved to Manchester from Nottingham Forest. We were told that, because of his admiration for his new club, he signed on for less than the £400,000 a year that he was offered by Blackburn Rovers. If the story is true, good for him. But bad for football. Wages like that - combined with the cost of creating all-seater stadiums - are pushing the price of a match beyond the reach of low income families. And that is only part of the problem.

The big clubs justify big wages by saying that, in a competitive sport, you must expect competition for the best players. But what sort of competition is it that gives a built-in advantage to the rich and turns every race into a steeplechase with obstacles which can only be surmounted with money? Everybody in football says that it is impossible to buy the championship of the Premier League or to purchase promotion from one of the lower divisions. Why then do managers spend these vast sums? Not, I think, as a sort of outdoor relief. In football, charity is just the name of the shield for which the cup winners and league champions play at the beginning of the season.

Given the outspoken partisanship of this chapter, let me make it clear that I am at best ambivalent when I read that Sheffield Wednesday have spent millions. Like a true supporter, what interests me is not the quality of the play but the result of the game. And if buying established internationals contributes to that end, I rejoice. But I do not feel the pride that engulfed me when we won matches with half a dozen players who were born only a goal-kick away from the ground. And I long for the days when our internationals were forged in Sheffield instead of being bought ready-made.

I have explained that those were the days when Wednesday's main ambition was to avoid relegation into whatever division happened to be below us. The season's target was 44 points and, after the game, our concern was for the fate and fortune of teams in straits as desperate as ours. Often our survival depended on their continual failure. We normally endured a frantic April and desperate May. But there was not even a touch of metropolitan sophistication to mar the club's reputation for cosy incompetence. The players all had last year's hairstyles and spoke not of 'set piece' but 'free kick'. They did not perform war dances, slide along the pitch on their knees or blow kisses to the crowd when they scored - not that it happened very often.

Wednesday will, I think, always remain a different sort of big club. It will never be owned by a single tycoon and champagne will only be served in the boardroom after spectacular and significant victories. Scampi, the real sign of football stardom, will be kept to an absolute minimum. That is why I have the real hope that, when I get to my next home game, all the old joy - associated in my mind with rain down my neck and, worse, down the back of my trousers - will return.

Only one possible hurdle stands between me and joyous reunion. If, when I arrive, I discover that (like Chelsea) we have installed a lift to connect the directors' box with the real world, I shall know that for me and the Premiership, it is all over.

NORTHERN IRELAND

CLIFFORD FORSYTHE (Ulster Unionist, Antrim South)

A former professional footballer in the Irish League, he played centre-forward for Bangor, Linfield and Derry City, gaining an Irish Cup-Winners medal with Derry in 1954.

Later Mayor of Newtownabbey, he was then elected to Parliament in 1983. The Ulster Unionist spokesman for Social Security, Transport and Communications, he is a member of the Select Committee on Social Security.

4

ULSTER UNITY

Clifford Forsythe

One of my earliest recollections is of football gear festooning the kitchen when the weather was too wet for outside drying. My father was Chairman of the local club, Carnmoney Church FC. My brothers, cousins and uncles all played and my mother provided a weekly laundry service.

That was my upbringing in Northern Ireland - in Glengormley in County Antrim, in a family totally involved with football. My good fortune in being from a football family was compounded by coming under the influence of school teachers and youth leaders who encouraged me in all athletic activities and insisted that I train hard to reach the level of physical fitness which would enable me to succeed. So many other boys and girls didn't have that privilege.

Fit for Football and Politics

That urge to be physically fit still remains with me today and helps to counter-balance the stress and late nights of parliamentary life.

The most disappointing memory of my football career was when I was selected for a youth international, but accompanying the letter of selection was a request for my exact birthdate. I duly received a cold formal note from the Irish Football Association advising me that I was seven days too old.

I began playing organised football at the age of 12. I progressed from the Church Lads Brigade to Minor, Amateur, Intermediate and 'B' Division Leagues, finally becoming a professional in the Irish League. My opportunities to be a spectator were therefore rather limited. I suppose my father's team was the only one I ever supported as a spectator - *before* I became a player. The only other team I followed was the Irish

FA team, now the Northern Ireland team. I recall with pleasure watching greats such as Jack Vernon and Peter Doherty, opposing and occasionally defeating Welsh, Scottish and English teams.

Those were the days when players from all over Ireland were eligible for selection by the IFA in the North. Another Irish team was selected by the Football Association of Ireland, the organising body in the Republic of Ireland - but bear in mind that, in those days, the Gaelic tradition prevailed in the Republic and soccer was not as widely popular as today. This easy state of affairs regarding selection ended when FIFA ruled that players would be eligible for one or the other team, depending upon where they had been born. Subsequent rule changes allowed the birthplace of parents - and, later, other close relatives - to count. Jack Charlton has, of course, turned this into an art form.

One Northern Ireland game that I did witness as a spectator was the 'Battle of Windsor' in December 1957. It should have been a World Cup qualifier against Italy, but the Hungarian referee, Istvan Zsolt, was stranded in fog at Heathrow. Some 50,000 irate fans booed the friendly - and some of the less-than-friendly play - which replaced the scheduled game. When the local referee blew the final whistle on a 2-2 draw, there was a pitch invasion. Danny Blanchflower, the Irish captain, allocated a team-mate to each Italian to secure his safe custody from the pitch and no lasting international damage was done.

Italy returned to Windsor Park the following month. This time, Harry Gregg, the Irish 'keeper, was fogbound at Manchester airport, but Norman Uprichard was on hand to play in a 2-1 win that took Northern Ireland to the 1958 World Cup Finals in Sweden - the only time that all four home nations have qualified.

Scottish contributors to this book reflect on the significance, to different degrees, of the religious divide. No chapter on Northern Ireland would be complete without some elaboration on its impact. Equally, though, no chapter by an old pro would be complete without his thoughts on some of the changes the game has seen - changes that have nothing to do with religion.

'I recall with
pleasure watching
greats such as
Jack Vernon and
Peter Doherty.'

The 'Battle of Windsor' - the
'friendly' that replaced the
scheduled World Cup qualifier

The real thing - the World Cup
qualifier, which Northern Ireland
won to reach the finals.

Football across the Divide

Some followers of Irish politics might refuse to believe that the question of religion or political persuasion never arose during my playing career - even though I played both for Linfield and for Derry City, whose followers are reputed to represent the opposite ends of the political spectrum. Linfield has always been associated with the Unionist community, while some people consider that Derry City has now replaced Belfast Celtic as the standard bearer for Nationalists. In my day, Derry played in the Irish League. Today, of course, they are a successful member of the Republic's League of Ireland.

I clearly remember standing on the terracing at Windsor Park watching them defeat Glentoran in the 1949 Irish Cup Final. Little did I realise that, five years later, I would lead the Derry City forward line at the same stage of the competition when, after two replays, we once again beat Glentoran. Of all the games I played, those three against Glentoran were my most exciting. That cup winners' medal was the most satisfying success of my whole career. It was principally teamwork, rather than individual brilliance, that led to our victory. But it certainly helped to have the legendary Jimmy Delaney - already a holder of **Scottish and English Cup medals, with Celtic (1937) and Manchester United (1948)** - as a team-mate.

The scenes following our victory are something I will never forget. A cavalcade in the late evening was immediately followed by a civic reception in the Guild Hall, where an appreciation of our efforts was thundered out by thousands of supporters of all shades of opinion. That is not to say that sectarianism among supporters has not been a factor in the postwar history of the Irish League. It has. Thus Belfast Celtic left the Irish League in 1948, and folded the next year, following a riot during a match against Linfield at the latter's Windsor Park home. The Celtic centre forward, Jimmy Jones, was pushed over a parapet and sustained a broken leg. The trouble is reputed to have started following a ground broadcast of the news that the Linfield centre half, Bob Bryson, had sustained a broken leg in a collision, earlier in the game, with a Celtic player. Onlookers felt that this provocative announcement was the spark to what became an ill-tempered game. I am glad to say that both Jimmy and Bob recovered to play many more games - Jimmy for Glenavon, his Lurgan, home town, team.

The Celtic, which was dominated by one family at the time - a bit like Glasgow Celtic, as Brian Wilson reminds us in his chapter below - felt they had no option but to withdraw from the league. That was, and still is, a great loss to the Irish League.

I have alluded already to Derry City's defection. Their ground, The Brandywell, was in the 'no go' area of the Bogside. While other teams continued to go there and play, games against Linfield had to take place at Coleraine's Showgrounds. This arrangement continued until 1972 when, following Ballymena's game at The Brandywell, rioters burned the visitors' team bus. Derry City felt obliged to leave the Irish League and were not allowed by the football authorities, for fear of a repeat performance, to return. So Derry applied to join the League of Ireland. Such was the sensitivity of the matter between the two national leagues that it took them several applications. The reorganisation of the League of Ireland in 1985 eventually opened the door to Derry who duly won the treble - of league and both cups - in 1989.

There remains a problem with Cliftonville. After the demise of Belfast Celtic, Cliftonville (The Reds) had become a focus of Catholic loyalty in the capital. Following the Irish Cup Final victory by their arch-rivals, Linfield (The Blues), against Ballymena in 1970, trouble occurred on the Antrim Road - near Cliftonville's Solitude ground - when Linfield supporters, returning to the centre of Belfast, clashed with local fans and other local residents. The police advised that games between Cliftonville and Linfield must not be played at Solitude. Since that time, Cliftonville's home matches with Linfield have been played at Windsor Park by kind permission of Linfield and the RUC. This arrangement has again been thrown into the melting pot by Linfield's 1994 withdrawal (for various reasons) of this facility. At the time of writing, the matter remains unresolved.

Such manifestations of sectarianism are spectacular but, I'm glad to say, rare. Indeed, it is unfair to dwell upon them. Notwithstanding my limited experience as a spectator, I am very well aware that the vast majority of supporters of all teams are interested only in the result on the field and follow their team, in all weathers, with a fierce dedication unequalled in other sports. I consider it an honour to have been welcomed, as a player, both by Derry City supporters in the Bogside and

49

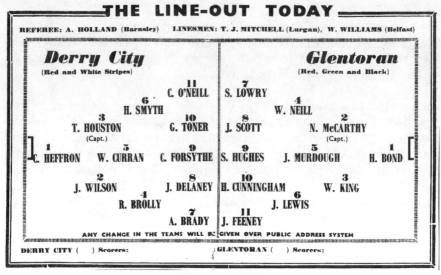

THE LINE-OUT TODAY

REFEREE: A. HOLLAND (Barnsley)   LINESMEN: T. J. MITCHELL (Lurgan), W. WILLIAMS (Belfast)

Derry City
(Red and White Stripes)

Glentoran
(Red, Green and Black)

```
                    11         7
                C. O'NEILL   S. LOWRY
            6                          4
         H. SMYTH                  W. NEILL
     3              10        8              2
  T. HOUSTON    G. TONER   J. SCOTT    N. McCARTHY
   (Capt.)                               (Capt.)
  1        5          9        9        5          1
C. HEFFRON  W. CURRAN  C. FORSYTHE  S. HUGHES  J. MURDOUGH  H. BOND
     2              8        10              3
  J. WILSON    J. DELANEY  H. CUNNINGHAM  W. KING
            4                          6
         R. BROLLY                  J. LEWIS
                    7          11
                A. BRADY   J. FEENEY
```

ANY CHANGE IN THE TEAMS WILL BE GIVEN OVER PUBLIC ADDRESS SYSTEM

DERRY CITY (   ) Scorers: GLENTORAN (   ) Scorers:

The Irish Cup Final 1954: Clifford Forsythe alongside Jimmy Delaney

WILLS'S CIGARETTES

J. DELANEY (CELTIC)

'... the legendary
Jimmy Delaney'

Been there!
Jimmy Delaney
had Cup-Winners'
medals with
Celtic (1937) and
Manchester
United (1948).

"TURF" CIGARETTES

JIMMY DELANEY
MANCHESTER UTD. & SCOTLAND
50 FOOTBALLERS Nº 38

The Brandywell and by Linfield fans at Donegal Avenue and Windsor Park.

And I can say, with absolute truthfulness, that throughout my career, players never at any time thought of each other as anything other than colleagues and fellow-players. There was no divide at any time, regardless of background or team. That happy situation remains today. And the camaraderie has extended beyond the pitch into my everyday life. I have fond memories of the congratulations I received from all sides of the political divide when I was elected to Parliament, as an Ulster Unionist, in 1983.

There've been some changes made

The joy of winning an Irish Cup winners' medal in 1954 included, as I say, the joy, and great privilege, of playing with the late Jimmy Delaney. Incidentally, his remarkable record of gaining cup-winners' medals in Scotland, England and Northern Ireland was almost extended in 1956, when he played for Cork Athletic in the Republic of Ireland Cup Final. I remember listening to the commentary on the radio as Shamrock Rovers came from behind to win 3-2.

Jimmy was a gentleman in the truest sense of the word. But, then, my boyhood heroes - like Stanley Matthews and Peter Doherty - were sportsmen in the same mould and set a glorious example to the youth of the country. Sadly, the wrong type of example is provided by too many of today's players.

It seems to me that football is now too professional and, except in a few cases, less sporting than in earlier days. Money has taken comradeship out of the game and TV over-exposure has been detrimental. Football is now a business and the philosophy of the game has changed, with too much emphasis placed on winning - even in minor, or children's, matches. And there is too much self admiration exhibited by goalscorers. The current fad for idiotic kissing and posing from players when a goal is scored says more about the players themselves than what has happened.

Kissing apart, any physical contact has now to be dealt with as a foul and goalkeepers seem to be too well protected. When I was playing regularly, it was clearly understood that, if you couldn't look after yourself, you had better not travel to some of the outlying parts of the province. But, while I experienced tough 'thou shalt not pass' tackling, it was generally fair and not designed to put an opponent out of action as with some of today's questionable tackles.

If players adhered to the rules, referees would require few yellow or red cards. I am quite relieved nowadays when I see referees controlling matches the way they did when I played, always up with the game and with a word at the right time to keep even the roughest players in check.

My solution to the abuse heaped upon referees would be to compel each and every spectator to undergo a referee's course followed by at least four junior matches in the foulest weather and no help from linesmen. This would imprint referees' difficulties upon even the most biased mind.

I am appalled at the vicious and vindictive criticism, from former players who now commentate for the media, of players, managers, coaches and officials. They seem to feel that only by carping can they parade their knowledge of the game. All done with the benefit of hindsight and slow-motion replays. What a travesty of sportsmanship and fair play! But perhaps one shouldn't expect any fairness from media commentators anxious to stir up controversy.

One could forgive those without any football experience but - like many other viewers, listeners and readers, I'm sure - I expect something more realistic and balanced from those who should know better. Retrospective trial by television is unfair to referees and bad for football.

The good of the game requires that the referee's word be final. That said, I enjoyed the occasion, as a player, when the opposing centre-forward, incensed by an offside decision, removed his glass eye from its socket and handed it to the referee with a suggestion that his need was the greater. In those days, goalnets were unheard of in junior soccer and the poor referee had to decide which side of the goalpost a ball had passed. Other hazards included women wheeling prams across a public

We're on our way to Windsor: Jimmy Delaney (on ground; striped shirt; partially obscured by his team-mate, Clifford Forsythe) scores with an overhead kick in the 1954 semi-final against Linfield.

And finally... Clifford Forsythe, kneeling, heads Derry into the lead in the first of the three games that it took to beat Glentoran.

pitch and the ball striking a tree before entering the goal.

Facilities have, of course, improved in the junior game. I sometimes envy today's young sportsmen and women their indoor sports halls and hot showers. Yet using 'behind a hedge' as a dressing room and washing down in cold water never did my generation any harm. It will be a sad day when young men and women allow deficient facilities to put them off striving for the top.

And I envy, yet applaud, the excellent training which is clearly evident in the fitness, stature, ability and stamina of present day youth - although I worry lest too much coaching remove, in some cases, the individual's capacity to think for himself or herself.

I have always admired the excellent people who give of their time to run football at the lower level, pleading, cheering and encouraging and generally helping young players to express themselves in their own way, before they fall under the influence of coaches, who may try, I repeat, to drill all signs of individuality out of them.

Other good developments include improved kit and a lighter ball. In my day, socks, pants and jerseys were heavy and weighed the proverbial ton when wet. And we wore heavy *Manfield Hotspur* leather boots, with leather studs fixed by very sharp nails. This brand of boot gave me my first taste of publicity when I appeared in a larger-than-life action photograph in a Belfast shop window.

Finally, the ball. The present plastic-covered ball, which I could still kick past the halfway line without too much effort, has replaced the heavy leather ball which, on a bad day, was like heading a sack of potatoes. There were many cases of minor concussion suffered by centre forwards.

A thought for spectators

As a player one sees a different side of football facilities. Players are well looked after and protected from anything which would distract them from the game on the field. On the other hand, my limited experience of grounds as a spectator is not favourable. I fully support the move to all-seater stadiums, as I believe that the paying customer should be treated with consideration and every inducement should be provided to win back family supporters. Overgrown terraces with dangerous underfoot conditions are unacceptable as is the prospect of standing for 90 minutes in pouring rain without cover. The difference between refreshments available for directors and friends and the facilities provided for the average spectator is colossal.

There has been an improvement in conveying information to spectators but only at some of the larger grounds. It always surprises me to see the difference between the approaches to American football grounds and ours. They have better car-parking facilities and, while the entrances to UK grounds generally manage to cope with those going *in*, one gets the feeling that clubs close their eyes to the free-for-all which develops when thousands of people try to leave the ground and car parks at the same time.

It is puzzling that with business people now having a big say in running clubs that such matters are not addressed. Of course, having said that, I admit that there are notable exceptions among the clubs.

And I admit that every year, on Christmas Day, I still take great pleasure in standing on a cold, windswept terrace, with my former football buddies, watching Northern Ireland's premier junior cup match, the Steel & Sons Cup Final.

Perhaps I am one of the game's spectators, after all. Changes notwithstanding, I am certainly one of its fans.

MANCHESTER UNITED

STAN ORME (Labour, Salford East)

A longtime resident of Sale, three miles from Old Trafford, he was an engineer in Manchester and a member of Sale Borough Council before becoming a Salford MP in 1964 (Salford West until 1983; Salford East since).

A Minister for Northern Ireland, then for Social Security, in the Wilson-Callaghan administrations of 1974-79, he served on Labour's front bench, 1979-87, as the principal spokesman, in turn, for Health and Social Security; Industry; and Employment.

Is a Vice-Chairman of the All-Party Parliamentary Football Committee.

5

GLORY, GLORY - WE'RE UNITED!

Stan Orme

When Manchester United became Premier League Champions for the second year running, in May 1994, with a magnificent team, a team of all nationalities blended together by Alec Ferguson which made them the outstanding team in Britain, my mind went back to the end of the Second World War.

A young Scottish soldier was offered the managership of Manchester United. A Scottish international, he was asked to inherit a club and a team that had to be rebuilt, with a ground which had had the main stand destroyed by bombs during the war. And so, until the the start of the 1949-50 season, they had to use the Maine Road ground of their neighbours. The new manager was, of course, Matt Busby.

The parliamentary contribution to the players' cause, of Ellis Smith, the Labour Member for Stoke, is acknowledged in William Mallalieu's chapter. A lifelong Manchester United supporter, he fought for a steel allocation to help build the new stand and was bitterly criticised for his efforts, as the argument was about rebuilding homes, not football stadiums. For a while when the club went back to Old Trafford, supporters in the main stand had to sit in the open air until the new stand was built. When one looks at the magnificent ground today, it is hard to envisage what a transformation has taken place.

As Busby's leadership and football nous began to take effect, his team reached the 1948 Cup Final, one of the best ever seen at Wembley. The 4-2 win over Blackpool was the climax to a cup run in which United won every game at the first time of asking and by at least two clear goals, yet never played on their own pitch.

The progress from there is, of course, well known and some of us have had the privilege of seeing that 1948 team, the beginning of the Busby Babes, the development of Duncan Edwards, the tragedy of the Munich

EDWARDS OF ENGLAND

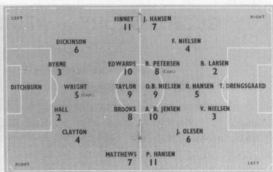

LEFT	FINNEY 11	J. HANSEN 7				RIGHT
	DICKINSON 6		F. NIELSEN 4			
	BYRNE 3	EDWARDS 10	B. PETERSEN 8 (Capt.)	B. LARSEN 2		
DITCHBURN	WRIGHT 5 (Capt.)	TAYLOR 9	O.B. NIELSEN 9	O. HANSEN 5	T. DRENGSGAARD	
	HALL 2	BROOKS 8	A. R. JENSEN 10	V. NIELSEN 3		
	CLAYTON 4		J. OLESEN 6			
RIGHT	MATTHEWS 7	P. HANSEN 11				LEFT

v. DENMARK - up-front, flanked by Matthews and Finney, Edwards scored twice in a 5-2 win.

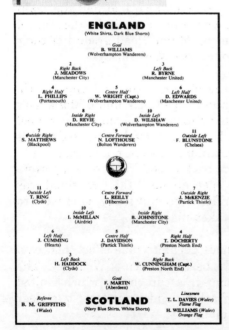

v. SCOTLAND (1955)
The youngest-ever
England debutant.

v. SCOTLAND (1957)
Scored from left-half
in a 2-1 win.

air crash, the rebuilding again, Denis Laws, George Best, Pat Crerand, Bobby Charlton ... one could go on and on.

The Greatest Of All

Rather than go on and on, I should like just to reflect on Duncan Edwards. Of all the magnificent players Manchester United has had during the period I have outlined, none is greater than Duncan.

He was, to my way of thinking, the complete footballer: two-footed, a magnificent tackler, superb distributor of the ball and a terrific shot. He had everything.

One particular match I recall with real joy was the first leg of the FA Youth Cup Final against Wolverhampton Wanderers at Old Trafford in May 1953. Duncan had made his first team debut the previous month, but, still only 16, remained eligible for the youth team. The game was played one Monday afternoon, with more than 20,000 spectators present. Players seemed to bounce off Duncan, as United won 7-1.

That was the start of five consecutive Youth Cup wins by the 'Busby Babes' and Duncan was eligible for the first three of them. By the time he played in the 1955 semi-final win over Chelsea, he had made his full international debut. Chelsea questioned whether a full international could play in the Youth Cup. He could. He did. And he set a fine precedent. When United won the Youth Cup for the sixth time in 1964, they fielded a first-team winger with two full caps for Northern Ireland. George Best.

I was at Wembley in April 1955 when Duncan, still only 18, played that first game for England - a 7-2 win over Scotland. At the Manchester industrial instruments firm where I worked as an engineer, some of us paid a few bob a week into a pool. By the end of the season - every season for 15 post-war years - we had bought ourselves a trip, whether to Wembley or Hampden, to see England v Scotland.

Again, I could, but won't, go on and on about those games ... Jim Baxter, one of the greatest defenders I've ever seen. Being in a Hampden crowd of 139,000 - most of whom seemed to travel to Wembley the following season. In Piccadilly Circus, Eros had to be boarded up, with a police guard inside the boards, against rampaging Scots. It wasn't hooliganism as we came to experience it, but the centre of London was a place to avoid when Scotland came to Wembley.

So it was that I saw Duncan again at Hampden in 1956 and at Wembley in 1957. In that 1957 game, he played at left half - and scored - in a 2-1 win. Tom Finney was at centre-forward. Stanley Matthews, who had won his first cap two years before Duncan was born, was at outside right.

Earlier that season, in the World Cup qualifier against Denmark at Molineux, Duncan was at inside-left, Finney on the left wing and the 41 year-old Matthews on the right wing. With Duncan scoring twice and United's Tommy Taylor getting a hat-trick, England won 5-2 and went on to qualify for the Finals in Sweden - where, of course, they had, post-Munich, no Edwards, no Taylor and no Roger Byrne.

Along with all the other tragedies at Munich, the loss of Duncan Edwards not only to Manchester United but to football in general is incalculable. We will not forget.

On 8 February 1958, the Saturday after Munich, United were scheduled to play Wolves at Old Trafford. The game was, of course, postponed but I went to the ground, anyhow. So did thousands of others. It was a quite extraordinary occasion - all those people just standing there, not speaking.

The Fifth Round FA Cup tie v. Sheffield Wednesday, due to be played the following Saturday, was also postponed - until 19 February. In the circumstances, United had been allowed to sign the cup-tied Stan Crowther from Villa and had paid Blackpool £8,000 for the 33 year-old Ernie Taylor. He had starred in the so-called 'Matthews Final' of 1953 - recalled in several chapters of this book - and had then had the misfortune to win his first, and only, England cap in the 6-3 defeat by Hungary.

Neither name appeared in the programme for that cup-tie. In fact, acting manager, Jimmy Murphy, had been unable to name a side, so the teamsheet in the programme was left blank. The team, including the two new signings and Munich survivors, Bill Foulkes and Harry Gregg,

*'Jimmy Murphy had been unable to name a side, so
the teamsheet in the programme was left blank'.*

Stan Crowther signs for
Jimmy Murphy, 54 minutes
before the kick-off,
in time to fill the
blank No.6 spot.

was announced, just before the kick-off, to a crowd of 59,848. I was one of them.

Sheer emotion carried United to a 3-0 win and all the way to Wembley - and defeat by Bolton. As Ann Taylor sombrely reflects in her chapter, it was hard for Bolton supporters to celebrate that win.

The rebuilding continued, as I say, for the League title in 1967 and the European Cup in 1968. Then the blank period, 26 years without a championship.

New enchantments

But then, in 1994, we had championships two years in succession.

One of the sad things about the 1994 achievement was that Sir Matt Busby did not live to see it. I often chatted to him after the game. He was never critical, always supportive and his presence was still a motivating force throughout the club. He was enchanted by the football that was being played by the current team, the development of young players like Ryan Giggs, the arrival of Cantona and the positive play of the whole team.

The 1994 World Cup reminded us that there is still much for British football to learn, not least the skill of the defensive players in teams like Italy and Brazil. I believe that we shall see that type of development at Old Trafford, as United gain experience in Europe. That experience includes, in the 1994-95 European Cup, a renewal of their acquaintance with Galatasary. The 1993 meeting in Istanbul brought me into the affairs of fellow-United fans in the behind-the-scenes diplomacy that Tom Pendry describes in the final chapter of this book.

It is, though, *as a fan* that I think of myself in relation to the postwar Manchester United. When one looks at the history of the club over this period, one is reminded of the saying of a national newspaper:

'All human life is here'.

The ups and downs are like the problems that we all face, the triumphs, the tragedies, the sweetness, the bitterness, the births, the deaths. I believe it is this sort of commitment that people have to their football club that reflects many facets of their own lives.

As I approach the ground on match day, I still get that tingle of expectation, of something around the corner which is going to be exciting and exhilarating. The match of course could be a disappointment, but there is always the next one to look forward to, always the next hill to climb.

Nothing is permanent and that particularly goes for success.

'Jim Baxter, one of the greatest defenders I've ever seen.'

'... the complete footballer. He had everything.'

NOTTINGHAM FOREST

KENNETH CLARKE (Conservative, Rushcliffe)

Having grown up 10 miles from Nottingham, his election, in 1970, for the Nottinghamshire constituency of Rushcliffe, brought him nearer to the City Ground.

After holding junior posts in the Heath Government, he shadowed Social Services and Industry in opposition. Then, from ministerial posts in Transport, Employment and Trade and Industry, he was Secretary of State, in turn, for Health, Education and the Home Department, before becoming Chancellor of the Exchequer in 1993.

6

FOREST FIRST AND FOREMOST

Kenneth Clarke

Most of my friends at school were Derby County fans and by rights I should have been a Derby fan too. As a child, I lived on the Derbyshire side of the Derby/Notts border, with Derby 10 miles away in one direction and Nottingham 10 miles away in the other.

In those early postwar seasons, Derby County were in the big time, a leading First Division side, one of the handful of clubs everyone knew and talked about. And even though they were in the Third Division (South), Notts County, too, had some star names.

County Records

So it was that, at the start of the 1947-48 season, Derby broke the transfer record by signing Billy Steel from Morton for £15,000. Notts County promptly capped it by bringing England's reigning centre-forward, Tommy Lawton, from Chelsea for £20,000, to play alongside the young Jackie Sewell.

Forest, amid all this, were down near the bottom of the Second Division. Yet I always supported Forest first and Notts County second. My father wasn't interested in football at all, but my grandfather used to take me in by bus, Forest one week, County the next. I think it was the name 'Forest' that made them my first team. They were also, as I say, in a higher division - just - though early in my spectating career, in 1948-49, Forest were relegated to Division III (South), which meant my first Nottingham derby.

The question of loyalty is perfectly easy. If Forest are playing County, I'll support Forest. If County are playing anyone else, I support County. Over the years I've probably grown less partisan, which is just as well because I don't just watch football in Nottingham. In any given year, I'd also like to see Leicester, Derby, Mansfield maybe, as well as some of the London clubs - though since becoming Chancellor I seem to have less time than in any other job I've done. In 1993-94, I saw just 10 matches - the lowest number since I was in short trousers. Among them were both the Nottingham derbies.

I had never believed for one moment the cliché that Forest were 'too good to go down' in 1993, but I was extremely relieved when we proved ourselves good enough to go back up again.

It's not that I can't cope with lower division football, mind you. If I'm doing weekend speeches or visits, I like to check what games are on nearby. A few years ago, I was up in the North West and managed to get in the first half of Stockport v Hartlepool, thanks to Labour MP, Peter Snape, who, as he reveals in his chapter below, was then a director at Edgeley Park. And, of course, I'm fairly used to watching the lower division stuff down the years, both at County and Forest. There was a time when both were in the old First Division, but for decades Nottingham was like Bristol, one of those towns that most people saw as second or third division when it came to soccer, incapable of getting clubs in the top flight.

I was at the game we won to get promoted to the First Division in 1957, a 4-0 win at Bramall Lane. That was our first taste of the top division, but even then I never imagined that we would go on to be one of the really big names in English football. Yet thanks to Brian Clough, that is exactly what we did. Clough has to be, quite simply, the best club manager since the war. He took two very ordinary Midlands clubs, first Derby and then Forest, and turned them into world beaters. To turn Nottingham Forest into a club that won the First Division championship and then the European Cup was a genuinely remarkable achievement. He would develop a side, take it to the limit of its potential, then break it up, bring in new blood and get even better.

He turned average players into good players. He took players other managers had found hard to control and made them tick. Like Bertie Auld, who went on to a great career with Celtic. And he took Viv Anderson, gangly and ungainly and not naturally skilful, and made him a great player. And look what happened to Des Walker after he left Forest. Lost without Brian.

The other amazing thing about Brian was the way he managed his own son, Nigel. Most people will find it hard to imagine how a father can manage a son or how a son can be managed by a father, but he did it. And Nigel is a nice, uncomplicated man who just thrived on being managed by Brian. I'm not saying he was perfect, though. I thought it was dreadful mistake to let Lee Chapman go. He may have looked our least skilful forward, but as soon as he'd gone, it was obvious that we lacked someone the other forwards could play off and come on to score goals.

As an outspoken Labour supporter, Brian's politics are pretty well removed from mine, so whenever we met, we tended to talk about football - not that either of us shirks a good debate. During the kerfuffle over Michael Heseltine's pit closures, Brian led a march past my surgery, which is a short walk from Forest's ground. At the time, Forest were heading for relegation and I threatened to lead a counter-march past the ground.

Brian Clough
'...simply the best.'

September 1947: £15,000   County records   November 1947: £20,000

Someone to Sing About

Being so well known, I get the occasional cat call thrown my way, but it is generally in good humour. I do, however, sit in the directors' box now, not out of status consciousness, but more because I can better guarantee that people won't come up and lobby me about something or other. When I go to a football match, I like to lose myself in it. I forget about politics and everything else besides. I like to get involved.

I always go to the Cup Final. Until a couple of years ago, I always went on the underground but my recognition factor has become a problem. We got absolutely jam-packed into a tube train and, although it wasn't nasty, it was a bit of a pain having a 20-minute journey with fans singing about you. Some of the songs were pretty good but it was a bit tedious nonetheless.

Yet I have never felt intimidated by crowds and I don't actually believe soccer violence was ever as bad as non-football followers sometimes imagined. I do not deny it was a problem and potentially still is, but the way some people talked, you'd visualise Saturday afternoon guaranteeing scenes of mayhem and bloodshed. I do remember occasions - particularly when I was living in Birmingham and going to St Andrews and Villa Park a lot - when violence was a real issue and one to which my children and I were occasionally too close for comfort. But, equally, you could go season on end without seeing a single incident to alarm you.

I was never involved in any discussions within Government about what to do about violence in the game. Mrs Thatcher ensured that Ministers who actually went to football had no say at all in developing the policies. I think she found it difficult to understand why anyone would want to go to a football match at all.

I wasn't keen on the ID scheme, which made us very unpopular, and I thought we handled the alcohol problem in a peculiar way, too. At one point, magistrates would grant a licence to some bars within the ground, but not those from where the pitch could be seen. This meant that any spectators could buy a drink - unless they were in the executive boxes. Executive boxes have never struck me as the best places from which to watch football, but nor do they seem to me to be centres of violence either.

It was clear, given the attention devoted to football safety and the public concerns, that something had to be done, but I think some of the things we did were unconvincing. When I first started going to football - back in the 1940s, as I say - the crowds were enormous. Even at Third Division County, you could get well over 30,000. It was so packed that if you arrived at all late, you'd be lifted down to the front with all the other small boys. Indeed, my first memory of football is of leaving the ground, very slowly, in the middle of a huge human mass shuffling its way out. Had there been lots of pushing or shoving, fighting or larking about, there would have been deaths every week. But behaviour was different, standards very different, and it didn't happen.

I never imagined that ID cards alone, or all-seater stadia alone, would deal with the problem. If people want to misbehave, they can misbehave in seats just as well as on the terraces. I remember the experience of Highfield Road, another ground I know well. When Coventry went all-seater, the hooligans started to hurl the seats about and they went back to terracing.

I was very pleased, at the 1992 election, that all the parties had agreed - as John Greenway explains in his chapter - that the two lower divisions would not be forced to meet the demands of the Taylor Report. I will concede to Lord Justice Taylor that we are now having built splendid stadia that might not otherwise have been built. But I do not think they have made one jot of difference to crowd safety. The report has also cost clubs huge sums of money and several of them have only just survived.

I don't believe violence has ebbed because of the various reports and legislation. I think it is more that gang violence, and football's role in it, went out of fashion. That is not to decry the special role the police have played in keeping rival supporters apart or the effect of closed circuit TV inside the grounds.

We have always been fairly lucky at Forest. The fans have always had a good record. I'm sure that was partly because the team played good clean football, too. In 20 years, we didn't have a player sent off. The only real trouble, at the height of hooliganism, was with visiting fans. I remember the police being totally unprepared for this. They resisted segregation because they thought it meant putting all the trouble-makers together. They resisted CCTV because they were worried it could not be used as evidence. And they resisted fencing because it stopped them getting in to arrest people. It took about two seasons for them to sort it out and they now have an excellent arrangement.

Police costs are a big problem, however. I've had people complain to me that when they're playing obscure friendlies, or a game in the Autoglass Trophy or somesuch, the costs of the police can exceed the gate. I was at Filbert Street when Leicester tried out their own trained security staff for the first time, and that seems to be working well all around the country now. You must have sophisticated crowd control, but in the end you must have the discipline of the crowd, too.

I'm one of the lucky ones who represents a seat which is home to my club. The suggestion that some MPs go to football matches because they think there are votes in it is aired in the introduction to this book. Such MPs are wasting their time. It's the kind of nonsense you might hear from people who don't know what they're talking about. But voters aren't stupid. Why should they imagine that just because an MP shares an interest - or pretends to - that he or she is any good as an MP? If there are MPs who go to a match just to be seen, but who don't actually enjoy it, I strongly advise them to give it up.

For my part, as I say, I get very engrossed in the game. I get worked up. My idea of relaxing is not to do nothing. It is to get involved in something. It has to be intense, whether it's watching football or cricket - or bird-watching for that matter.

I get much more involved in club football than internationals. The worst game I ever saw was probably the World Cup qualifier, in 1993, between England and San Marino at Wembley. It was a total farce. Six-nil, ten blokes standing around the area just trying to stand in the way. I can't get switched on to internationals in the way I can with League and Cup football. If I was running a club, I would be club before country every time. I wouldn't release my players to play some silly friendly, or take on San Marino and risk a broken leg.

Not that I could ever have been a football manager, as I was never very good at spotting talent. I saw the young Gary Lineker play for Leicester a few times and I'd have had him down as a reasonable Second Division centre forward. I was wrong.

Spotted Youths

The two exceptions to my talent-spotting failure were Trevor Francis and Laurie Cunningham, at Birmingham and West Brom respectively. They were brilliant. Francis was in a class of his own. The last time I saw him play he was player-manager at QPR and he scored a hat-trick. Here he was, a relatively old man in footballing terms, as brilliant as when I first saw him as a teenager.

The game has changed out of all recognition and in many ways for the better. Money is a bit of a problem and I didn't like the way the Premiership was started to stop money being shared at all levels of the game, but you can't have too many hang-ups about the game's commercialisation. It is a business.

I like the competitiveness of sport. I like the speed. When I played as a schoolboy, you had a big leather ball, big boots, great big shin pads. On wet days it was sometimes difficult to kick the ball from one end of the mudbath into the other. The game today is horrendously fast. The top players are athletes. Their technical skills are genuinely impressive. Sometimes it is too fast, too furious, and the skills don't match. But when it's good, there is nothing like it.

When it's really good, you realise why Jack Dunnett, former Labour MP and former chairman of Notts County, became the first person to leave politics to spend more time with his football.

71

NORWICH CITY

MICHAEL CARTTISS (Conservative, Great Yarmouth)

A teacher (1961-69), first in London and then at his former school in Great Yarmouth. Agent for the Great Yarmouth constituency (1969-82), he became its MP in 1983.

A Great Yarmouth councillor (1973-83; Conservative Leader, 1980-82), Norfolk County councillor (1966-85; Education Chairman, 1982) and member of East Anglian Health Authority (1982-85).

7

PLENTY TO SING ABOUT WITH THE CANARIES

Michael Carttiss

'What are you doing here?', several people bedecked in yellow and green called to me as we queued outside the Hillsborough ground, 'shouldn't you be electioneering in Yarmouth?'

'That's in the bag! I hope I can be as confident about Norwich winning today', I replied.

It was 5 April 1992, the Sunday before the General Election. We were in Sheffield for the FA Cup semi-final against Sunderland. Without taking too much for granted at the time, I had no doubts then about John Major's victory, nor that I would be re-elected MP for Gt. Yarmouth. Being at Sheffield to cheer the Canaries on to the Cup Final had to be a priority that particular afternoon. In any case the Conservatives in Great Yarmouth don't canvass on a Sunday.

Although we had defeated Sunderland in the Milk Cup at Wembley in 1985, they were a tough Second Division side, sure to provide Norwich with sterner opposition on the football field than John Major was facing at the hustings.

Once inside the ground, I found myself seated, by some administrative error, amongst a sea of red-and-white scarves, but there was a tradition of good-natured friendship, going back to that Milk Cup meeting seven years before, between Norwich fans and our northern rivals. Even if I had not been surrounded by them, I had no problem in admitting that Sunderland deserved their victory that Sunday afternoon.

Memories are made of bliss

Football memories, like all memories, can taunt and tease as so often they lead us to misrepresent the present as they glorify the past. The football seasons in which we live now have everything in them: fears of relegation, magnificent moments, missed opportunities and everything that is good and bad. We tend to look back, though, through 'rose coloured spectacles'. The worst moments we have lived through with our respective clubs seem to disappear into the shadows and warmth of those old standing terraces.

My first visit to Carrow Road, as far as I can remember, was when I was about 10 or 11 years old. An uncle took me to see a Third Division (South) match, maybe three years after the Second World War. I have always been proud of my birth place, the fine City of Norwich, so it was natural for me to be a Canaries fan. Though born in Theatre Street within sight of City Hall, from early infancy my home has been at Filby, the village where my mother and our forebears were born and bred.

Norfolk is a superb County. It has the premier seaside resort of Great Yarmouth with its port and offshore gas industry; ancient market towns, charming villages and our unique Broads. For football supporters in Norfolk, the fortunes of the Canaries will play an important part in your life, even for those whose allegiance lies with the 'big clubs'. Norwich City Football Club is the sole standard bearer of the league football flag in a large and disparate County. I have found the events at Carrow Road to be a major unifying factor, whether in the home, office, factory, shop, boathouse or farm.

That was certainly the case in January 1950, when the Canaries, still in Division III (South), met Portsmouth in the Third Round of the FA Cup. Pompey were then at their peak - First Division Champions and on their way to a second successive title. Norwich held them to a 1-1 draw at Fratton Park, but went down 2-0 in the replay at Carrow Road, watched by a record crowd of 43,129.

That huge crowd was controlled by a handful of police officers and stewards; only a fraction of the number deployed in the recent past for crowds much less than half that number. The atmosphere on those big occasions could only be described as electric and only rarely was there any crowd trouble. It did not matter that there were precious few seats and very little cover, for these deficiencies were made up for by the warmth, togetherness and comradeship of being packed together with a common purpose, or am I putting on my 'rose coloured' spectacles

74

again?

I don't think so, though perhaps I am forgetting the lack of acceptable toilet facilities and little opportunity to buy even a cup of tea in those days. It was during my early days of watching the Canaries that the post-war soccer boom reached its peak. As previous chapters testify, there was plenty to get romantic about in the late 1940s and early 1950s. Attendances of 25,000 to 30,000 and beyond were commonplace at Carrow Road, for Third Division football.

A complete cottage industry had grown up around Carrow Road as thousands of bicycles were stored in gardens, yards and sheds as supporters made their way to the ground. Hundreds of others were stacked and unlocked in piles at locations around the ground with an almost cast iron guarantee that they would be there after the match.

Winners of the 'Friendly Final' 1985
Back row *(l-to-r)*: Donowa, Bruce, Woods, Watson, Deehan, Devine.
Front row *(l-to-r)*: Barham, Mendham, Haylock,
Channon, Van Wyk, Hartford

Away Days

National service in the Royal Air Force took me away from home in 1956 and, after that, apart from a brief period as a student teacher back in Gt. Yarmouth, the early sixties found me enjoying life in London, a 'Mecca' for so many of my generation brought up in the provinces. As a student at Goldsmiths' College, I had 'digs' in New Cross where the local team was Millwall - quite a colourful bunch of eastenders they were!

Later I was teaching in Waltham Cross, not far from the Tottenham Hotspur training ground. Many of the pupils, parents and staff there were Spurs fans. They were then a very successful, glamour side. While I was not tempted to transfer loyalty from the Canaries, Tottenham, of all the London clubs, has a special place in my football memories.

My time away from Norfolk coincided with one of the most difficult periods experienced at Carrow Road. It was during the 1956-57 season that it became clear all was not well. The attendances of the post-war boom years had tailed off, although, even in that season when Norwich finished last and had to seek re-election, the average home gate of almost 13,000 was the fourth highest in the division. Perhaps more remarkably they even had the fourth highest 'away' gate.

As their season fell apart, it emerged that the club was unable to find the cash to pay the weekly wages bill of £500. The Norfolk News Company (now Eastern Counties Newspapers Ltd) stepped into the breach and helped the club with the money to carry on. It was clear, however, that the Canaries were in deep crisis and a fight was on for their very existence.

Ironically, the installation of a new set of floodlights costing £9,000 helped plunge them into financial darkness. Liabilities totalled £20,000 on top of an annual loss running at £10,000 (This is the club that sold a player, in 1994, for the record sum of £5,000,000). Several prominent businessmen, under the chairmanship of the Lord Mayor of Norwich, Alderman (now Sir) Arthur South, formed an appeal committee and a new Board under the chairmanship of Geoffrey Watling was elected. The task was enormous, and to add to the financial problems, City finished bottom of the league and were forced to seek re-election. Supporters rallied to the cause and, by the end of the season, nearly all the appeal money had been raised and a new manager appointed.

If we Canaries supporters expected recovery to be slow, how wrong we were! One of the greatest periods in the club's history was about to unfold as the team finished eighth in the Third Division (South) in 1957-58, and thus secured a place for the following season in the newly formed Third Division, when the regional split in the bottom half of the Football League was ended with the creation of fourth and third divisions.

The 1958-59 season started quietly enough. With City winning just six of the first 19 games, there was no indication of the drama and sensation to come. For Norwich were to miss promotion to the Second Division by a 'whisker' and stand on the threshold, in the FA Cup, of becoming the first Third Division side to get to Wembley - in the days when playing at Wembley meant your club were Cup Finalists at last. On the Cup trail they were to beat mighty Manchester United (managed by the late, great Sir Matt Busby) at Carrow Road before a crowd of 38,000, and then dispose of Tottenham Hotspur and Sheffield United before losing to Luton Town in a semi-final replay at St Andrew's.

No-one will ever know exactly how many City supporters turned out for that Cup run, but more than 105,000 watched the two matches against Tottenham. This still well-remembered soccer success for Norwich coincided with my year as a student teacher at the Greenacre Secondary School in Gt. Yarmouth. Cup fever gripped Norfolk in 1959 and, for me, it remains one of the highspots in the club's history.

The quality of football which had been the hallmark of the cup run was carried over into the 1959-60 season. On 27 April 1960, Norwich clinched promotion to the Second Division when they beat Southend United at Carrow Road. The cup run and promotion in successive seasons were fitting rewards for a club and its supporters which three years previously had been on the edge of bankruptcy and at the foot of the Third Division (South).

Home Draw

In 1964, I returned to teach at the school where I had once been a pupil in Gt. Yarmouth - the Technical High School - renewing my relationship with Carrow Road. The motor car and motor coach were much more in evidence and the number of cycles had considerably decreased. The attendances were somewhat down but Carrow Road remained a social, warm and friendly place to be.

No account of Norwich's footballing fortunes could possibly omit Ron Saunders who joined the club in 1969 as Manager. In the 1960s, the Canaries had provided only average Second Division football. It required someone with the capabilities and qualities to go the extra mile. Saunders was a strict disciplinarian and what the players lacked in skill they made up in fitness. He was unyielding but never asked more than he was prepared to give himself. Slowly and surely he stamped his authority on the team and, although unpopular in many quarters, he was to take the City to two notable firsts.

In the 1971-72 season the Canaries clinched a place in the First Division amid unforgettable scenes at Leyton Orient's Brisbane Road ground. The next season Ron Saunders led the Canaries onto the Wembley turf at long last for the League Cup Final. The Final was a disappointment. Spurs were the deserved winners - much to the satisfaction of my old friends, and ex-pupils at Waltham Cross!

Unswerving in his devotion to the club since 1957, Geoffrey Watling handed over the chairmanship in 1973, to Arthur South, a dominant figure in Norwich politics. The reorganisation of local government in 1973 saw Mr South, as he was then, in two new roles: as Norwich FC Chairman and as the Labour Opposition Leader on the new Norfolk County Council. I had been on the old County Council and was elected to the new authority for the whole of Norfolk, becoming the Council deputy leader. Arthur and I also served together on the newly-created Norfolk Area Health Authority, of which he became Chairman. Despite very different political convictions, he and I became friends, not least because of the conviction we shared in Norwich City's destiny for greater achievements in the football world.

Unfortunately the profile on the terraces was changing as hooliganism and violence became the order of the day at many a game. The friendly rivalry which had previously existed was changing as many young thugs were more concerned with what was happening off the pitch than on it. While there was undoubtedly a number of reasons for this behaviour it was clear that the pitiful facilities and conditions at most grounds did not help the situation.

It seems to me that those who controlled the game at national and club level then made the mistake of over-reacting by erecting huge fences, caging supporters in, and employing armies of police officers to keep two groups of supporters apart. The comment that this exacerbated the situation may come from the benefit of hindsight, but what is not hindsight, as far as I am concerned, is that the Football Spectators Bill was no answer to that problem. I opposed it from the outset.

The idea that no-one could get into a football ground without an electronic membership card to activate a turnstile was obviously absurd. When that legislation was being debated in Parliament, I did not need to test the various devices different manufacturers brought to a House of Commons committee room to realise the whole membership scheme was quite unworkable. I never understood then, nor now for that matter, why the Rt. Hon. Margaret Thatcher, as Prime Minister, committed herself personally and so adamantly to that policy. Whatever my esteemed leader at that time knew about international affairs, and running the country so successfully, she clearly knew nothing about football grounds. I said at the time that such an intelligent person as Mrs T. could surely work out for herself that the whole idea was doomed to failure. Lord Justice Taylor's report on the Hillsborough disaster consigned that ridiculous scheme to the wastepaper basket, fortunately!

While most of the time Carrow Road escaped the disorder problems experienced elsewhere, segregation and searching of many supporters became the order of the day. Although hooliganism clearly had an effect on overall attendances, Carrow Road remained the place for me to be on match days. With one of the best playing surfaces in the country, Carrow Road was now graced by the best teams in the country. Although in truth the City found the going difficult, our position in the top flight - apart from two spells in 1974-75 and 1985-86 in the old Second Division - demonstrated the steady progress that had been made over my years as a supporter.

On 24 March 1985, some 40,000 supporters travelled to Wembley for the final of the Milk Cup against Sunderland. That final became known as the 'friendly final'. Before the kick-off a 60-a-side soccer match between rival supporters took place in the car park. The fans also mixed freely outside and inside the stadium, as I recalled at the beginning of this chapter. It was a hopeful sign that the hooliganism and disorder problems that had dogged England at club and national level could be turned round.

Norwich won the match by the only goal but, together with other English qualifiers, the club found itself excluded from European competition after the dreadful events of 29 May 1985 at Heysel Stadium. It was a cruel twist of fate that, after all their efforts, Norwich were deprived of a place in the UEFA Cup competition.

The Football Business

In the autumn of 1985 problems associated with building a new City Stand, to replace the one that had burned to the ground in 1984, led to the resignation of the board. When a new board was elected Robert Chase was appointed Chairman. In recognition of the contribution they had made over the years, Geoffrey Watling was appointed Life President and Sir Arthur South, Honorary Senior Vice-President.

By then, the constituency where I and my family have always lived and worked had sent me to Westminster as MP for Great Yarmouth. Being at Carrow Road, in touch with events on and off the pitch, on a Saturday has been an important relaxation from the world of politics.

For me, going to a football match is about being one of the crowd, and not on 'centre stage', as is usually the case for a politician in his or her constituency. Unkind observers might add that shouting at the referee on a Saturday afternoon makes a change from shouting at the Labour Party on the Commons green benches during the week. As the Chief Whip in Michael Dobbs's *House of Cards*, Francis Urquhart, says, 'You might say that, but I could not possibly comment'.

I mention watching football on Saturday afternoons, but now we have league games, as well as the additional fixtures, Sunday afternoons,

Monday evenings, Wednesday nights, etc. Mainly because of Sky TV. I realise football has to attract financial support, and those famous 'market forces' dictate that TV coverage goes to the highest bidder. Watching the top English clubs on TV is now confined to the minority, and the FA deal with Sky TV is not good news for hundreds of thousands of youngsters, whose families cannot afford, or won't abide, the dreaded dish stuck on the side of their house. It may bring in money for football, but what will be the long-term outcome for those thousands of young fans?

The contemporary youngster is becoming more familiar with the celebrities in Italian football by courtesy of Channel 4, than with our home grown stars. TV seems to have brought us 'The Premiership', a ridiculous name for the top division, upon which Roy Hattersley has adversely commented elsewhere in this book. Who on earth thought that one up? Was it the same 'spin doctor' who invented green shirts for premier league referees? Referees now have the look of one of the reserve team who has strolled into the first team game by mistake, rather than the authoritative image that the traditional black kit gives even the poorest referee, and without the pyjama blue and white edging that Endsleigh League officials have now.

'Mike Walker had taken them within touching distance of the highest pinnacle in league football...'

'Is Robert Chase, the Canaries' controversial Chairman, the man to take them further?'

Back to Norwich! Where does the club go from here? Is Robert Chase, the Canaries' controversial Chairman, the man to take them further? If the past eight years are a benchmark, then there will be no shortage of either controversy or success for Robert Chase.

He has been supporting Norwich City ever since he was seven years old. As he progressed from an apprentice bricklayer to a businessman in his own right, that support became tangible in the shape of sponsorship for the Youth Team. Since he was elected Chairman he has not missed a game at home or away. Coming from the next village to mine, Robert Chase's family have for generations had their roots firmly embedded in the Norfolk soil, and he and I have been friends for a long time. His success at Carrow Road, not without its controversial aspects, has been no surprise to me.

Mr Chase has never made any secret that his most important objective was to put the club on a sound financial footing: he recalls his first task was to pay the club telephone bill himself, so that he could use the phone on becoming chairman. Now the club's finances are amongst the most stable in the Premiership.

A second objective was to improve the facilities at the ground for supporters and he will justifiably show you a stadium which of its type and size is second to none in the country. He recognises the job is not finished, but is particularly proud of the new Stand for the Disabled completed in 1988 in which up to 115 disabled supporters are accommodated free of charge in completely weather-proof surroundings.

Robert Chase had the vision to anticipate the Taylor Report and Carrow Road became one of the first all-seater stadia in the country. Though this was not welcomed by every supporter, by acting swiftly, he was able to maximise grants from the Football Trust and save the club thousands of pounds. The pitch was re-laid, complete with a modern drainage system and undersoil heating. Crowd management and safety at Carrow Road has also been a high priority under the Chase regime.

Building a stadium with first class facilities, and actively encouraging family groups back to the game, is only part of the Chairman's strategy.

The Community Department at the club, which is operated in conjunction with the Norfolk FA, reaches out into the schools and youth clubs of the County involving the youngest members in all that is best about football.

In the season Robert Chase became Chairman, Norwich returned to the then First Division. Over the next six seasons they finished three times in the top five before becoming a Premier club in 1992. The Canaries have battled through to two FA Cup semi-finals and performed in three unforgettable UEFA Cup ties in Europe in the same period.

It has been well remarked by a season ticket holder, Mr W Bayliss of Redgrave, writing, in July 1994, to our local newspaper, that

> *'football today is no longer a sport but a business, and I congratulate Robert Chase on the way he has turned the club round and if the club can continue as it has then I shall be pleased to support them and hope the Chairman is there for many more seasons. Well done Mr Chase, and your team ...'*

Well done, indeed!

Into Europe

'Well done' has to be the understated verdict too on Norwich's entry into European football in the 1993-94 season.

Mike Walker had taken a team built and fashioned by his predecessor, Dave Stringer, and coached and encouraged them to within touching distance of the highest pinnacle in league football. For most of the 1992-93 season they led the Division but faded in the last four matches and had, seemingly, lost any chance of playing in Europe. Fate this time, in contrast with 1985, was on the club's side as ex-Canary Andy Linighan's late FA Cup Final replay header past ex-Canary, Chris Woods, of Sheffield Wednesday, gave Arsenal the cup 'double', thus ensuring that Norwich would be in the EUFA cup draw for 1993-94.

The team's six games in their first season of European football will have an especial place in the annals of the club. The 'throwing to the

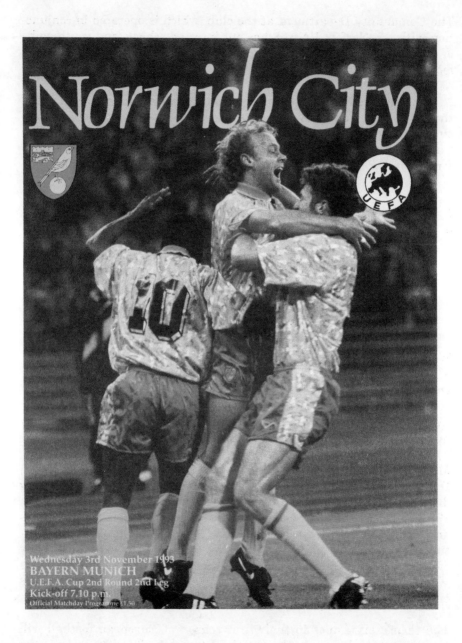

Norwich City

Wednesday 3rd November 1993
BAYERN MUNICH
U.E.F.A. Cup 2nd Round 2nd Leg
Kick-off 7.10 p.m.
Official Matchday Programme £1.50

lions' which was widely forecast never looked like happening. In all six matches the team offered a marvellous mixture of flair, flexibility, intelligence and passing skills and demonstrated to Europe that British footballers could still play the game the way it was meant to be played.

Off the pitch the quite unbelievably well-behaved Norwich supporters were redressing much of the balance relating to football hooliganism, and it is a testimony to each and everyone of them that they did much to restore the pride of English football supporters.

The dream of European honours for Norwich ended in that mighty San Siro Stadium, but the club, from a County more famous for dumplings and turkeys, had proved they were a match for any team.

'On the ball, City!'

'...their first season of European football will have an especial place in the annals of the club. Norwich proved they were a match for any team.'

The programme cover (*opposite*) for the UEFA Cup, Second Round, second leg v. Bayern Munich shows Jeremy Goss celebrating his goal in Norwich City's 2-1 win in the first leg in the Olympic Stadium in Munich. A 1-1 draw at Carrow Road earned City a Third Round tie against Inter Milan when *'the dream ended in that mighty San Siro Stadium'.*

STOCKPORT COUNTY

PETER SNAPE (Labour, West Bromwich East)

A former railwayman and regular soldier, he was a regular footballer during his six years in the army. After becoming the Member for West Bromwich East in February 1974, he trundled up and down both wings for five seasons with the Westminster Wobblers.

Despite many years of hospitality from West Bromwich Albion FC, he has remained faithful to his home-town club, Stockport County, where, since the mid-1970s, he has been a fund raiser, director and Vice-President.

Re-elected five times, despite embarrassing scorelines such as Stockport 5 West Brom 1 (February 1993).

8

ON EDGELEY

Peter Snape

It was grim post-war 1948. Ration books and fuel shortages. At 5 o'clock on Saturday afternoon the familiar introduction to *Sports Report*. Eventually, in the League Division III (North),

Stockport County 1 Gateshead 2

'Your father won't be very pleased, will he?'

Within a few minutes, the crash of the back gate and in he came with a face like thunder. Tactlessly I asked

'Can I come next week, dad?'
'I'm not going again and nor will you either'.

But he did and I did. In his case for over 50 years, almost literally to the day he died. For, 24 hours earlier, he saw Stockport County beat Scunthorpe 3-0 in a First Round FA Cup tie in 1977. In my case as supporter, Director and Vice-President. Anybody can support the likes of Manchester United or Arsenal - but Stockport County?

Joining the County Set

The first game to really stick in my memory was one which at the last minute I was not allowed to go and see. It was Stockport v. Liverpool in the Fifth Round of the FA Cup in 1950. To avoid the crush of a record crowd, I was sent reluctantly to the long-gone Curzon cinema in nearby Turncroft Lane. Although it was two miles or so from Edgeley Park I still clearly remember hearing the roar from the near 28,000 crowd as Alec Herd opened the scoring for the County.

Liverpool, who won that game 2-1, feature strongly in the cup memories of County fans. We held them 1-1 at Anfield in the FA Cup Fourth Round in 1965, before going out 2-0 at home. And, in 1985-86, when Liverpool had just won the League Cup four seasons running, we met them in the two-legged Second Round, drawing 0-0 at Edgeley Park, then losing the away leg 2-0. I made sure that I was there on all those occasions.

My first involvement, other than as a spectator, came in the early 1950s, when my father was a Collector for the Supporters' Association Pool. I remember the two of us walking through the terraced and cobbled streets of Portwood to 'pay-in' at the Association's offices near the old Tiviot Dale Station. Alas, successful as it was for a time, the Association eventually collapsed in some acrimony after a dispute between its members and the Board of Directors about how the cash raised should be spent.

In these days of near universal car ownership, it seems strange to recount that in those days it was possible to see both players and bowler-hatted directors travelling on one of the fleet of special buses which ran from the town centre to the ground on match days. I remember finding myself sitting behind centre-forward, Bill Holden, shortly before he scored a brilliant solo goal in a 3-0 cup defeat of First Division Luton Town in 1958.

In the late 1950s, as railway workers, both my father and myself were eligible for reduced-rate staff tickets which we used to follow the club around the country. We were, I suspect, better travellers then the players were, given the number of times we returned empty-handed from lost soccer outposts such as Workington and Barrow. It was especially agonising for me in my signalling days at the two Edgeley Junction signal boxes behind the ground. From the No. 1 box I could see only half the pitch (invariably the wrong half), while Edgeley No. 2 was immediately beind the pie stall and, although I could hear the roars, I could not see any of the action. Usually, however, my mate would take pity on me and enable me to slip over the fence by the Labour Club so I could catch the last 15 minutes or so.

The club pioneered Friday night football in the early 1960s and my signal boxes were regularly adorned with stickers declaring *Friday night,*

'The first game to really stick in my memory...'
Joe Scarborough's evocation of that memory includes the signal box *(left)*, which was later to provide Peter Snape with an 'especially agonising' view of Stockport County.

County night, much to the occasional annoyance of visiting top brass. It was about that time that I unofficially closed a nearby branch signal box for a couple of hours one Saturday afternoon to watch a cup-tie. It was with a mounting sense of horror that I realised that one of my supervisors was standing very close to me in the crowd. Fortunately, he chose not to see me and my colleagues both covered up for me and kept the trains moving.

Into the Board Room

Following my election to Parliament in 1974, I was regularly invited into the Board Room - much to the delight of my father when he accompanied me. After all, the drinks in there were free. A change of Chairman brought in local man, Freddie Pye, and he asked me, together with Director, Andrew Barlow, if we would help with the formation and running of a new fund-raising organisation which we named the 'County Bounty'. My first task was to sit in his office with a copy of the local *Yellow Pages,* attempting to drum up some financial support and sponsorship from understandably reluctant local firms. As we had sought re-election to Division IV twice in the previous three seasons, many of the calls I made were brief, succinct and to the point.

I had no luck with the local council, either. None of the three political groups was very interested in the club or its fortunes. I once drove up from London to meet representatives of the council, to find that only one had actually turned up. Frustrating indeed when one sees what councils like Swansea and Lewisham have done for their clubs. One councillor once wrote me a fairly indignant letter after I had commented, on a local radio station, that the town's fame rested either on Stockport County or the London and North Western Railway's floodlit viaduct. The council has never recognised that the team's result on the BBC World Service was and is one of the few mentions Stockport gets world-wide. Hopefully, a new Chief Executive will prove to be more anxious to make and retain contact.

Stockport's newspapers and the locally-based radio station, Signal, have always been much more supportive. In my younger days, Bert Stewart and Len Noad, in the *Express*, and Tom Turton, in the *Advertiser*, gave detailed and exciting match reports. Over the years the club has had more struggles than rejoicing to report.

After we had finished 92nd in 1965, Manager Jimmy Meadows, with a side including stalwarts like Matt Woods and Eddie Stuart as well as prolific goal scorer Jim Fryatt, took us to the Fourth Division Championship within two years. The first trophy the club had won since 1936 and the last we were to win for nearly 30 years.

Yet nothing ever truly disillusioned Stockport's faithful hardcore supporters and I have met County fans all over this country and occasionally in some surprising parts of the world. Around 1977, for example, while being conducted, along with the British Ambassador, around the Tokyo Trade Fair, I was delighted to be greeted by an exhibitor who asked me 'Didn't I see you at Edgeley Park last Friday?'

Come 1982, the then Secretary rang me to ask if I would like to join the

Board. For me this really was a dream come true. I knew that my father, if he had still been alive, would have been as proud of me as a Director of his football club as he had been when I had first been elected to Parliament. My first task was to prevent the Inland Revenue putting us into the bankruptcy court. I wrote numerous letters and took a trip to their headquarters in Hastings. It took a face-to-face meeting with the late Nicholas Ridley, the then Treasury Minister, to save us on that occasion. It was the prelude to some years of acrimony for the club.

Manager Eric Webster regularly worked miracles, plucking talent from obscurity only to see good players sold on cheaply at the first opportunity. He signed Mick Quinn on a free transfer from Wigan and had to sell him within 18 months to Oldham. Quinn's successor, John Kerr, was virtually given away and then Mark Leonard was quickly sold for next to nothing. Board Room rows about the club's policies or lack of them eventually led to a special Board Meeting in 1986. I had been asked by the Sports Editor of the *Stockport Express*, in a call to the House of Commons, about the impending transfer of yet another of our players. I had said straight out that 'as usual, I had been told nothing about it'. This provided Vice-Chairman, Dragan Lukic, with the excuse he sought to get rid of me. I was thrown off the Board and told that I was 'not welcome on the ground'.

About Mr Lukic I will say only that knowing him for around 20 years gave me great insight into the everlasting hatreds in the Balkans. But while they could keep me out of the Board Room, they could not stop me from standing again on the terraces and they did not.

The famous Wolves were at that time languishing in the Fourth Division and, determined to give a literally two-finger salute to some of those who had wielded the axe, I hired a box at Molineux to watch the County game. Alas, never was money more ill-spent: the ground was falling apart and thick fog rendered the view of play impossible. Dragan Lukic, the director I was most anxious to harangue, did not turn up and the club had no licence to sell alcohol. After we'd heard a faint cheer, word came back that the great Frank Worthington had opened the scoring for us, which at least lifted the gloom somewhat. A combination of near beer and non-alcoholic wine proved to be less than a boost to the celebration of the 1-1 draw.

Down - but not out

Starting with the 1986-87 season, the tradition of applying for re-election was replaced by the automatic relegation, to the Vauxhall Conference, of the League's bottom team. That season opened disastrously. It looked as though Stockport would be the first club to drop out in this way. Over 100 years of history were about to come to an end. The 180 miles round-trip from my home south of Birmingham, to watch 'up-and-under' football on a pitch resembling a badly-ploughed field, became less of a pleasure week by week. However, we survived and the 1990s have brought a real upturn both in the club's fortunes and in my own involvement.

In 1989 the new Chairman, Brendan Elwood, invited me to become a Vice-President. Under his stewardship and with talented Manager, Danny Bergara, we escaped from the old Fourth Division as runners-up in 1991.

Even better was to come when, in 1992, we went twice within seven days to Wembley, sadly to lose to both Stoke City in the Autoglass Final and to Peterborough in the play-offs. It was nevertheless a wonderful moment for all 18,000 or so of us who were present when Danny led the team onto that famous pitch. Stockport County at Wembley - who would have believed it?

Certainly not Bert Millichip, the Chairman of my constituency team - West Bromwich Albion, the famous 'Baggies'. The Albion Board always made me welcome although there was initially some leg-pulling about my affection for a team few expected to see. When I became an MP in 1974, Stockport were a few seasons into what was to become a 21-year stint in Division IV. The Baggies had just started a brief spell in the old Second Division, but they were back in the top flight from 1976-86, flying high with three seasons in Europe.

Bert Millichip once asked me, during one of their successful cup runs, whether I was coming to Wembley if they made it to the final. Jokingly, I replied that I would only go to Wembley to watch 'the County'. Much amusement all round, although none of us knew then

'... a well-written, punchy publication which I have to conceal
about my person while in the Board Room'.

that Stockport would get there before the 'Baggies' did.

The 1991-92 season found both teams in the same division. A week before the General Election, they met at Edgeley Park. My constituency agent, an Albion loyalist, came with me and sat fuming in the 'Home' directors' box as Stockport won 3-0. For once I declined to comment to the Sandwell office of the *Express and Star*. Worse was to come for Baggies' fans as Stockport won 5-1 the following season. I thought that I might have to keep away from the Hawthorns for a little while but the welcome remained just as warm - although I didn't rub it in. It was a pleasure, however, to follow West Brom to Wembley for the 1993 play-off final. For me, it meant two trips to Wembley - as in 1992. The week before, I had seen Stockport lose in the Autoglass Final - an occasion recalled, in some detail, in Joan Walley's chapter on their conquerors, Port Vale.

It was also, of course, Vale's turn to come straight back to Wembley for a second final. It was good to see Albion beat them and secure promotion to Division I. I look forward to slipping surreptitiously into their ground again once we eventually get ourselves promoted, hopefully this season.

We should have made it in 1994, but again lost in the play-off final at Wembley - this time to old foes, Burnley. Rough-house tactics and pathetic refereeing did for us. Given Burnley's histrionics, County fans can be forgiven for wondering whether the team choreography had been directed by Lionel Blair. However, we have been there, we know our way there and we intend to be back there again.

Fans, fanzines and ruffled feathers

The creation of the sort of atmosphere that brings back and retains support has certainly been helped by the fans' having such a professionally-produced fanzine. The *Tea Party* is a well-written, punchy publication which I have occasionally to 'conceal about my person' while in the Board Room. It is sometimes critical of the directors' decisions, although a spell on a Football Club Board would provide a salutary and frustrating lesson in economics. Critics and carpers should consider that. Compared with some of their predecessors, Brendan Elwood and his colleagues have worked wonders at Edgeley Park, a feat not always recognised in the *Tea Party* pages.

It has been a memorable near half century now for me. Watching Jack Connor scoring five goals twice, winning a local newspaper competition when aged 13 for picking Stockport County's best post-war team, seeing us lead 2-1 against Manchester United at Old Trafford in a League Cup game. Laughing at Bradford City's goalkeeper kicking his own cap into the net in sheer frustration after Len White's third goal in a 7-1 massacre at Valley Parade.

What memories! And, hopefully, plenty more yet to come.

LLANELLI, SWANSEA CITY and LIVERPOOL

MICHAEL HOWARD (Conservative, Folkestone and Hythe)

Llanelli born and bred, he became a barrister, a fan of football and baseball (New York Mets) and a Conservative candidate in Liverpool (Edge Hill, 1966 and 1970).

Elected to parliament in 1983, he held various ministerial posts, before becoming Secretary of State for Employment (1990-92), Environment (1992-93) and then for the Home Department.

9

THREE INTO ONE CAN GO

Michael Howard

Doubtless the majority of football followers believe that REAL supporters could only ever support one team. ·Confronting that view in his chapter below, David Evans plausibly defends his position, shared by a few other contributors to this book, as a supporter of two teams.

My defence needs to go one better: I consider myself to be a real and passionate supporter of *three* teams: Llanelli, Swansea and Liverpool.

Other than on the rare occasions when they have met, I have never faced any difficulty arising from split loyalties. And when they have met, I have always found it easy to know which team I was supporting. When Llanelli met Swansea in the Welsh Cup, I supported Llanelli. When Swansea met Liverpool in a First Division game, I supported Swansea.

Shanks for the Memory

The first such Liverpool v Swansea encounter took place at Anfield on 3 October 1981. It was a memorable occasion in that it was Liverpool's first game following the death of Bill Shankly. That was the finest Swansea side I had ever seen, composed largely of ex-Liverpool players drawn there by manager John Toshack. They included Ian Callaghan, Phil Boersma, Tommy Smith and Ray Kennedy. During the minute's silence, Toshack removed his track suit top to reveal a No. 10 Liverpool shirt. At the time, many saw it as a bid for the manager's job, a gesture in the worst possible taste. I have always liked Toshack and I still believe it was a genuine show of respect and affection for the greatest club manager that ever lived.

I suppose if Swansea had established themselves in the top flight, split loyalties might have posed more of a problem, but sadly, they never did. If you are brought up near a less successful league team and you hanker after a big club that has prospects, you can quite easily support two teams. My third team, Llanelli, was the one I watched most as a child. The ground, Stebon Heath, was quite close to where I lived, and my father would take me there on a Saturday. It was exciting if sometimes lacking in skill, though we did have the pleasure, in the 1950-51 season, of seeing the great Jock Stein as our centre half. To this day, I can use that piece of information as a conversation stopper. Fellow-enthusiasts of Welsh non-league football - like Alex Carlile writing below - may be expected to revel in this piece of history, but not a lot of people know that Jock Stein played for Llanelli.

Coming from South Wales, I should by rights have been a rugby follower. I was educated at Llanelli Grammar School, which was seen by many as the rugby king of Welsh schools, but I always preferred soccer. I was almost kicked out of school in the mid-to-late fifties, when I organised a soccer team. The game simply wasn't recognised. I love good rugby, and when you have a good open game with three-quarters in full flight, there are few things to beat it. But as a general rule, I think soccer is more fluent than rugby, and more fluid. You get more dour rugby games than you get scrappy goalless draws in football.

I cannot get to as many games as I would like these days, but towards the end of the 1993-94 season, I went to see the Liverpool v. Chelsea game, as a guest reporter for the *Sunday Express*. I was glad to have that last chance to see the Kop before it was demolished. I have many happy memories of the Kop. As a young man, I tried to become Conservative candidate for Liverpool Edge Hill. When I appeared before the selection committee, they asked me what links I had with Liverpool. Ever since I was a lad, I said, I've supported Liverpool FC. I was sure it was a good card to play but it was immediately clear I'd made a terrible mistake. They were Evertonians to a man. I still regard it as my greatest achievement that, despite such an error, they selected me. I then had years of combining politics with sport. I held surgeries every Saturday morning, and went to stand on the Kop in the afternoon. That was the team of dreams:

Lawrence; Lawler, Byrne; Strong, Yeats, Stevenson;
Callaghan, Hunt, St John, Smith, Thompson.

CLIFF JONES

IVOR ALLCHURCH

MEL CHARLES

'... the best attacking line-up I ever saw at the Vetch Field.'

'Billy Liddell was the player who turned me towards Liverpool...'

'Toshack was the only manager to get Swansea to the top flight...'

I fought two General Elections there, in 1966 and 1970. I'm the only living Conservative to have fought two General Elections in Edge Hill and survived. By the end, that great team was giving way to another, the Toshack-Keegan vintage, and to an era that gave birth to my favourite sporting headline of all time. When Liverpool won the European Cup in 1977, the *Liverpool Echo* proclaimed that

Keegan sends them Moenchen Sad Back

There was no comparable Swansea side, though when I went home from Cambridge, aged 22, to revise for my bar exams, they had perhaps the best attacking line-up I ever saw there - Ivor Allchurch, Terry Medwin, Cliff Jones, Mel Charles. Toshack was the only manager to get them to the top flight, and I was at the Vetch Field for their second home game, a 5-3 win against Notts County.

That was a very emotional day, but for real raw elation, one memory stands out and remarkably it was at a game that Liverpool lost: the 1971 FA Cup Final against Arsenal. I'd been unable to get a ticket but a friend called on the Friday night to say he had one and would I like it. I had to pay over the odds and when I got to Wembley I discovered that it was a terrific seat, close to the half-way line. But as the ground filled, I realised I was surrounded by Arsenal fans. So I went and stood at the entrance of the end that was going to be the Kop. A man came by on crutches and I said to him: 'You can't go on there on those. You need a seat'. 'I'd love a seat', he said, so we swapped tickets.

The game went into extra-time and Steve Heighway gave us the lead. The ten minutes after that were mass elation of a quite inexplicable and unbelievable kind. Only the birth of my children could really compare in terms of emotion. Then Arsenal equalised, Charlie George scored their winner and it all ended in tears.

Heighway was probably my all-time favourite player, though Chris Lawler, Kevin Keegan and Ivor Allchurch would run him close. Billy Liddell was actually the player who turned me towards Liverpool, even though I never saw him play. I read about him and I liked what I *read*. He was a great figure.

The game then is clearly different to the game now, though I believe standards have remained as high. Of course the game has lost something through becoming such a huge business, but I don't see how it could have been avoided. In the old days of the maximum wage at £20 a-week the players were obviously much more part of the community. Once that arbitrary wage went, the market could decide, as in so much else. Top players ARE paid a great deal of money but I would argue that they're worth it. They have a great talent, which they can employ only for a few years, and I would say they are worth far more than pop stars who earn a great deal more. I suspect that football is less important to the national life than it was before the war or immediately after the war. Most people led very humdrum lives with not a lot of colour or excitement. Football was the main provider of such excitement for millions whereas today there are many different forms of entertainment, so it is not so central to people's lives. But if you remember how we all felt when it was clear there would be no British side in the World Cup finals, you understand just how important it is.

UK Could Rule, OK?

That was a real blow and if it is not to be repeated in future, I think we should move towards having a UK team. It is a shame that Ryan Giggs, Mark Hughes and Ian Rush may never play in the World Cup Finals, despite getting so close with Wales. As part of a British team they would get there but of course national vested interests and bureaucracies keep getting in the way. There is no logical objection. Welsh people selected to play cricket for England aren't made less Welsh by playing. The British Lions rugby team excites just the same passions in British supporters as the national sides arouse among English, Scots, Welsh and Irish followers. I feel just as British as I feel Welsh and if we had a British side, it would be there, and possibly winning. We have so much talent and it is tragic that none of it will be seen on the world's greatest stage.

As for the manager? Until recent times, I'd have said John Toshack was the man for the job. I was surprised though, and disappointed, that he didn't last the course with Wales. Perhaps it's a job for Kenny?

ARSENAL AND YORK CITY

JOHN GREENWAY (Conservative, Ryedale)

A former London policeman and Arsenal fanatic, he now lays down the law in the directors' box at York City, where he is the club's president.

The MP for Ryedale in North Yorkshire since 1987, he is a member of the Home Affairs Select Committee and Vice-Chairman of the All-Party Parliamentary Football Committee.

10

ON THE SPOT WITH YORK CITY AND ARSENAL

John Greenway

Is there anything new to say about football ?

We could relive my playing career - never before seen in print. It need not take long, especially if I include a goal-by-goal analysis of my scoring achievements.

The fact is that I only ever scored one goal in competitive football. It was in a Northwich and District Junior League match, in 1963-64, when I was in the sixth form at Sir John Deane's Grammar School, where rugger was worshipped and soccer banned. With other football-crazy schoolmates, I played for an under-18 team, sponsored by a local shipyard. I was the right back, the perfect position for a left-footer. But, in this particular game, I was playing up front where I couldn't give away any more goals.

Another feeble strike at goal was inexplicably lobbed straight back to me. I swung my right leg and made a perfect, on-the-volley contact with the ball, which sailed into the top corner. Well, it was something like that. We duly lost the match 6-2. I was roundly bollocked for missing half-a-dozen sitters and promptly dropped. Even then, it was how many you missed - or let in - that mattered most. But the usual player shortage at this level ensured my early re-instatement to the No. 2 shirt and we finished the season runners-up.

I still have the medal to prove it and bring it out occasionally at football dinners in a defiant gesture of self-ridicule. That medal is the only thing I have ever won in my life apart from elections.

Yes, I was useless at football. Yet, as colleagues in the York City directors' box will tell you, that has not disqualified me from treating them to non-stop, kick-by-kick, totally partisan commentary.

Getting The Bug

I've always been a football fanatic. I blame my dad. He used to take me, as a lad, to watch Witton Albion, then playing in the Cheshire League at the Central Ground, Northwich. In recent years, the ground has gone - to make way for a Sainsbury's superstore - and Albion have enjoyed a brief spell up in the Vauxhall Conference, alongside local rivals, Northwich Victoria.

The great rivals for my dad's affections were Arsenal. If Witton were away, we would tune into Raymond Glendenning on the radio. I vividly remember listening to the 1952 Cup Final. Arsenal v. Newcastle. Wally Barnes was stretchered off early on. Lishman hit the bar near the end before Newcastle scored a late winner. Dad was close to tears and I had got the Arsenal bug. Arsenal mattered. Witton Albion mattered. Football mattered. In that order.

Arsenal had giants. Swindin, Barnes, Forbes, Mercer, Compton, Logie and Lishman. They won the Championship in 1953 by the narrowest of margins - how exciting that must have been for devotees who could do sums - but the game I remember from that season is the Cup Final, the first match which so many of my generation watched on television.

Mum and Dad had bought a 9" Bush TV to watch the Coronation, come June. Dad insisted that the set be installed a few weeks early - just in case. Half the street came to watch Blackpool beat Bolton 4-3. A chap called Matthews could dribble with the ball like no one I had ever seen before - and I dare say since.

Sometimes, my dad would treat me to Arsenal away matches. There were plenty of them within easy reach of Northwich. I remember a trip to Maine Road. Here was the Arsenal of Dodgin, Groves, Holton, Tapscott and, of course, Jack Kelsey, probably the best goalkeeper I ever saw. Arsenal won 3-2. Dodgin and Groves could dish it out - Man City's second goal was a penalty for a Dodgin up-ender.

We were sitting in the main stand. The chap on my left swore at every breath. This was a language I had never heard before - foul, spiteful and full of hatred. They swore at Witton. But not like this. In the end dad said something and they nearly had a punch-up.

ALEC FORBES
ARSENAL & SCOTLAND
50 FOOTBALLERS №30

*'Arsenal had giants...
Forbes, Mercer,
Compton
and Lishman'.*

JOE MERCER
ARSENAL & ENGLAND
50 FOOTBALLERS №1

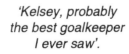

John Kelsey

*'Kelsey, probably
the best goalkeeper
I ever saw'.*

LESLIE COMPTON
ARSENAL
50 FOOTBALLERS №7

D. LISHMAN
ARSENAL
50 FOOTBALLERS №40

Despite this unhappy episode, if I saved my pocket money I could go to any ground I wanted. The crowds were huge. Yet the atmosphere was always friendly. You could stand at the Stretford End or on the Kippax and support Arsenal. Then, in the early sixties, it turned nasty. I remember a match at Blackburn. A policeman spotted my red and white scarf. 'Over here, son'. Before I knew it, I was in a pen with about 500 Arsenal supporters. On another occasion, I took my younger brother, David, to Turf Moor. It must have been in 1962-63, when Burnley, who had been making a habit of finishing in the First Division's top three, were playing newly-promoted Liverpool. The atmosphere was hostile and we were surrounded by scouse. It was pretty frightening and not what we were used to.

On the train home that Saturday evening, we noticed scores of navy blue-and-white scarves. Bolton Wanderers v. West Ham United. A 7.30 kick-off. Time to take in another match! In those days you could watch football - Cup Finals apart - only by going to games.

Although they promised much, the Arsenal of that era never won a thing. Yet they had some great players. The best of the lot was George Eastham, who rocked the football world, in 1960, by taking Newcastle to court, so that he could play for Arsenal. His case was also taken up, of course, at Westminster - notably by Philip Goodhart who recalls the occasion in his chapter below.

Eastham was my teenage idol. He challenged the establishment and that impressed me. He also went from the north to London out of a love for Arsenal. Why couldn't I do the same?

The Metropolitan Line

My hopes of gaining a place at a London music school came to nothing. I joined a bank instead. I hated that. But I liked London. So, on my nineteenth birthday, in 1965, I applied to join the Metropolitan Police.

During my five years as a West End cop, Arsenal re-established themselves at the top of the English game. True, they lost two League Cup Finals: to Leeds in 1968 and - as Nigel Jones recalls in some detail - to

Swindon Town in 1969. But, then, on an unforgettable night at Highbury, the 1970 team beat Anderlecht 4-3 on aggregate to win the European Fairs Cup.

The following season, I scarcely missed a match, home or away, as Arsenal won the double. That Charlie George extra-time goal to win the 1971 Cup Final may have reduced Michael Howard to tears, but it was sheer joy for me. Little did I know that, 22 years later, I would be at Wembley as an official of another club - York City - writing their own little bit of soccer history.

In 1971-72, *Match of the Day* witnessed another incredible goal by Charlie George in a tremendous 2-2 draw at the Baseball Ground. It was the FA Cup Fourth Round. And it was the time of the miners' strike, the three-day week and power cuts. So the replay at Highbury had to be played on the Tuesday afternoon with a 2 p.m. kick-off. By now a life assurance inspector in the West End, I skipped work to go to the match, worried lest I be seen in a thin attendance. Over 63,000 had the same idea. I have never seen Highbury so full, even on a Saturday - and all for a dreadful, goalless draw.

A Ray Kennedy goal put out Derby in the second replay at Filbert Street. But Arsenal eventually lost to Leeds on the big day. Bob Wilson, injured in the semi-final, had to give way to a young lad called Geoff Barnett. He, too, came from Northwich and had played in a very successful Mid-Cheshire youth team. Sadly, he couldn't stop Allan Clarke scoring the only goal.

The following Monday evening, Leeds played at Wolves. A draw and they'd be champions. They lost 2-1. So Liverpool needed to win at Highbury to pip Derby for the title. The game ended 0-0. Liverpool had a goal disallowed for offside right at the end. It didn't look offside from the North Bank.

In the queue for the tube, two girls, both Liverpool fans, were standing next to me: one crying buckets; the other trying to console her.

> *'Never mind kid ... it's only a game'.*
> *'It's always bloody Arsenal!'*

What a prophecy! When it matters, Arsenal always seem to beat Liverpool, especially at Anfield when all you need is a 2-0 win to become league champions.

The Arsenal double team never realised its full potential and, following an FA Cup Semi-Final defeat by Sunderland in 1973, the team seemed to disintegrate.

Not For Always 'Bloody Arsenal'

Things were changing dramatically for me, too. I had started broking insurance, mostly advising doctors and dentists, with a nation-wide client base. With Sylvia expecting our third child, we decided to head back to the North. York, a suitable mid-way point between my family in Cheshire and Sylvia's in Whitby, seemed to have everything to offer. Inexpensive housing, good schools and less than three hours to London by train.

York City were also on the up. In 1974, they won promotion to Division Two. I became a Bootham Crescent regular and, as the insurance broking business prospered, a season ticket-holder with my younger son, Anthony - *en route* to becoming President of the club.

Like his dad, Anthony has become obsessed with York City and Arsenal. His older brother, Stephen, never quite caught the soccer bug. He was fine when York City were winning but relegation seasons were another matter. I recall a dismal afternoon in 1975-76, when a crowd of 11,000 saw York beaten 4-1, at home, by Sunderland. They were on their way up. We were on our way down to Division Three.

One of the York fullbacks, Derrick Downing, lived two doors away. At one point in that match, he slipped in front of our goal, fell on the ball and then picked it up. An obvious penalty. Another goal for Sunderland. To make matters worse, it was raining cats and dogs and, with most of the York ground open to the elements, we got well and truly soaked. In years to come, I'd be able to help put that problem right.

York slid straight through Division Three. There followed several seasons in Division Four. In 1980-81, they had to apply for re-election for the seventh time in their history. By 1982-83, things were looking up again, though. Eighteen wins in 23 home matches, with 59 goals scored. It was tremendous entertainment.

If only they could stop leaking goals on their travels! The following season they did. A remarkable improvement in away form - nobody minds going to Aldershot if you win 4-1 - and another 58 goals at home. They won the Fourth Division with a record 101 points.

Then, in 1984-85-86, York City experienced the kind of FA Cup glory of which dreams are made and legends born. And I was to experience the excruciating agony of the two teams I loved playing each other in a Fourth Round tie at Bootham Crescent. The only previous FA Cup meeting between Arsenal and York had been in 1974-75. Following a creditable draw at Highbury, York lost the replay 3-1, after extra time. At that stage, I'd not established any great attachment to York City. But this 1984-85 business was different.

As often happens in end-of-January cup ties, the weather was atrocious. Snow had been cleared from the pitch, leaving a frozen surface which was just playable. An Arsenal team of 11 internationals - including Kenny Sansom, Brian Talbot, David O'Leary, Paul Mariner and Charlie Nicholas - didn't relish the conditions. They seemed to fancy their chances of a 0-0 draw and a replay at Highbury. But, late in the game, the volatile Steve Williams had a dig at a York player, outside the box, before bringing him down inside. Penalty. Keith Houchen scored from the spot to put York through and Arsenal out.

To say I had mixed emotions was an under-statement. I was livid with Arsenal's inept performance. York City were marvellous on the day and fully deserved their win. I felt elated for everyone at the club.

The next round saw Liverpool at Bootham Crescent - cup fever had struck the City of York. It was like 1955 all over again when York had unluckily lost an FA Cup semi-final replay to Newcastle United. Early in the second half, Ian Rush scored for Liverpool and they began to turn on the style like the European champions they were. But York stuck to their task and got a late equaliser to take the tie back to Anfield.

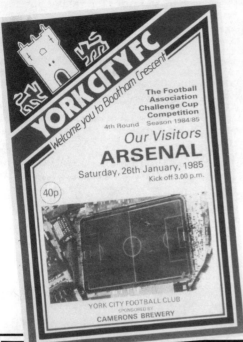

'... the two teams I love playing each other'.

TEAM CHECK

Red/Navy Blue	YORK CITY	v.	ARSENAL	Yellow/White
	MIKE ASTBURY	1	JOHN LUKIC	
	STEVE SENIOR	2	VIV ANDERSON	
	ALAN HAY	3	KENNY SANSOM	
	RICKY SBRAGIA	4	BRIAN TALBOT	
	JOHN MacPHAIL	5	DAVID O'LEARY	
	SEAN HASLEGRAVE	6	TOMMY CATON	
	GARY FORD	7	STEWART ROBSON	
	MARTIN BUTLER	8	STEVE WILLIAMS	
	KEITH WALWYN	9	PAUL MARINER	
	KEITH HOUCHEN	10	TONY WOODCOCK	
	GARY NICHOLSOLN	11	CHARLIE NICHOLAS	
	HUGH ATKINSON	12	IAN ALLINSON	

Referee : **MR. D. SHAW** (Sandbach)
Linesmen : Red Flag : **MR. D. B. SCRIMSHAW** (Cheadle Hulme)
Yellow Flag : **MR. R. A. HART** (Darlington)

'An Arsenal team of 11 internationals didn't relish the conditions'

In the replay, City were overwhelmed and suffered their biggest-ever FA Cup defeat. A young supporter who couldn't make the trip to Liverpool rang Radio York to ask the score. 7-0 came the reply. *Who to?*

The great thing about football is there is always another day, another season and another chance. Incredibly, that chance came in 1985-86, with another Fifth Round, home tie against Liverpool. It was my birthday. And City put on a birthday show. On the hour, they took a deserved lead. It lasted four minutes until Jan Molby equalised from a penalty, after a York fullback was adjudged to have handled.

The replay at Anfield was rather different from the year before. To be blunt, York were robbed. With 25 minutes to go and the scores level, York centre forward, Keith Walwyn, collided with Grobbelaar, Hansen and Gillespie but managed to poke the ball over the line. Everyone in the ground, including the BBC commentary I later discovered, thought the goal fair. But the referee, Howard Taylor, blew for a foul, the game went into extra time and Liverpool ran out 3-1 winners. That season Liverpool won the double. They say that only Arsenal are lucky!

When he hung up his whistle, Howard Taylor became a York Vice-President. There are no hard feelings in football.

To Parliament and President

At the end of the following season, York escaped relegation by one place and I was elected to Parliament. But, in May 1988, York dropped into the basement again. The team was struggling, but the club was well run and its survival was never seriously under threat.

On the wider soccer scene, travelling England supporters had disgraced themselves, the game and their country once too often and Margaret Thatcher seized on the idea of a national membership scheme. David Evans explains, in his chapter, why he was so keen on it. But I never doubted that it would ruin clubs like York City. Our then Chairman, Michael Sinclair, was also Chairman of the Third and Fourth division clubs, known in league circles as the Associate Members. He invited me to become the Club's President. I was initially worried that this might cause me some embarrassment if, having opposed the member-

111

ship scheme, I then had to vote for it in the House of Commons. However, having slept on it, I could see that there was no option but to oppose the scheme and vote against the Football Spectators Bill in Parliament.

I was galvanised in my opposition by a stupid remark from Nicholas Ridley, the Secretary of State responsible for the legislation, when he received a deputation from the All-Party Parliamentary Football Committee (APPFC). The work of this committee, of which I've been the Vice-Chairman since 1988, is outlined in the chapter by Tom Pendry, who founded it with my Tory colleague, Jim Lester. Both of them were there that day, along with Menzies Campbell for the Liberals and Labour's Joe Ashton, now the APPFC Chairman.

I argued that the smaller clubs should be exempt from the scheme; otherwise, I could not support the legislation. 'Whenever did you support the Government?', Ridley asked. My record since the election had been exemplary. I was incensed and complained to the Chief Whip. Anyway, it made voting against the Bill that little bit easier. Being charitable, I have since thought that the Secretary of State mistook me for a Labour member. Tory MPs are supposed to prefer cricket and rugby, rather like the school I went to.

We failed to stop the legislation being passed, but the campaign against the membership scheme continued. Then came the Hillsborough tragedy and Lord Justice Taylor's backing for all that we had said about the scheme. Identity cards were dead, but we now faced the prospect of converting the York ground into an all-seater stadium. Financially, that would have been impossible. So the new cause was to exempt the bottom two divisions.

I was able to contribute to this effort - with two other fans, Joe Ashton (Sheffield Wednesday) and Alan Meale (Mansfield Town) - during 1990-91, when the Home Affairs Select Committee looked into the policing of football hooliganism. One of our recommendations was to reprieve the smaller league clubs (with a capacity below 10,000) from having to put in seats throughout their stadia. After the 1992 election, David Mellor, who had been appointed Secretary of State for the new Department for National Heritage, listened carefully to all the arguments - including another forceful presentation from the APPFC - and agreed to exempt

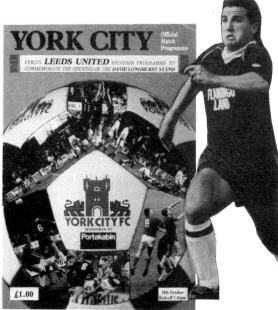

'It's at moments like this that you discover that football clubs are like just one big family'. Scunthorpe United fan, Fiona Pound, raised £1,032.13 for the David Longhurst Stand Appeal. Her employer, British Oxygen, doubled it (a company policy when employees fund-raise). She presented the £2,064.26 to David's father, Vic Longhurst (*left*) and John Greenway, chairman of the appeals committee.

'...Leeds United kindly brought their entire first team, free of charge...'

Inset: David Longhurst

the bottom two divisions.

That doesn't mean that our smaller grounds don't need improvements. They most certainly do and we need to ensure that the Football Trust continues to have the resources it needs to help fund them, once the Premier League and First Division clubs have become all-seater. The Trust helped to finance York's David Longhurst stand. Much of the money was generously donated by the fans themselves, in support of the club's scheme to put a roof over the Shipton Street end of the ground, as a permanent memorial to David.

York's most expensive-ever signing, David had collapsed on the pitch just before half-time in a home game against Lincoln City, in September 1990, and died instantly. The autopsy found that David had suffered an extremely rare heart condition. It's at moments like this that you discover that football clubs are like just one big family. Every single person connected with the club made the journey to David's home town of Corby for the funeral.

It was a very proud moment for me, as chairman of the appeals committee, when Leeds United kindly brought their entire first team, free of charge, to play a gala match, at the start of the 1991-92 season, for the official opening of the David Longhurst Stand. I meant it when I said that nothing I had ever been involved in before had given me so much satisfaction and pleasure.

The stand has made a tremendous difference to Bootham Crescent. And we have since built a new family stand which has helped increase family attendances.

If lower league soccer is to survive, though, it must also continue to receive financial support from the more prosperous part of the game. That's the big worry. Although York City have enjoyed two marvellous seasons, we can't survive on match receipts. The effect of the National Lottery on our own well-supported lottery is also a cause for concern.

Excitement and Incitement

On the pitch, there's not a lot wrong with the game. There are professional fouls but there always were. The refereeing can be inconsistent but twas ever thus. The game is faster and players are fitter and it's often the lack of time and space which causes them to make mistakes.

The promotion play-offs have added a great deal of extra excitement at the end of the season - especially if your team manages, in successive seasons, to make the play-offs for different divisions. It should have been enough for an Arsenal fan in 1993 that his team had twice beaten Sheffield Wednesday to become the first club to win both major Cups in the same season. But I had the added excitement of returning to Wembley, for York's Third Division play-off final against Crewe. There's another irony. Crewe were the nearest league club to my Cheshire home. I saw Witton Albion win the Cheshire Senior Cup there.

With York and Crewe level after extra-time, we were into a penalty shoot-out. Shades of the European Cup Winners Cup Final, in the Heysel Stadium in 1980, when Arsenal lost to Valencia on penalties. Not again, please!

York's goalkeeper, Dean Kiely, saved one of the Crewe efforts. It was left to York's young full back, Wayne Hall, to stroke the ball into the corner of the net and win York promotion. It was every bit as memorable and exciting as that Charlie George winner in 1971. And I was just as emotionally drained.

Indeed, I might have been content with a calmer 1993-94 season, with York consolidating their Division Two place, while Highbury staged a few European encounters. But no! First, Arsenal went all the way in the Cup Winners Cup, with me missing out on a trip to Copenhagen for the sake of a parliamentary vote. Then came another play-off climax for York.

Stockport County lay between City and another date at Wembley. In the first game at Bootham Crescent, York had several good chances to score and should have had more than a goalless draw to show for some fine play. I missed the second leg at Stockport - more votes at Westminster - when City went down to a late County goal.

I checked the scores, on CEEFAX in the Commons library, with Peter

Pike - MP for, and fan of, Burnley. He seemed more than a little surprised at Burnley's 3-1 win at Plymouth. I would have put money on a City v. Argyle final.

Despite our obvious disappointment, feeling at the club is one of having done rather better than we generally expected. Fifth in Division II is York's fourth highest placing ever in the Football League.

Having declared, at the outset, my lack of football expertise, I won't attempt to analyse the reason for our success. What I do know is that the club is run by lovely people, dedicated, loyal and professional. We have a first class youth policy and we don't spend money we haven't got. Best of all, there is a happy spirit at the club. I just wish that more of our supporters would come to matches. Over 10,000 went to Wembley for the play-off final in 1993, yet we barely average 4,500 at Bootham Crescent.

York's decision not to join the anti-racism initiative, jointly launched in 1993-94 by the Commission for Racial Equality and the Professional Footballers Association, has been misunderstood. Some people seem to forget that I am a member of the Home Affairs Committee - as I mentioned earlier in respect of its position on all-seater exemptions - which has twice, of late, urged measures to tackle football ground racists. Thus, in the 1990-91 session, the Committee called for the speedy implementation of the Taylor recommendation to create a specific offence of racialist chanting at sports grounds. This was duly achieved in the Football (Offences) Act 1991.

Reviewing, in 1993-94, the way this new power had been used by the police, the Committee noted the policy - of the Association of Chief Police Officers, the Home Office and the football authorities - of increasing the share of policing that is entrusted to stewards, who are not empowered by the 1991 Act to arrest racist chanters. The Committee has accordingly asked the three interests involved to consider how best to enforce the Act at grounds policed by stewards.

Yet none of that means that every club need take part in a high-profile campaign. At York City, this could make a relatively small problem infinitely worse. Both our Chairman and Club Secretary have used the public address system to tell fans that racist chanting will not be tolerated at the ground and, thus far, this has proved extremely effective.

The Arsenal of the Smaller Clubs

In 1965, when my love of Arsenal took me to London, York City won promotion from Division Four. Their home record was the best in the club's history:

P 23   W 20   D 1   L 2   F 63   A 21

In his *Complete Record* of York City, the club historian, David Batters, recalls the sentiments of the then chairman, Hugh Kitchin, when, to celebrate that 1965 success, everyone at Bootham Crescent went to the York Mansion House as guests of the Lord Mayor:

> 'We *feel that York City FC is a respected club in soccer circles and we treasure a comment from the late Tom Whittaker, when Arsenal Manager, that he regarded York City "as the Arsenal of the smaller clubs"'.*

I can't argue with that.

Full references to the two reports of the Home Affairs Committee and to the club history are given in the further reading at the end of this book.

MOTHERWELL and BOLTON WANDERERS

ANN TAYLOR (Labour, Dewsbury)

Motherwell-born and Bolton-bred, she entered Parliament in 1974 for Bolton West and became an Assistant Whip. Lost the seat in 1983, returning to Westminster, in 1987, as MP for Dewsbury.

Having shadowed Education, as Deputy to Neil Kinnock, she was, in turn, the Shadow Minister for Housing, Environment and Home Affairs, before becoming Shadow Secretary of State for Education in July 1992.

11

WELL OF MEMORIES FOR A HAPPY WANDERER

Ann Taylor

Marx may have said that 'religion is the opium of the people' but football has probably done more than religion to prevent a revolution in Britain.

The outburst of energy, each and every Saturday afternoon, must have been a genuine outlet, over the years, for the pent-up frustration of 'the masses'.

I am not talking of the players who may or may not run up and down the pitch for 90 minutes. I am talking about those who suffer much greater stress and expend just as much energy - even if much of it is nervous energy. I am talking about the fans.

If you'd worked a long five days and Saturday morning, you would have had good reason both to slump asleep on Saturday afternoon and then to spend the evening angrily discussing your lot - rates of pay, hours of toil or the drudgery of working life - in the pub or club. As it is, or as it has been for the whole of this century, Saturday evening conversations have been dominated by frustrated grumblings not about work but about sport. In terms of a contribution to the stability of the established order of society, sport - and, in particular, football - has to be high on the list.

And football provides an outlet not only for those who follow it as a sport. Along with horse racing, it is a major excuse for betting. Any assessment of the escape route-safety valve factor in sport should include the millions who fill in their football pools forms, each week, and avidly check, as the scores come in, to see if their magic formula of birthdays and house numbers has secured their escape into a new world of luxury. Like many others, I can remember being crouched around the radio, at tea-time on a Saturday, trying to fill in the scores as they came in, only to be told by my grandfather to wait until the

*'... with their Wembley appearances in 1953 and 1958,
Wanderers remain part of Cup Final folklore.'*

Nat Does It: Lofthouse scores the first of his two goals in the 2-0
win that Ann Taylor could not entirely celebrate - for reasons reflected
in Stan Orme's chapter above. Note Crowther's presence at No.6
- again, see chapter 5.

classified results or I might put one on the wrong line. As if I would! I knew the responsibility I had not to raise or dash hopes of rewards to come by some trivial mistake.

All of this was carried out in an atmosphere of reverence which gave me a respect for football which has never diminished. I knew football was important before I knew football was to be enjoyed. And just as I knew I was Labour before I knew what the Party stood for, so I knew which teams I supported and which teams I hated.

Learning to Love

I know I should be able to recall my first match but I cannot. I don't even know if it was at Motherwell or Bolton. And that is not negligence on my part. It's due to the fact that both teams were part of my life from a very early age.

I was born in Motherwell, within shouting distance of Fir Park, where 'Well' play. And, for the first few years of my life, I not only spoke with a Scottish accent but was Scottish. Before I started school, though, the family moved to my mother's home town of Bolton. My father obviously felt no conflict of loyalty in supporting Bolton Wanderers: after all, they were never likely to play against Motherwell. And I absorbed his attitudes to football in the same way that I absorbed his interest in politics.

In the mid-1950s, Bolton Wanderers were, as today (on a good day), a side to be reckoned with. If today's team has caught the imagination with its cup runs - ask Liverpool, Everton, Arsenal and Villa - the 1950s Wanderers, with their Wembley appearances in 1953 and 1958, remain part of Cup Final folklore.

As John Greenway reflects, in his chapter, the Coronation, in 1953, was a wonderful excuse for investing in a television set. And even if you couldn't afford one, there might be a neighbour who could. The scene that he recalls, where half the street came to his home for the Cup Final, must have been repeated many times over. But not in our street. My family huddled round a radio set at my grandparents with my uncle and aunt - everyone trying to listen and comment, sometimes at the same time, on events we couldn't see

121

'I knew we should have played ...'
'That Blackpool bloke is a dirty player'
'That ref is not on our side'

And all of this, as I say, when none of these 'commentators' had seen a ball of the match. Nor had they heard everything. Lots of the match was lost to us, as different adults took turns in telling everyone to 'shut up' so that they might hear. The only moments of real silence were the split second after the crowd's crescendo. Then, everyone held their breath to see if the ball was in the net or not.

The result sticks in the mind of many outside of Bolton and Blackpool. It was, after all, not just a match between two towns but the Lofthouse v Matthews final. No-one in Bolton - whether they had *seen* the evidence or not - believed that the result was anything but a travesty.

By the time of Wanderers' next final in 1958, I was no novice to football. It was then that I was guilty of a generosity which I resented for many years. Bolton's run was going well and my father went to queue for a ticket for the semi-final. I went with him. We stood for hours on Manchester Road, in a queue which was incredibly orderly and peculiarly silent. It probably looked like one of those grim Russian queues for bread - except that they are usually mainly of women, while this queue was of men in identical raincoats and flat caps. I persuaded my father to buy a second ticket for me, which wasn't too difficult, but when we got home my mother was not best pleased.

The following Saturday was the Spring 'bring-and-buy' at my junior school on our council estate on the northern side of Bolton. Jollied along by my parents (my father having defected), I was persuaded that cup matches were not like other matches (true), that I was too big to sit on my father's shoulders (true), that at 10 years old I wouldn't be able to see a thing (untrue). So it was that in a rash moment - I still can't quite believe it - I volunteered my ticket for the school raffle, much to the general delight but to my later anguish.

And so it was that I did not see the Bolton v. Blackburn semi-final at Maine Road. What rankles even more is that my husband was taken as a boy by his father. Perhaps that is why I am so keen to take my son

BOLTON WANDERERS - FA Cup-Winners, 1958
Back row: W. Ridding (manager), Hartle, Hennin, Hopkinson, Higgins,
Edwards, B. Sproston (trainer).
Front row, players only: Birch, Stevens, Lofthouse, Parry, Holden, Banks.

MOTHERWELL - Scottish Cup-Winners, 1991
The squad that took Motherwell to Hampden
and brought tears to Ann Taylor's eyes
Back row: McCart, Burley, Philliben, Cusack, Ainslie, Maxwell, McKeown,
Paterson, Kirk, Cooper, Angus. *Middle row; players only:* Reilly, McGrillen,
Bryce, Tannock, McNair, Gardener, O'Donnell, McLean, Candish, Burke.
Front row: T. McLean (manager), Griffin, Gahagan, Russell, Boyd, Mair,
Arnott, O'Neil, Dolan, T. Forsyth (coach).

123

to the big matches for *his* team. Like everyone in Bolton, I watched and savoured the 1958 cup victory - access to TV had spread considerably since 1953 - although Munich took the edge off the pleasure of beating Manchester United.

In the years that followed, I saw more matches at Burnden Park than anywhere and remained loyal despite the vagaries of their performance. The Nat Lofthouse era was a difficult one for any team to follow (the 'Lion of Vienna' was forced to retire, following injury, in December 1960) and the frequency of those glories has never quite been equalled.

But all's Well ...

Meanwhile, north of the border, Motherwell were quite a team to be reckoned with. Living in Bolton and without a car, and before there were motorways over Shap Fell, I did not get to many Motherwell matches, except on occasional Hogmanay visits and on annual trips in August - I was always staying with my Granny in Scotland at the start of the season - and at Easter. By the age of 12 or 13, I was confident enough to go to a match alone if there were no adult, or a younger cousin, to dragoon into coming along.

These were days when visits to Motherwell were rarely a disappointment. Big crowds to watch a team with big names. We stood behind the goal on a banking which seemed high and steep until I returned as an adult. At Easter 1960 my father hired a car. We left Bolton, as soon as the booking allowed, at 9.30 a.m. and drove north in appalling weather, over Shap Fell to Glasgow for my first visit to Hampden. Motherwell played Rangers in the semi-final and we arrived late and found all the gates firmly shut and a great deal of 'ooing' and 'awing' from the crowd.

We raced around the ground looking for an open entrance until my father spotted a steward, slipped him some money and we were in. We weaved our way high onto the embankment and watched Motherwell lose. I stayed with my grandmother but my father drove back next day in snow so bad that he had to keep the window open so that he could reach out and brush the snow off the windscreen because the wipers couldn't cope. He still thought it was worth it and so did I.

Those were the days ...

> ... the days of Ian St John, Pat Quinn, Willie Hunter, Andy Weir and his brother, of Bert McCann.

> ... the days of hope - of the First Division championship and cups - and of late season disappointments.

> ... the days when our Sunday paper, in Bolton, was the *Sunday Post*, so that we could read of Motherwell and their rivals.

My mother still claims that I cried when Ian St John was transferred to Liverpool in 1961 (and not because the fee was only £35,000 - a huge sum then, enough to buy one of the best stands at any ground). I was certainly 'gutted', as my hero worship could not be dented, but I simply could not comprehend the necessity (apparently obvious to everyone else) of any move at all. I felt hurt and rather bewildered but adjusted slowly as I heard the Liverpool jokes. The old ones may be the best; but, at 14, I thought it hilarious to learn of the church placard asking

> *'What will you do when the Lord cometh?'*

and of the scribble beneath:

> *'Move St John to inside-forward.'*

I was able to see Ian St John play on occasion at Burnden Park. I think my admission that Ian St John caused me a conflict of loyalties when Liverpool played Bolton made me incomprehensible to my now husband. What I really wanted was for Bolton to win but for St John to get a hat-trick. So, 4-3 would have been an acceptable score.

My football attendance did wane, I must confess, first when I had to get a Saturday job to pay my way; then when I went to university; and then when my Grandmother died and my Scottish visits became infrequent. My interest didn't diminish and was maintained by that all-absorbing occupation of watching football on TV. In the late 1960s, there was far less than now but enough to keep the football spirit alive.

Elected and Promoted

By the early 1970s, however, I was back in Bolton on a more regular basis, as a Parliamentary candidate and then as MP. I cannot actually claim all the credit for the success of Bolton Wanderers at this time but suffice it to say that when I was the Member for Bolton West, Wanderers were promoted to the First Division (when it *was* the first division) in 1977-78.

Being an MP provides few real perks but I have to admit that sitting in the directors' box for football matches is one that really counts. Indeed, I cannot for the moment think of any others. The fact that my husband and I, my father and I, or my brother and I, could sit centre stage - and I could even tell the directors what we thought at half-time - provides fond memories. And it wasn't just home matches.

As well as the obviously local opponents, we followed Bolton Wanderers to the likes of Elland Road - parking in the middle of a roundabout much to the concern of my youngest brother - and the City Ground. The latter visit was reciprocated when Brian Clough came to open our Labour Party office before a match at Burnden Park which Forest subsequently lost - maybe because of the lack of, or brevity of, the pre-match talk: who knows?.

Most of all, we kept trying to see Bolton Wanderers win in London. And it just didn't seem possible. Time after time, they threw away matches in London as if they were jinxed or as if the team had failed - as the fans used to put it (or, rather, in a polite version of how the fans used to put it) - to recover from a night out on the town. I saw many Bolton Wanderers games in London, particularly against Spurs. In 1977-78, they were among Bolton's rivals for promotion and were drawn at home to us in the Cup. Inevitably, Wanderers lost the league game; but we did manage to draw the cup-tie (and finish the job in the Burnden replay).

Spurs were, and are, supported by quite a few people in the House of Commons, including some of my then colleagues in the Whips Office and the boys (as our civil servants were called) who ran the admin side of whippery. At this time, the Labour Government was on a knife edge, surviving without a majority, but business for a Monday was never sorted without jibes and counter-jibes about Saturday's results. Even in politics, you must have a sense of priorities.

The Spurs team had its stars - Hoddle, Villa, Ardiles - but Bolton were not without their superstars. Our only problem was that they were not consistent superstars. I challenge anyone to deny the sheer absolute brilliance of Frank Worthington, the intelligent artistry of Willie Morgan or the work rate of Peter Reid - until he broke his leg that bleak New Year's Day in 1979.

These were heady days. Frank Worthington was the First Division's leading scorer, with 24 goals, in 1979, scoring over head with his back to the goal more than once and taking a pride in scoring the impossible. And Willie Morgan more than redeemed himself for the ridiculous back pass against Luton, at the end of the 1976-77 season, which had denied us promotion.

I had moments of fame in this as well. In 1978, I presented one of the first cheques, if not *the* first, from The Football Trust for ground improvements at Burnden Park. Later, the local 'paper came to photograph me looking at some of the new seating and safety measures. I was persuaded to don a Bolton Wanderers kit for the snapshot, which the 'paper enterprisingly sold to the *Daily Mirror*. I'm not sure it is wise of any MP to end up on page 3 - even if fully kitted out in a Bolton Wanderers strip.

And, to cap it all, one Christmas I went to the office of the Manager, Ian Greaves, to give him a bottle of whisky and who should be sitting there, as a visiting TV commentator, but Ian St John. So overcome was I that I acted like a child presenting flowers to royalty, with bulging eyes and wobbly knees. I thrust the bottle at Ian Greaves and turned and bolted, tongue-tied in a mixture of awe and disbelief.

After that, it was downhill all the way. Bolton Wanderers went back down to the Second Division in 1980 and then down to the Third in 1983. My empathy extended to losing my seat in 1983, allegedly because of a boundary change but, in reality, in line with Wanderers' fortunes - yet not before I had given birth, in August 1982, to my son,

Andrew, who attended his first match at Burnden Park when two weeks-old.

Son and Football Lover

There have been compensations and highlights since then, with those scintillating 1993 and 1994 cup runs and promotion to the now First Division in 1993. Yes, I was there, and with my husband and son and youngest brother. And I hope my son, though not quite able to share my teams, will continue to get as much enjoyment from football.

The signs are good. Andrew wanted, and was able, to go with me to one of the greatest events of my life.

On 18 May 1991, we went to Hampden Park for the Scottish Cup Final between Motherwell and Dundee United. It was an incredible experience which would have made anyone forget the rest of the world. Motherwell, glorious as ever in Claret and Amber, went into the lead and then went 2-0 up. Then, because football is football, United pulled one back and then another and before you knew it Motherwell were 3-2 down. I can still feel every moment and - not least - the sympathy of my (then eight year-old) son.

Motherwell had all the play yet couldn't get that goal. But then - unbelievable relief - they equalised and the match went to extra-time. The Motherwell goalkeeper, Alastair Maxwell, was challenged and badly hurt, but played on despite reported broken ribs. We needed heroes. And it happened. Motherwell got the winning goal and tears came to my eyes, which earned puzzled looks from my son.

I had waited over 40 years. My father, who had thrilled to Motherwell's last cup victory in 1952 and told so many tales of Motherwell in the late 1920s and early 1930s - when they won the championship in 1932, were runners-up in 1927, 1930, 1933 and 1934 and were third in other years - had not lived to see the victory.

But his grandson was there to be injected with a commitment that will surface, as necessary, in years to come.

*'The Motherwell
goalkeeper,
Alastair Maxwell,
played on despite
broken ribs...'*

*'... one of the greatest
events of my life.'*

This cover shows Dougie
Arnott (Motherwell, *left*) and
Maurice Malpas (Dundee
United), plus the brotherly
managers, Tommy McLean
(Motherwell, *bottom*) and Jim
McLean (Dundee United - as
profiled in Chapter 17)

CELTIC

BRIAN WILSON (Labour, Cunninghame North)

Having grown up in Dunoon - a mere boat, train and tram ride from Celtic Park - he studied in Dundee and Cardiff, becoming a journalist and the founding Editor and Publisher of the West Highland Free Press.

The author of the centenary history of Celtic, he was elected for his Strathclyde constituency in 1987. Has been an Opposition spokesman since 1988, initially on Scotland and, since 1992, on Transport.

12

LIFE WITH THE LIONS

Brian Wilson

Kennoway, Hogg and Morrison; Geatons, Lyon and Paterson;
Delaney, MacDonald, Crum, Divers and Murphy.

These were the names to which I was spoon-fed as an infant - surely an
extreme, but effective, example of childhood conditioning. They formed
the legendary team which won the Empire Exhibition Cup for Celtic in
1938. By the time the Coronation Cup was taken in 1953, I was old
enough to feed myself. But the important fact was implanted deep in
my psyche that this maintained Celtic's record of having won every trophy they had ever competed for.

Legends and lean years, pre-Lisbon

For the next, formative decade, legends and boasts were essential. For
I grew up in the leanest of Celtic years. I was already a bit of an oddity
as a Celtic supporter from an otherwise robustly Church of Scotland
background. There were very few of us in those pre-Lisbon days.
Although he was an elder of the Kirk, my father had an affinity for all
things Irish, which extended most emphatically to Celtic Football Club.
The two most treasured books which I recall from childhood were a
bound volume of the Dail debate on the 1922 Treaty and William
Maley's history of Celtic's first half-century.

Bonnar, Haughney and Rollo; Evans, Stein and McPhail;
Collins, Walsh, Mochan, Peacock and Fernie.

That Coronation Cup-winning side was still on duty, when I started to
be taken to games at Celtic Park. Always, I was instructed, the shrine
should be referred to by its proper name; never 'Parkhead'. That was
almost as bad form, in my father's book, as calling the Six Counties
'Northern Ireland'.

We lived in the Clyde resort of Dunoon, and travel to Glasgow - which was rarely countenanced for any other purpose - involved a steamer trip to Gourock, the train to Central Station and a tram or train journey to the ground, through the tenements of the East End. It was an expedition worthy of the destination, a place in the Celtic Park stand. The first game I saw Celtic play was against Raith Rovers. I vividly remember the 3-0 scoreline and a few other crucial details. On checking back the record-books, I found that this game took place on 10 October 1953, when I was two months short of my fifth birthday. Such a gentle introduction to actually seeing the great names in green-and-white hoops merely encouraged a false sense of infallibility. After a couple more league games, my brother and I were taken to a big occasion - the Scottish Cup semi-final of 1955, against Airdrie.

I can still summon up the sense ot trauma which ensued when, straight from the kick-off and without a Celtic player touching the ball, it lay behind Johnny Bonnar and Celtic were a goal behind. The record-books confirm the time of the goal at 15 seconds. This was impossible. What was a six year-old to do in the face of such injustice? I burst into tears. (It ended as a 2-2 draw and Celtic won the replay).

Nobody who supported Celtic or Rangers in that era could, I suppose, escape the wider connotations which these badges carried. We were taught to understand that Celtic, while proudly Irish in origin, had never exercised discrimination in the employment of players; hence there was no barrier to our supporting them. Had not John Thomson - the martyred goalkeeper - been a Protestant? And was not Jock Stein one? No further proof of Celtic's ecumenical Olympianism was required. The alternative Rangers brew of Union Jacks and distorted Protestantism was rendered correspondingly unattractive. It was a simplistic set of generalisations, from which to extrapolate any wider opinions. It also did an injustice to most of the Rangers supporters I grew up with, who were no more or less products of their conditioning than I was.

Between my fifth and 16th birthdays, Celtic won neither League nor Cup. It was a period which tested loyalty and encouraged stoicism. These years were lifted by just one solitary event - the League Cup Final of 1958 in which, for reasons which defied rational explanation,

Celtic beat Rangers by seven goals to one. That kept us going until the good times came. Indeed, to this day, the scrawled scoreline - *7-1* - is short-hand for other terms of abuse directed against the old enemy. Tactics were fairly loosely based in those days, but another saving grace which we clung to was the belief that Celtic strove for high standards of skilful, attacking football, while Rangers relied on physical force. Cyril Horne of the *Glasgow Herald* enthused on the 7-1 game:

> 'With a display of such grandeur as has rarely graced the great, vast ground Celtic proved conclusively the value of concentration on discipline and on the arts and crafts of the game ...'

Of Rangers, he pinned responsibility on

> 'those who have, encouraged by results at the expense of method, not discouraged the he-man type of game that has become typical of the side in recent years'.

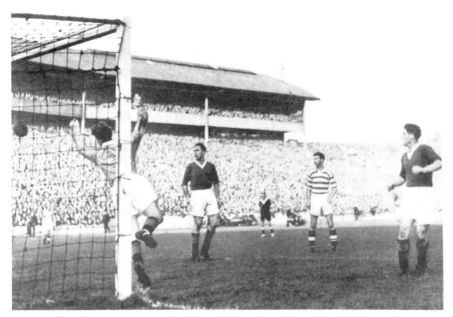

'... for reasons which defied rational explanation, Celtic beat Rangers by seven goals to one'.
Here's one of the reasons - the fifth goal, from Neil Mochan (out of picture).

This was the stuff we wanted to believe. Naturally, I was brought up to understand that Horne was the only Scottish football writer who gave Celtic a fair crack of the whip. To prove it, he had even been banned from the Ibrox press box. Years later, I was told a story which had at the time dented Horne's credibility just a little. The great Charlie Tully (the man who scored twice from successive corners) had dropped in to visit Bob Kelly, the Celtic chairman, as a certain class of player apparently did in those days. As he walked up the drive, he looked in the window to find the entire Kelly family plus Cyril Horne gathered around the piano, singing *Wrap the Green Flag Round Me*. Tully being Tully, he told the entire football world!

Kelly was the driving force behind Celtic at this time, although Jimmy McGrory was nominally the manager. It was a relationship incomprehensible by modern standards. When I was writing the Celtic history - of which more below - I came across an entry in the board minutes when arrangements were being made for a game with Rangers:

> *'The secretary intimated that a band was necessary at half-time according to our agreement with the magistrates of Glasgow. Mr McGrory was to take up this matter'.*

In contrast, there was a well vouched-for story of the Celtic bus making its way to a match at Airdrie when Kelly spotted the reserve goalkeeper standing at a bus-stop. He was taken on board and Kelly enthused over the spirit of the player, who was prepared to make his own way to Airdrie to see Celtic play. By the time the bus reached Broomfield, he was in the team!

Celtic supporters were well aware of the balance of power at Celtic Park, if not the more absurd details. Not for the first or last time in the club's history, hostility turned towards the board as fortunes continued to plummet in the early 1960s. Yet, at this time, the players who would eventually acquire the cloak of greatness were being assembled at Celtic Park under the title of the 'Kelly Kids'. Another of the virtues which we were brought up to admire was the fact that Celtic reared their own talent, rather than buy up the most effective of their opponents. What was needed was one man to pull it all together, and it became increasingly apparent that the supremo in question must be Jock Stein.

And so to Lisbon ...

From the moment of Stein's arrival, Celtic supporters acquired a new spring in their step. We knew that success could not be far away and didn't have long to wait for confirmation. Celtic's long drought ended on 24 April 1965, when they beat Dunfermline at Hampden in front of a 108,000 crowd.

Fallon, Young and Gemmell; Murdoch, McNeill and Clark;
Chalmers, Gallagher, Hughes, Lennox and Auld.

The Kelly Kids had come good. For a 16 year-old who had suffered the agonies and taunts of the lean years, the new era was more than welcome.

The extraordinary, and often over-looked, fact is that, of the team who later won the European Cup, 10 were already at Celtic Park when Stein arrived in 1965. They were almost all ordinary, working-class lads from the west of Scotland. I have often wondered whether he could have worked the same miracle if he had inherited a different set of players. How strong was the power of this extraordinary man to inspire, influence and bring out the best in players who might otherwise have been good but never part of a European Cup-winning team?

Few Celtic supporters could have cared less if Stein was a Hindu or a Knight of St Columba. But for my father, it was a source of deep, additional satisfaction that the great man came from a Protestant background - the ultimate exoneration of his own tenaciously-held belief that discrimination played no part in Celtic's affairs. Indeed, Stein had a wonderful answer to the question of whether, given two players of equal ability, he would sign the Catholic or the Protestant.

'The Protestant, of course - because Rangers couldn't sign the Catholic!'

At Dundee University, which I went to in 1966, we formed a Celtic supporters club. It was to turn out to be the greatest season of them all. The game I remember above all others was the second leg of the European Cup quarter-final with Vojvodina of Yugoslavia. Celtic were one goal down from the first leg but, euphoric with the season's success, everyone in the 75,000 crowd assumed that the deficit would be quickly cancelled out and the Yugoslavs overtaken. It was a tense game, and it took until the 58th minute for Stevie Chalmers to equalise. The tie seemed to be heading for a hazardous play-off in Brussels - in those days, there were no penalty shoot-outs - when Celtic launched one last great assault.

Charlie Gallagher - my favourite player of that era and now a Glasgow taxi-driver - sent over a perfect corner from the right and Billy McNeill cannoned it home with his head. I was right behind the goal and can picture yet the power of that header and the explosion of joy which followed. Indeed, if I had to name the two Celtic snap-shots most firmly etched on my memory, I would settle for that unexpected Airdrie goal, a dozen years earlier, and the Billy McNeill header which - we all instinctively knew - was the most vital moment in the ultimate European campaign. A couple of weeks later, we watched Celtic build up a 3-1 home lead against Dukla Prague, and that was enough to take them through to the final against Inter Milan.

Simpson; Craig and Gemmell; Murdoch, McNeill and Clark; Johnstone, Wallace, Chalmers, Auld and Lennox.

I can't claim to have been there. The night Celtic won the European Cup in Lisbon, I was, as I say, a student in Dundee - and in the middle of my first year exams. The Kenneth Wolstenholme commentary and the black-and-white view of the goals going in, from Tommy Gemmell and Stevie Chalmers, are etched on the mind forever. The quite small number of us who were established as Celtic supporters celebrated as fully as we could afford. But I remember it also as the night of the great turning-point, when everyone in Scotland and beyond, except the most intransigently opposed, was willing to be a supporter of the 'Lisbon Lions'.

Celtic had won the European Cup with a home-bred team, probably the only club ever to do so right down to the present day. Celtic had won with the traditional, exhilarating style of attacking football. Celtic, in fact, had won for everything we had been brought up to believe about them. Before the game, Stein had told Hugh McIlvanney of the *Observer*,

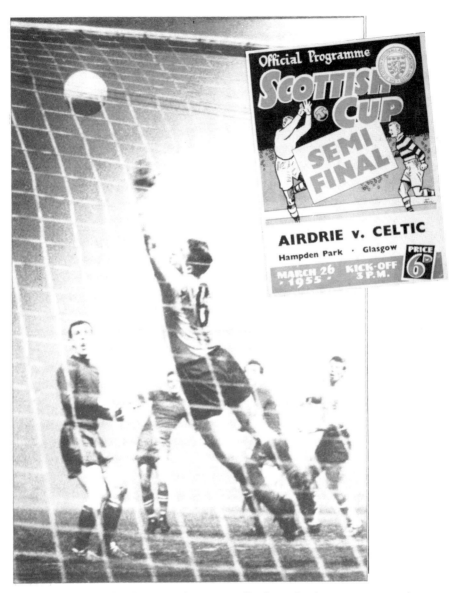

'... the two Celtic snap-shots most firmly etched on my memory' -
Brian Wilson's first 'big occasion' - the semi-final of 1955 - and
the header by Billy McNeill (*right, dark strip*) that eliminated Vojvodina...
'...the most vital moment in the European campaign'.

> *'We don't just want to win this cup. We want to win playing*
> *good football, to make neutrals glad we've won it, glad to*
> *remember how we did it'.*

His every wish had been fulfilled and we worshipped him for it. Nine
league titles in a row were to follow. Just as the years from childhood
to adolescence had been marked with the agonies of failure, so the next
decade became characterised by the assumption of success.

The Jigsaw of History

During that period, I wrote about football for part of my living and
would freely admit to never quite breaking clear of being a fan with a
type-writer. I suppose that's why Celtic asked me to write the centenary history of the club - an opportunity which I leapt at. I was given
access to the club's records and spent many hours in the office of the
White accountancy firm in the centre of Glasgow, reading through the
minutes of countless board meetings.

An extra dimension was added to all sorts of stories which had become
part of Celtic folklore. For instance, the jigsaw of events which had led
to Jock Stein becoming manager fell neatly into place. There were also
plenty of hints at why, organisationally, Celtic were already beginning
to fall far behind Rangers by the mid-1980s. One classic entry from a
board meeting in June 1983 revealed that Sunderland had phoned
Celtic Park to offer Ally McCoist for £210,000. Manager Billy McNeill
was on holiday and, as a result, 'the significance of the call was not
appreciated and no action was taken'. So they phoned lbrox instead.
The rest is history.

My main satisfaction in writing the book lay in the discovery of much
more about Celtic's origins than had previously been published. The
whole story had descended into the realms of fairytale, in which
Brother Walfrid started the club to feed the Catholic poor of Glasgow's
East End. While that was certainly an element, the other figures and
motives involved were more interesting to me. By and large, the big
men in Celtic's establishment were also leading figures in the Irish
political movement in Glasgow. And just as they quite deliberately

chose to eschew, as a name for the club, the Catholic exclusivism of 'Glasgow Hibernians', so they were also prominent in leading the Irish community into the fledgling Labour movement. In general, those who argued for Celtic to be a purely Catholic club would also have favoured the creation of an Irish Party in Scotland - with enormous implications for future political developments. It was no accident that the name 'Celtic', which linked the common Scottish and Irish inheritance, was chosen. Celtic the bridge-builders - it fitted in with what I had been hearing, virtually from birth!

The centenary fell in 1988 and Celtic marked it by winning the League and Cup double. With 15 minutes left in the Scottish Cup Final at Hampden, Celtic were a goal down to Dundee United. I would have to admit that the impact on book sales did cross my mind. Then Frank McAvennie struck twice to provide a perfect climax to the centenary celebrations and the book sold 25,000 copies.

Sadly, the intervening years have been less happy. Celtic's archaic ownership structure, which effectively vested power in two families, eventually came under successful challenge. Players and managers, as well as directors, have come and gone at an unprecedented rate. There have been no great teams and precious few high points to remember. An ill-starred plan to shift the club's home to Cambuslang never left the drawing-board and, in my view, should never even have got that far.

Supporters' patience has been stretched to the limit, and optimism about the future is still based largely on faith and hope rather than anything more tangible. But wasn't it just the same in the dark days of the early 1960s, just before Jock Stein arrived?

Well, not quite. But it's a straw worth clinging to. And, so far, the auguries are good.

The full reference to the centenary history is given in the further reading at the end of this book.

SCOTLAND

GORDON BROWN (Labour, Dunfermline East)

A graduate, and doctor, of Edinburgh University, he lectured there and in Glasgow, before becoming a journalist with, then Editor of, the Scottish Television Current Affairs Department. Was then elected to Parliament in 1983, for a constituency that includes part of Fife, where he grew up.

Has been on the Opposition Front Bench since 1985, alternating between Trade and Industry and Treasury matters, becoming Shadow Chancellor in 1992.

13

WHY SCOTLAND MEANS THE WORLD TO ME

Gordon Brown

On the night of 18 June 1982, along with thousands of other Scots football supporters, I was in Seville. Scotland was playing Brazil. I stood on the terrace behind the Brazilian goal and watched as David Narey drove the ball into the top right corner of the net. It was joy, pure joy, for the Scottish team, for the thousands of us there on the terraces and tens of thousands more at home.

In the searing heat of a Spanish summer, Scotland - synonymous with its football team, of course - was doing well against the world's best. For just for one moment Scotland was on top of the world. Out there in the heat, could the team that trained in the rain, under the grey skies of home, now go on and do the impossible?

Whatever the feelings of that moment, it couldn't and it didn't. Brazil went on to score four and I still remember the anger I felt for weeks about a comment made on TV by Jimmy Hill back in London. In his view our brush with greatness was merely a 'toepoke' - as if Narey's shot were an accident.

Tours with the Tartan Army

Both before and since I've followed our national team. I've travelled far for Scotland - the team has helped to open up the world for me. In 1990, I was one of the Tartan Army that went to Italy, for an all too brief visit to the World Cup. In Genoa, as the Italians prepared for a Scottish invasion, I saw Scotland beat Sweden 2-1 - two great Scottish goals followed by the almost inevitable soft goal thrown away by our defence - and the Italian police were prepared for trouble. There was none. The nearest thing to it came from the Swedish supporters, who drank a lot and then generally fell asleep.

Denied my chance to go to America in 1994, I am already planning my visit to France for the next World Cup finals in 1998. I have followed Scotland's World Cup ambitions ever since I was a schoolboy. I was one of thousands of teenagers who stayed off school when Scotland had to beat Italy to qualify for the 1966 finals in England - and failed to do so. As schoolboys, we were serious about Scotland. According to local legend, the headmaster in the adjoining school belted the boys in the morning for playing truant in the afternoon. He punished them in advance because he knew he could rely on them - to support Scotland.

You start young, and you can't give up supporting Scotland. You can't walk out simply because they are playing badly. You'll be there, irrespective of standards, performance, bad luck and the usual - mainly defensive and goalkeeping - errors that come from nowhere to snatch defeat from the jaws of victory for Scotland yet again. Once disappointed before, twice we turn up, and as optimists. Scotland's like that.

My passion for football started a long time before I ever got to see the national team play. I grew up in Fife, part of which I now represent at Westminster. My earliest football memories are of Stark's Park, the Kirkcaldy home of Raith Rovers. Indeed, my introduction to market forces was a season spent attempting to sell programmes outside the ground.

It was my father - a Church of Scotland minister but a keen follower of our national game - who first took me along to football matches, and together we travelled around Fife, seeing the local teams play. All my schooldays I turned to the sports pages long before I turned to news or politics.

Those 1960s games were my first exposure to Cowdenbeath's unique style. The team is much loved and its home record in the 1993-94 season - a long run of bad luck when it failed to win at Central Park until it beat Arbroath 1-0 on 2 April - made it famous throughout Britain.

Such reputations are by definition temporary; in the Scottish League life goes on. A new season puts the old one firmly in the past: who knows what glories now await the 'Blue Brazils' of Cowdenbeath? Their ground is better than ever - cruel local humour about an all-seater stadium and a three-piece suite notwithstanding. As the local

'"Slim Jim" Baxter, one of my heroes'.
Denis Law hails a Baxter goal (one of his two) at Wembley in 1963 -
another Scottish win, 2-1.

'There's that 9-3 defeat at Wembley in 1961'
(*Left*) Frank Haffey watches the seventh England goal go past him.
(*Right*) Haffey leaves the Wembley pitch - allegedly
contemplating leaving the country.

143

MP, I was delighted to receive an invitation to the official opening of the ground improvements, so can now conclusively deny this calumny.

Small World

It's sometimes said - enviously, and usually in England - that Scotland is so small that we all know each other: so it's hardly surprising that I've had the the chance over the years to meet some of the managers of the national squad. I remember meeting Jock Stein during the seventies, by which time his reputation was secure, thanks to the efforts of Celtic's Lisbon Lions, as celebrated by Brian Wilson in the previous chapter. I met Tommy Docherty years after his brief tenure in charge of the squad; I only wish that his results with the team had been as impressive as his subsequent charity fund-raising.

And I met Alex Ferguson, before his departure for Old Trafford, when he was still the toast of Scotland for his achievements with Aberdeen during the eighties. He struck me immediately as a man who had never lost touch with his roots in Govan, the working class area of Glasgow where my father was a minister in the thirties and forties. He gave the impression that no matter how high he climbed, his feet would remain firmly on the ground.

Andy Roxburgh was altogether different in his approach. I always suspected that, as a former primary school headmaster, he brought useful skills to the management of our more volatile international players. But perhaps his greatest achievement was to lower the expectations of the Scottish football-following public to a realistic level more in keeping with our small population and our real status in the footballing world.

Yet the fanaticism that has characterised Scotland's following - of which I can claim to have been a part for many years - of the national football team still demands some explanation. You need only to recollect the scenes of delirium among the Scottish fans when the team beat England 3-2 at Wembley in 1967 - when they tore up bits of turf to take home as a living memento - to realise that clearly there was a lot more at stake than the result of 22 men kicking a ball around.

They took a lot more turf after the 2-1 win in 1977. There's a pub in central Scotland that displays a lump of Wembley turf to commemorate victory over England. I wouldn't be at all surprised to hear that some of the hundreds who took a lump had, in the heat of the moment, eaten a bit. Some, I know, even jumped onto the crossbar and broke that up too. One - anonymous since he has failed to confess it in this book - is now a colleague, an MP and a respectable citizen. If you don't count Saturday afternoons.

It's often argued in Scotland that the problem with the team's following in the 1970s was that they were expecting the national squad to carry the burden of national pride, for a country that was denied its own parliament. And certainly, if English nationalism flowered on the playing fields of Eton, then Scottish nationalism has had one recurrent expression - on the pitch at Hampden. Which perhaps explains, in the context of the United Kingdom, why many Scots' pride in the team's performances has been enhanced periodically by the sheer joy of defeating the English at the game they regard as their own.

That's why 1967 was surely one of the greatest hours of the boys in blue. I was 16 then, but I still remember watching the humbling of England - on the very pitch on which they had been crowned only a year previously as the champions of the world - by the skills and audacity of 'Slim Jim' Baxter, one of my heroes. It was both a Home International and a European Championship qualifier. In Scotland, though, that day is still thought of as the real World Cup decider. I feel similarly about the 2-1 win at Hampden, in 1976, when Dalglish slid the winner through the legs of a disbelieving Clemence.

But such rare triumphs must be judged in an historical context in which disappointments and defeats at the hands of the English are legion. And I don't mean Flodden, Culloden and all that. There's that 9-3 defeat at Wembley in 1961. I will never forget listening on the radio, listening ever more incredulously as goal after goal went past Frank Haffey, the unfortunate goalie who said he'd have to emigrate. Nor would I dwell on our team's performance at Wembley in 1975: suffice it to say that England just slipped past us with a sneaky 5-1 win.

But as someone who was actually there at a lot of the games, I think that it's also fair to say that there were some other non-political reasons to account for the fans' fanaticism. In 1974, we managed not only

145

'Archie Gemmill scored the goal of the tournament'.
But a 3-2 win over Holland - the eventual runners-up in 1978 - was not enough to take Scotland to the next stage in Argentina.

Among my Souvenirs: The Tartan Army comes out *with* the pitch in 1977.

to be the only team from Britain to qualify for the World Cup finals in West Germany, but we also managed to go out of the tournament without losing a single game. Players like Bremner, Jordan, Holton and Harvey were worthy of some fanaticism.

In 1978 - a national disaster for Scotland that many would compare with the Darien Scheme - part of the fanatical support generated by the team's qualification for the finals in Argentina must surely be explained by that extraordinary personality of the team's manager - the irrepressible Ally McLeod. Who else would have had the brass-neck to organise a Victory Party for thousands of the supporters at Hampden - before the team had even set foot on Argentine soil? In fact, come to think of it, perhaps he knew more about Scotland's relative strength than the rest of us. And even once the team had suffered the indignity and agony of the games against Peru and Iran - and Johnston's early, forced departure - we still had our moment of glory, when Archie Gemmill scored the goal of the tournament. For a few brief, flickering moments the impossible - Scotland beating Holland by the three clear goals needed to go through - seemed to be happening. But alas, once more it was not to be.

Knowing our own strengths - and weaknesses

The 1980s have proved to be a harsh journey of self-discovery for the Scotland follower. What we've discovered is that we're really not World Beaters and should therefore relish the chance to play among the world's best every four years. Yet, if our weakness at international level has sometimes been brutally exposed, Scottish football still has some great strengths.

George Foulkes illustrates, in his chapter, what the game can mean at the grassroots across his Ayrshire constituency. That goes for communities the length and breadth of Scotland. Wee boys still have kickabouts in the street, dreaming of glory. Old men in pubs will tell you what they have seen and what might have been. Middle-aged men like myself watch and hope.

Who knows? ... Some day ... And, if worst comes to worst, we still beat England sometimes.

147

BURNLEY

ALEX CARLILE (Liberal Democrat, Montgomery)

Born in Burnley, he qualified as a barrister in London, before moving to the Welsh Borders. Having contested Flintshire East in 1974 and 1979, he was elected to Parliament, for Montgomery, in 1983. Has been the spokesman for his party on several issues, mainly Legal Affairs until 1990, then Trade and Industry, Wales, Employment and Health.

A member of the Select Committee on Welsh Affairs, he is Leader of the Welsh Liberal Democrat Party.

14

VINTAGE CLARET AND WELSH RAREBIT

Alex Carlile

Our house was on Manchester Road, Burnley. The town is surrounded by moorland hills, cold and blown and patterned with dry-stone walls. Our house was Trafalgar House, a reminder of Nelson's great victory in the year of its building. Below Trafalgar Street stood Nelson Square. From victorious early nineteenth century optimism the Industrial Revolution developed a town of local strength and close community. At the focus of that community were The Clarets, Burnley Football Club, one of the founder members of the Football League. It was the Clarets that gave Burnley the feel and confidence of a big town.

I was first taken to Turf Moor when I was seven, by old Harry Hargreaves. The crowds were large, often 25,000 plus. The first match which I ever saw was between Burnley and Luton Town in the First Division. Colin McDonald, probably one of England's finest ever keepers, played in goal for Burnley. From the age of seven onwards, I was a regular. With Harry Hargreaves I used to stand behind the goal at the open end of the ground, often hearing more than I could see. When I arrived home after the match they always knew the score - the cheers and groans carried all the way, half a mile across the town from the ground, which nestled in a corner of Burnley centre.

Lord Above

Burnley football was ruled with an iron rod by a rough, tough and able butcher called Bob Lord. To the footballing authorities, he was an unwelcome rebel. To us Burnleyites, he was someone who knew how to keep a small club at the top. The youth policy which he set up produced a series of great players, many of whom were later sold to bigger clubs at no cost to the quality of the Clarets. A lesson which Bob Lord could give to modern clubs is the importance of local loyalty: although he could be ruthless and at times showed disloyalty to some of his best players, under Lord's chairmanship the club always had a fiercely local quality. And the names of the players were redolent of the North - Brian Pilkington and Albert Cheeseborough were among the best of Bob Lord's young discoveries.

His greatest achievement was undoubtedly the Football League championship winning side of 1959-60, managed with compliant skill by Harry Potts. As the tabloids of the 1990s trumpet the qualities of today's millionaire super-heroes, I often wonder what they would have made of the likes of Jimmy McIlroy, Ray Pointer, Jimmy Adamson and Alex Elder. McIlroy was surely one of the greatest inside-forwards of all time: a balletic, lithe, lightweight player, he mesmerised defences with his ball control. There were no histrionics, yet when he had the ball on the ground, there was theatre in the air. He was a truly Irish player - his feet had wit; and defences feared him. Fulham were another great side of the same era, particularly because of the skills of Johnny Haynes; Blackburn Rovers, then definitely Burnley's poor relations, had Bryan Douglas; Spurs had the brilliant John White; Manchester United had the fabulous Bobby Charlton, probably the finest all-round player I have ever seen. Yet McIlroy had something possessed by none of them: an uncanny sense of where the ball was and where it should go next. A signed copy of his light, but interesting, *Right Inside Soccer* remains on my shelves; and McIlroy has not deserted Burnley, where he is a leading sports journalist.

Of course, there was much more to the Burnley Championship side than Jimmy McIlroy. Great goalkeeping was a Burnley tradition. Colin Macdonald was followed by Adam Blacklaw, who won international recognition for Scotland and was one of the most reliable of goalkeepers. The full-backs were the smooth and suave John Angus and the elegant Alex Elder: Elder was once picked in a world representative eleven, a true mark of his quality. Among the half-backs was one of the best of all uncapped players, Jimmy Adamson: his subsequent, and not unusually distinguished, spells in management will never remove the memory of a mid-field control which makes most of today's players look like park amateurs. And there were others - the dashing Ray Pointer, his shock of red hair striking the ball goalwards; Jimmy Robson, the butt of many jokes yet nevertheless a prolific, if gangling, goal scorer.

Sometimes, I feel almost overcome by nostalgia for a Burnley football

League Champions 1960. Back row *(l-to-r)*: Elder, Robson, Cummings, Blacklaw, Miller, Angus and Pointer. Front row *(l-to-r)*: Connelly, McIlroy, Adamson, Pilkington and Meredith.

Division II Play-Off Winners 1994: Back row *(l-to-r)* :Wilson, Williams, Farrell, Deary, Parkinson, McMinn, Peel, Lancashire and Beresford. Front row *(l-to-r)*: Joyce, Davis, Eyres, Pender, Heath, Thompson and Mark Leather (physio).

team which once was but no longer is. Today the ground is much smaller in capacity. Yet it remains potentially a big club. Its crowds were among the highest in the new Second Division and greater than many in Division I, promotion to which was secured in the 1994 play-offs - and you shouldn't believe all that Peter Snape tells you about those in his chapter.

The town continues to regard The Clarets as the flagstaff for Burnley. They can count on my continuing support.

Moving on to Montgomery - football all the way

Since I left Burnley to go to university, I have continued to watch football whenever possible. I have tried supporting various other clubs - Chelsea when I was a student; Crystal Palace under the skilful management of Steve Coppell; Chester when I lived there; Wrexham when they were in the old Second Division for all too brief a period; and Shrewsbury Town. Yet childhood loyalty is hard to lose and I never felt drawn to another league club.

It was my home in Montgomeryshire that drew me inexorably to another team with its own Turf Moor - that is to say, a small but handsome stadium near its town centre, the town itself surrounded by hills, and with a club structure based upon local people and local support. This led me to Llanidloes Town, whose ground is at Victoria Avenue, Llanidloes.

I was first taken to Llanidloes Town by Dick Thomas, the President. He is no millionaire football club chairman. However, his is the essence of Llanidloes. In the early and mid-1940s, he used to organise the washing and setting out of the kit. He was the club groundsman for 20 years and the trainer for two; a linesman for several seasons; and has been, at the time of writing, a committee member for nearly 50 years. He acts as a gate-man at home matches and secures sponsorship - including my own modest contribution to help buy the ball once per season.

Llanidloes Town is one of the oldest clubs in Wales, currently in one of the local leagues but aspiring to return to what is now the Konica

League of Wales. The date 1875 on the Grandstand probably reflects the year when football was first played in the town. Prior to 1939, the ground had a private owner whose dairy cattle grazed on the pitch between matches. This created obvious difficulties, although it probably gave Llanidloes something of an advantage over visiting teams: at least they knew in advance where the cow pats were. Eventually, through the generosity of a successful local businessman and Alderman, Sir George Hamer, the ground was bought and secured for the town.

The history of Llanidloes Town evokes football of a bygone age. In 1906-07, they lost 3-2 after extra time in the Montgomeryshire Challenge Cup Final to The Royal Welsh Warehouse. They won the trophy for the first time in 1912-13 and many times thereafter. They have been frequent champions of the Mid-Wales League and won the Welsh Amateur Cup as recently as 1965.

Welsh football has had a chequered history over recent years. Of late Llanidloes Town have not enjoyed great fortune. However, the quality of the ground, the determination of the committee and the support for football in Llani make me very hopeful that we shall soon see them back near the top of the Welsh game.

Many characters have played for Llani. One whom I have met is Eirwyn Williams, who came from Tonypandy, to keep goal for the club, in the 1930s. On one occasion, he saved two penalties against Oswestry Town in the Welsh Senior Cup: unfortunately he does not remember either, as he was suffering from concussion at the time. On another occasion, he had just released the ball, preparatory to taking a goal kick: an eleven year-old supporter of opponents, Newtown, rushed on to the pitch and kicked the ball into the goal - and the goal stood! Llanidloes lost 2-1. Locals swear that this story is true.

Williams kept goal for Llanidloes on and off between 1933 and 1951. He has told me of other celebrated Llanidloes players - notably H.B (Gurra) Mills and Jack Lloyd. Mills was the last Llanidloes player to win a cap for Wales.

Victoria Avenue has had its share of other odd incidents and special memories. During the last war, there was a prisoner-of-war camp at

'... small but handsome... surrounded by hills.'
Victoria Avenue, home of Llanidloes Town FC.

Welsh Amateur Cup-Winners 1922: This historic photograph of Llanidloes includes
Sir George Hamer (standing furthest left), who was later to buy the ground for the
club, and Jack Lloyd, the captain, whose knees embrace the trophy.

nearby Newtown. A team of Italians and Germans was made up from the camp and came to Victoria Avenue to play Llanidloes Town. The local players found the Germans very pleasant, but the Italians less so. There was a fiasco in the middle of the match, a brawl involving the Italian prisoners. Troops had to come on to the field to bring about peace.

Less controversial was the appearance, in a Llanelli shirt, of Jock Stein. Michael Howard records, in his chapter, how the man who was to go on to manage Celtic and Scotland had a season at Llanelli. They still talk of his 1950-51 visit to Victoria Avenue.

To visit Llanidloes Town is to see pride amid the struggle of modern football. In addition to Dick Thomas, there are local characters like the Chairman, Byron Hughes, and advertisers like the High Street Cobblers and Les's Cycle Shop, for whom the advertising is an act more of faith than commerce.

Although I still look first for Burnley's result, I hope that one day I may have the opportunity of seeing Llanidloes, albeit within the smaller Welsh context, emulating the success of The Clarets in 1959-60. Following both these teams has not always been unalloyed pleasure and has often been associated with failure. Nevertheless, they are to me the essence of what football should be - a game, part of the tribal loyalty of a community, an entertainment, sometimes a passion.

The full reference to Jimmy McIlroy's autobiography is given in the further reading at the end of this book.

LIVERPOOL

DAVID HUNT (Conservative, Wirral West)

Having been to school in Liverpool, he studied and practised law in Bristol. Was locally and nationally active, in the early 1970s, in youth organizations, when he served on the Advisory Committee on Pop Festivals.

Returned to Merseyside, in 1976, as MP for Wirral (subsequently Wirral West). Following junior posts in successive Thatcher Governments, he was Secretary of State for Wales (1990-93) and for Employment (1993-94), becoming Chancellor of the Duchy of Lancaster in 1994.

15

FAN ACROSS THE MERSEY

David Hunt

It was something of a dream come true to arrive in the House of Commons back in 1976, as a newly-elected representative from my beloved Merseyside. Although I was born in North Wales, it is Liverpool, where I was brought up, that has always been my home city; my centre of gravity.

Admittedly, my Wirral constituency is on the 'wrong' side of the river, where Tranmere Rovers are the local team. But, for many inhabitants not just of the Wirral and North Wales or even North-West England, Liverpool is not merely the centre of gravity, but the 'centre of the universe'. The reason for this is very simple: *football!* And the epicentre is, of course, Anfield and Liverpool FC.

In my youth, although I played a lot of cricket, the sporting lifeblood of my family, and of my city, was always football. During my lifetime, the city of Liverpool has had its ups and downs, and there have been times when the future has seemed quite bleak. But we have always come through, not least because our football clubs have given us a real reason for pride and for optimism. Supporters of Manchester United find that the name of their city is known across the world thanks to the 'people's game'; they rarely acknowledge that the same is true of Liverpool.

Notwithstanding, a Liverpool-supporting, Conservative MP, must surely be permitted to draw two parallels with the fortunes of Liverpool FC: those of Merseyside; and those of the Conservative Party.

The Quality of Mersey

In the last few years, Liverpool FC has seemed to mirror some of the travails of our city. The marked decline in performance on the pitch has seemed - wrongly in my view - to send the message that we in

Liverpool just aren't world-beaters any more. Our recent foray back into Europe showed that we have lost the right admixture of youth and experience for the time being; and humiliating exits from the FA Cup, in successive recent seasons, both of them at Anfield itself, show that ours is no longer a 'fortress to be feared'.

As I say, the Wirral has its own team in Tranmere Rovers. Their tremendous development, during the same period, has both intrigued me and cheered me immensely. Indeed, there has been a pronounced shift in the relative positions of our teams on Merseyside. It is just as hard to recall that Everton could win the Football League 10 years ago as it is to recall that Liverpool could achieve the same only five seasons ago.

But let us reflect on, and rejoice in, how far Tranmere, once very distant cousins, have come in recent years. I cannot predict how long this shift will last: it must have some connection with the prohibitive costs

'Images of Hillsborough'
Everton fans add to the tributes on the gates of Anfield.

of essential ground development for clubs with huge grounds like Anfield or Goodison Park. For instance, Liverpool's Centenary Stand, opened in 1992, cost £8 million. The persistent success of Wimbledon, against the odds, has been greatly helped by the ground-sharing arrangement at Selhurst Park, where the full costs of ground development have been borne by Crystal Palace.

There is, however, no point in reflecting on what sort of team we might have bought at Liverpool with the money spent on renovating, say, the Kop. The images of Hillsborough, which none of us will ever forget, must remind us of the importance of ground safety. We have seen a tremendous amount of work and effort - in upgrading standards of safety and of comfort, too.

That said, can there be a Liverpool fan in the world who does not mourn the passing of the old Kop terraces? I recall Ken Dodd reflecting on that vast, swaying mass:

> *'I'll swear they must all wear suede shoes ... otherwise, how do they do it?'*

Soon, there will be a whole generation supporting our clubs, to whom the Stretford End or the Kop will evoke not that almost organic mass of humanity which we have known, but banks of rather expensive seats.

I just pray that the changes don't result in the club's losing its tremendous community spirit as a result - even though being an MP has, in certain respects, cut me off from all that. If I don't share Ann Taylor's view that sitting in the directors' box is the only perk of being an MP (though perhaps that's how it feels in Opposition), I have been able to enjoy what can be both a perk and an obligation - not to mention an embarrassment.

I still remember that terrible moment. A derby match. And Liverpool scored against the oldest enemy, Everton. I leapt to my feet and started screaming, shouting, laughing and cheering. Then, suddenly, I looked around. I wasn't on the terraces. This was the directors' box, with rows of elder statesmen, seated solemnly and gazing at me in amazement. These were the perils of promotion!

THIS IS ANFIELD   Thus goes the famous legend at the end of the players' tunnel at Liverpool. Traditionally, that slogan had the same sort of effect on visiting players as a sign saying *'This is the Whips' Office'* at the House of Commons. My earliest memories of Liverpool really making the running in the League were in the days of Bill Shankly. What was so striking about what he developed at the club after arriving in 1959 was the quite palpable team spirit: the sense of shared success, determination to win and willingness to fight - allied, of course, to an attacking, flowing and skilled style of play.

We all too rarely hear about team spirit at the big clubs these days - ask today's youngsters about team spirit and they will think of Wimbledon's Crazy Gang, Oldham or even Barnet. But team spirit is too important, in football as in politics, to be the exclusive preserve of the equivalents of Kidderminster Harriers and the SDP. I am not proposing that Liverpool sign him, but they must understand what Vinny Jones represents - and why Graeme Souness's Liverpool never beat Joe Kinnear's Wimbledon. Kinnear is a great motivator and we all need them, in every walk of life. But, then, Tommy Smith and, in his day, Graeme Souness provided the same inspiration to the team and the same threat to the opposition.

Although the clubs are in many respects clearly poles apart, and despite the sales of the former years, a small number of clubs in the top flight - including Arsenal, Wimbledon and Liverpool - have one interesting thing in common: if you compare the squad photographs of 1993-94 with those of, say, four years previously, many of the personnel are unchanged. At Blackburn or Newcastle, on the other hand, you might find only *one* common face. Our players at Liverpool should know each other's strengths and weaknesses by now; perhaps familiarity has bred contempt, but it is a poor reflection on them if it has. With a settled squad, and players with the potential of Redknapp and Fowler, Roy Evans clearly has an opportunity to turn things around. But he will achieve that only if his players are a cohesive and energetic unit.

If Roy does find the sort of success which Liverpool had begun to take for granted, he will, of course, join a remarkable list. Of the 10 most successful football managers in England since the war, no fewer than three were at Anfield: Bob Paisley, who tops the table with 14 trophies; Bill Shankly, who laid the foundations, with seven; and Kenny Dalglish

THIS IS ANFIELD. And this is the second coming of Ian Rush - returning from Juventus, in August 1988, to sign for Kenny Dalglish *(right)*.

with five. Bob Paisley and Kenny Dalglish were League Champions with Liverpool as both player and manager. Each of them, and Bill Shankly, played in, and managed, FA cup-winning teams. That is an incredible list of achievements.

Metaphor and Against

Football metaphors abound in parliamentary debate - even among Members who are indifferent to football. The Liberal Democrat leader, Paddy Ashdown, may have disappointed his colleagues (as Nigel Jones reports in his chapter) when they canvassed his support on football matters, but he still talks of 'level playing fields' - an especially odd metaphor for the MP for Yeovil (although they have one now, I'm told) - and of 'own goals'. And my Cabinet colleague, Stephen Dorrell, recently warned Labour against 'playing the ball across their own penalty area'.

And so it goes on. But the parallels go beyond mere metaphor. For me, two parallels, in particular, stand out: politics, like football, is a team sport that depends upon harnessing local loyalties; and both of these activities are having to adjust to changes in tastes, management styles and marketing.

I've had my say on team spirit already. When we see defenders in a football match hurling hysterical abuse at each other, we see the discord which, unchecked, can bring a club to its knees. I, personally, am reminded of the fractiousness and bitterness in Labour Party ranks in the early 1980s and what they portended.

Like Liverpool FC, of course, the Conservative and Unionist Party has a pretty amazing record. We have our occasional mid-season wobbles, but we have never even flirted with relegation; our 'home' record is exceptional; and we have a fine history of holding on to narrow leads. Just ask the marvellous David Amess in Basildon or the equally marvellous Peter Thurnham in Bolton! It has always been said of the Conservative Party that loyalty is its 'secret weapon'; indeed, that is a pretty open 'secret'. Much the same was true of Liverpool FC; but loyalty - real dyed-red-in-the-wool loyalty - is not such a common commodity anywhere in football these days.

Yet football clubs, and political parties, must never lose their roots in localities and in communities. A club's scouts, and a political party's local councillors, perform the same sort of function. They make an institution responsive and representative. For the supporters, both politics and football are voluntary and expensive activities; and we must court their enthusiasm and support.

Red and Blue Together - We Shall Not Be Moved!

Since I was born in 1942, the Conservative Party has had a working majority for a total of 35 years. And Liverpool has been the dominant force in English football for most of the past 30 years. In the 1980s, in particular, Liverpool domination and Conservative domination went together. The Conservative Party has maintained its success by responding to change, not in a reflexive or panicky fashion, but by allowing itself periods of reflection and analysis, and by taking a reasonably objective and long-term view of how economic and social trends are to be reacted to.

Some contend that this is better achieved in opposition - the equivalent of arguing that a team needs to be relegated once in a while to get its affairs back in order and to regenerate. Both are specious ideas: the business, the motivation, the very stuff of both football and politics, boil down to one thing. *Winning.*

From the vantage point of a football club, several irreversible changes are now clearly discernible. The record attendance at Anfield, for a start, is 61,905 - for an FA Cup Fourth Round tie with Wolves, back in 1952. For 1993-94, the capacity at the ground was down to 45,054 - and rare, indeed, were the occasions when that sort of figure was attained. Tastes have changed. And clubs with average gates as low as Oldham's 12,000 or so and Coventry's 15,000 have shown that they can compete with the best.

The trend towards home-viewing of live matches, and the growth in 'Pay-TV', confirmed by Sky, shows how money taken at the turnstiles is diminishing in relative importance. Indeed, I believe that the Manchester United Club Shop takes more in a year than Wimbledon take at the turnstiles. The Tottenham experience is a salutary warning

JAMIE
REDKNAPP

STEVE
McMANAMAN

'If Redknapp and McManaman continue to develop...'

against excessive diversification, but that is clearly the direction in which clubs will move, be they large or small.

Finally, both football clubs and political parties need youth development. The main reason I foresee Manchester United dominating English football for so long is their exceptional youth policy, a highly successful throwback to the great Matt Busby's methods in which Stan Orme revels in his chapter. The last Liverpool player to win a PFA Young Player of the Year Award was Ian Rush, back in 1983, and he is now well into a highly-productive Indian Summer. We have had PFA players of the year more recently, but, like the Championships, they too have dried up.

The development of youngsters' talents was, of course, a major responsibility of mine while I was Secretary of State for Employment, 1993-94. It is also an important consideration for political parties. If our youth movements do not have active memberships, and radical but responsible views, the future looks far less promising. But 'youth activism' has found other channels in recent times and that is our loss. I could not help reflecting on this, when, having unwittingly failed to hand over 'protection money' on a recent visit to Anfield, I returned to find my car trashed by a group of urchins. That is not what we mean by enhancing opportunities for our young people!

After the World Cup of 1990, the game of football reasserted itself, with varying success, as our national game without peer. I hope that the 1994-95 season will demonstrate that we have been similarly galvanised, despite the great British absence, by the 1994 Finals. But fervour towards our national team cannot conceal the fact that every fan's primary, burning loyalty is towards his or her club team. So, if the resurgence of the game is to reach new heights, what we really need, above all, is to see the European Champions' Cup back here in England. Is it too much to hope for, I wonder, that it will be Liverpool who bring it back? If the likes of Redknapp, McManaman and Fowler continue to develop as they have been, that may well come to pass.

Even if it doesn't, I can only agree with that living legend, Elton Welsby, who once sagely remarked that

'football today would certainly not be the same if it had never existed'.

FALKIRK

Est. 1876
FALKIRK F.C.

DOUG HENDERSON (Labour, Newcastle North)

Opposition Spokesman on Local Government and Secretary of the British Russian Group.

A former Fife and Glasgow amateur footballer, he retired, with a groin injury, from the Westminster Wobblers' midfield. A timid climber and a poor cross-country skier, he is a 2.46 marathon runner who still runs, cross-country, for Cambuslang and Elswick Harriers.

Enjoys a glass of beer at Durham County Cricket Club and occasionally at the Oval/Lords (when the Whips can be deceived).

16

BOUNCING BACK WITH THE BAIRNS

Doug Henderson

'Too good to be relegated' said the press, as we lost yet another Scottish Premier League match in March 1993.

But my instinct told me differently. I had seen it coming in January, as Aberdeen knifed through our butterlike defence and I said so, after the loss of the third goal, to my son, Keir. Then aged six, he was oblivious to the portending horror, as his loyalties lay - and still lie - firmly with Newcastle United. He is proud of his Geordie origins, having been born a few months after I moved to Newcastle. The *quid pro quo* for being accompanied by father to St. James' Park is, on occasions, to join the long-standing sufferers at Brockville Park, Falkirk.

Yo-Yo Club

Relegation is commonplace for the 'Bairns'. We went down in 1950-51 before I was out of nappies. Our relegation, in 1958-59, was an acute embarrassment at school in Fife. My classmates either followed the local team, Raith Rovers, or succumbed, like many Scottish 'provincials', to sectarian tendencies and supported Glasgow Rangers. But, by the time of the next drop, in 1968-69, I had learned to rationalise the consequences of my addiction.

Readers who recall that the Scottish League consisted, throughout this period, of but two divisions, might wish to remind me that what goes down must have come up: relegation could so regularly be achieved only by being promoted every bit as often. True, but when did loyal fans dwell on the good times?

Anyhow, a good spell in the early 1970s was followed by relegation, again, in 1973-74. Then, with the creation, in 1975-76, of the Scottish League as we were to know it until the end of the 1993-94 campaign - of

Premier, First and Second Divisions - the Bairns promptly subjected me to the ultimate indignity of relegation, in 1976-77, to the new Second Division.

So it now needed a double bounce to get back to the top. Promotion to the Premier League came eventually in 1985-86. But, since I became a Member of Parliament in 1987 - for Newcastle-upon-Tyne North - we have twice been bounced out again. The baiting in the House of Commons Lobby more than matches the humiliation experienced at school in 1959.

My research assistant said to me, four days before the General Election in 1992, that she could not take any more of the pressure and stress. I told her this was nothing. My mind and body had had to endure far worse - every Saturday, for nine months of the year, and often on Wednesdays as well - for the last 35 years .

It's now 37 years. My life sentence dates back to 1956-57, when Falkirk won not only the Scottish FA Cup, but the undying support of a seven year-old, living 50 miles away in Fife. I've tried to find a more honourable explanation in family ties. Tracing a distant relative from Falkirk provided a tenuous link. Then, in 1972, I met Jan Graham who hails from Denny, a mere seven miles from Falkirk. While those roots added to the innumerable attractions of my wife-to-be, my devotion to the struggles of the South Enclosure gained me badly needed 'street cred' among my male in-laws-to-be - sufficient to compensate for my left political views and the length of my hair.

And yet, on those depressing Saturday nights after a fourth successive defeat, one questions one's sanity. Would it not have made life much easier to have supported Rangers? Or why not use the excuse of my exile in England and give my total commitment to Newcastle United? Who could blame me for switching loyalty not only to my constituents but to my son? Addictions are not, of course, so easily treated.

Falkirk are a medium-sized, Scottish provincial club, mostly drifting, as you'll have gathered, between the bottom of what is now the Premier Division and the top of the First Division. Occasionally, we creep into the middle of the top League. In 1970-71, when Alex Ferguson was our leading scorer, we finished seventh out of the top 18.

THE CUP FINAL LINE-UP

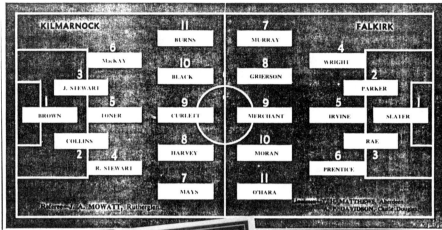

'... Falkirk won not only the
Scottish FA Cup, but the
undying support of a
seven year-old, living 50
miles away in Fife'.

Every few years we have a great find. But, inevitably, star players are transferred to ease the financial situation. Sir Matt Busby, when asked to name a World Star XI in the early 1960s, included Alex Parker, who had been sold to Everton in 1958. John White, our last full international to be capped while registered as our player, left for Tottenham in 1959. Gary Gillespie went to Coventry in 1977, while Stuart Kennedy (1976) and Gary Smith (1991) both joined Aberdeen.

My first game was a 2-1 win at Raith Rovers on 20 December 1958. But matters did not progress as well throughout the season. With one game remaining we had 26 points, as did Dunfermline. In the last game of the season we drew 2-2 in the return match with Raith Rovers, after missing a penalty, and Dunfermline beat Partick Thistle 10-1. We were relegated. The fact that we went down after getting the highest number of points for a relegated team in the old First Division was no consolation.

We were, of course, again relegated with a high points total in 1987-88, when league reconstruction required that three teams go down.

Heady days remembered

Football fans of my generation look back with nostalgia at the size of the crowds in those heady days. In 1956-57, on the way to that Scottish Cup win, the home ties against Aberdeen and Clyde drew 16,269 and 20,000, respectively, a remarkable achievement in a town with a population of 40,000 and a hinterland of a little over 100,000.

By the late 1960s, I was playing football most Saturdays and saw very few matches - typically before home gates of 7-8,000. I recall, with great affection, our successful season of 1970-71 when I was a student in Glasgow and, as I say, we finished seventh. And we reached the semi-finals of the League Cup. 'Tiger' McLaughlin, the attack-minded left back who was later transferred to Everton, emerged as a great star. Our goalscoring inside-forwards were two future managers of Scotland: Alex Ferguson and Andy Roxburgh.

Falkirk had signed Roxburgh from Partick Thistle in 1969, as we were reminded during a 1-0 home defeat by Thistle in 1992-93. At half time, Scotland's then Manager presented some local school footballers with a magnificent trophy. The chant went up from the young lads in the crowd:

> *He's just a Thistle reject,*
> *He's just a Thistle reject,*
> *Ha-ha-ha-ha, ha-ha-ha-ha!*

Yet most of them would not have been born then. To the uninitiated, many football chants must sound inane. But, to those in the know, so many of the ditties provide a resumé of the club's history, which even the young fans are expected to have learned.

In the late 1970s and early 1980s, we reached rock bottom. But the enthusiasm of the South Enclosure, whence I have long enjoyed spectating, remained undented. If individually we were pig sick, collectively we found solace in our predicament. The luck of the cup draw brought us many a chance to mock visitors from a higher League and we could take great comfort in the guarantee of a trip to Hampden - not, of course, for the Cup Final, or even a semi-final, but for the away League match against Queen's Park.

During this 'low' period, I saw few matches. Saturdays were mainly spent cross-country running in winter and hill-racing in summer. But I returned to my addiction in 1984-85 and have been permanently afflicted ever since.

Addiction confirmed

During these last 10 seasons of renewed addiction, I have breached, only occasionally, a firm rule. Taking part in running is given priority over watching football. Every August, I carefully identify some Saturdays for running and others for football spectating. No other use of a Saturday afternoon is considered. This formula now means I average around 25 matches a season. In 1993-94, I was two over par: 13 Falkirk; five Newcastle; and nine others - including a New Year's Day match at Stranraer, when most other Scottish fixtures, including our own against Stirling Albion, were postponed.

Sunday football has helped, though, to create space for multiple sporting activities at the weekend. Thus I recall taking in the away defeat
by Hearts in the Scottish Cup Quarter-Final on a Sunday afternoon in
March 1992, after turning out for Elswick Harriers in the North of
England Cross Country League on the Saturday. And many Newcastle
matches also take place on a Sunday to satisfy television schedules.
This has frequently enabled me either to run or to see Falkirk on a
Saturday and then take my son to St. James' Park on a Sunday afternoon.

But why do I stay with my addiction? I have explained that I have no
geographical obligation, and only a retrospective familial excuse, to give
Falkirk my support. Nearly all my life I have had to travel to both
home and away games. As a kid, as I say, I travelled from Fife. Then,
as a student and in my earlier adult days, I had to make the journey
from Glasgow. Since 1985 I have lived in Newcastle, a 260 miles
round-trip from Brockville Park.

The constant fear of the charge of betrayal keeps me hooked. If I
deserted them now I would feel ungrateful for the pleasures of the good
times in the past - even if they were few and far between. Desertion
would offend the memory of John White. It would erase the historic
euphoria of the 7-3 win over Clyde on 8 December 1962, when inside
left Hugh Maxwell - playing only his second home game - scored all
seven goals. I would be condemned outright as a hedonist who was prepared to revel in the delights of the Scottish Cup win in 1957 and the
more successful days of 1970-71, but not prepared to stand by the club
in the more frequent days of mediocrity. But, perhaps worse, if I
deserted, I would have forgone my right to be there if, by chance, great
days returned. It is that fear more than anything else that feeds the
addiction.

From time to time, though, one is reminded that there are those who
have it just as bad. I recall meeting Campbell Christie, the General
Secretary of the Scottish TUC, behind the stand before the second last
League match on a Wednesday night in the promotion season 1990-91.
My proud boast was that, as a measure of my commitment, I had trav-
elled, that morning, from working for a Labour victory in the
Monmouth by-election. I had flown to Edinburgh, met a lobby group

from the brewing industry, hired a car and arrived at the ground by 7.15 p.m. Dismissively, Campbell told me that he had flown back from a meeting in Seoul. Our boasts were both rewarded with a 4-1 victory. I did not admit to the Parliamentary Whip's Office the nature of my evening commitment and I am sure they would have been even less impressed if they had known that the match was actually live on Sky TV in England.

Campbell later became Club Chairman, taking over, towards the end of the 1992-93 season, as a neutral figure who attempted to bring together two opposing factions in the Board. The majority faction, 'The Deans', then forced him off the Board in March 1994. The wrangles continued until the new owner, George Fulston, took control a week before the end of that season - following a 3-0 win over Hamilton, the previous club he owned. I backed the 'Save the Bairns Group', led by Campbell, who felt the previous owners did not have the best interests of the club at heart.

Viewed in the context of the great swathe of the history of Scottish football, team performances have been relatively successful since the promotion season 1985-86. Crowds have been good in the modern context, averaging over 6,000. The humour, banter and boasts of the South Enclosure are a constant source of amusement and entertainment.

My favourite chant is from 1990-91. At the beginning of that promotion season, we had signed Simon Stainrod from Rouen for £100,000. He rewarded us well with goals, style and even literate interviews on Scottish television. In the crucial away match at Airdrie, in March 1991, he scored a spectacular third goal from 30 yards. Section B of the Airdrie end (a mini-version of Arsenal's now extinct North Bank) abused us with the outburst 'He's just an English bastard'. Our away support of over 4,500 erupted with the response: 'Graham Taylor - Come and get Stainrod!'

Like all football crowds, though, the South Enclosure can occasionally offend. I recall the 1992-93 visit of St. Johnstone, when abuse was hurled at their sweeper, Sergei Baltalcha. He was accused of being a Serbian. But the intellectual end of the enclosure disagreed, alleging that he was a 'Commie'. The error remained uncorrected. In actual fact, he is a Ukrainian citizen and has, as far as I know, given no grounds for any belief that he has any links with the now disbanded Central Committee of the Soviet Communist Party. The former Dynamo Kiev and USSR defender is now, of course, the manager of Caledonian Thistle, admitted to the expanded Scottish League - of which more below - in August 1994.

Too Good To Stay Down

Relegation does not cure an addiction. I was back in the South Enclosure, with my son and two nephews, for the opening game in August 1993 - a 3-2 win over Dunfermline, in what turned out to be a season that was kind to us.

At 3.45 in the morning of 13 December, I was listening to the World Service on my short wave radio in a hotel room in Kursk, where I was an observer at the Russian Elections. I jumped in the air to celebrate our 3-0 victory over St. Mirren in the B & Q Cup Final. There had been a turn-out of 14,000 fans at Fir Park, Motherwell, to watch the final of this competition for Scottish First and Second Division sides.

But better things were to come. The Reserve League was won by early May. Then, despite the Boardroom troubles, we won a two-horse race with Dunfermline to bounce back to the Premier League as champions, clinching it on the last day, 14 May 1994, with a 1-1 draw at

SCOTTISH FIRST DIVISION

AIRDRIE	0	ST MIRREN 2
		Bone 53, Hewitt 67
HT: 0-0		Att: 1,600
AYR	0	CLYDEBANK 0
HT: 0-0		Att: 1,706
DUMBARTON	0	STIRLING 0
HT: 0-0		Att: 887
DUNFERMLINE	1	FALKIRK 1
O'Boyle 34		Shaw 52
HT: 1-0		Att: 13,357
HAMILTON	9	BRECHIN 1
Clark 7, Ward 14, Bapptie 33		Millar 64
McCLean 49, Duffield 58, 72, 88,		
89 (pen), McIntosh 78		HT: 3-0 Att: 1,007
Sent off: Calmey (Brechin) 76, Brown (Brechin) 89		
MORTON	2	CLYDE 0
Mahood 60, 63		HT: 0-0 Att: 1,190

	P	W	D	L	F	A	W	D	L	F	A	Pt
1 Falkirk	35	12	4	2	35	14	8	7	2	28	14	51
2 Dunfermline	35	13	2	2	49	15	9	4	5	27	14	50
3 Airdrie	35	8	6	4	26	17	8	4	5	21	15	42
4 Hamilton	35	9	5	3	35	15	5	7	6	20	28	40
5 Clydebank	35	8	4	5	23	24	7	6	5	24	16	40
Mirren	35	8	3	7	24	20	7			24		38

26 March 1994 - when the Dunfermline v. Falkirk clash attracted 13,357 - more than twice the total of the First Division's other games put together.

Clydebank. We had lost only one League game in the last 32 - a record!

Thereupon, the Scottish League was again reconstructed into four divisions of 10 clubs. We replaced St. Johnstone, Raith Rovers and Dundee among the elite. I felt sorry for Dunfermline, for both clubs were streets ahead of the rest in the league. The second away match at Dunfermline, on 26 March, which ended in a 1-1 draw, was a nerve-wracking affair but a tribute to the commitment of both sides. So, too, was the size of the crowd: 13,357 - some 11,651 more than the next highest attendance in the Scottish First Division that day.

Our manager, Jimmy Jeffries, takes particular credit for motivating the players for that game. For, the night before, all the Boardroom divisions and machinations had become public.

In my view, Scottish football needs a larger Premier League if full-time football is to be extended beyond 10 clubs. I predict growing support for this position. We will probably need further reconstruction if we are to be spared the drop in 1995.

But such thoughts were far from our minds as we celebrated into the night on 14 May. We were euphoric as we drove back down the A74 to Newcastle, overtaking the phalanx of buses, bearing Rangers supporters celebrating the Premier League championship after a tame 0-0 draw with Dundee. Waving our scarves, we taunted them:

> *'We're blue, we're white*
> *We're Premier League dynamite*
> *Falkirk Bairns! Falkirk Bairns!'.*

DUNDEE UNITED

MIKE WATSON (Labour, Glasgow Central)

Became MP for Glasgow Central in a June 1989 by-election, following which he was immediately signed up by the Westminster Wobblers. A regular ever since, he has represented them at Wembley, Goodison Park and Old Trafford, venues to which he could never aspire during a playing career that reached semi-professional level in both England and Scotland.

Author of *Rags to Riches,* the official history of Dundee United, whom he has followed widely throughout Europe, perhaps a reflection of the fact that he specialises, in Parliament, in foreign affairs, particularly overseas development aid issues.

17

SUPPORTING THE ARAB CAUSE

Mike Watson

If not quite unique, it must have been one of the most remarkable matches of the 1950s.

Throughout that decade, goals were scored at a rate which would have contemporary fans drooling at the mouth. A match which produced fewer than four was a rarity and Dundee United alone recorded results of 9-2, 8-1, 7-3 and 4-4 during that 1959-60 season. Yet the first football match to be graced by my presence, on 24 October 1959, finished United 0, Albion Rovers 0.

My grandad used to disparage such matches: 'ach, nae goals, nae fitba'. And who was I to question the judgment of this former Partick Thistle player of the 1920s? At 10 years of age I wouldn't have appreciated the standard of play served up, but then, I didn't care. The roar of the crowd (all 4,500 of them) and the sense of being in on something really important proved a hypnotic mixture and I was hooked.

Terrors of Tannadice

We all know that offspring are supposed to adopt the footballing allegiance of their fathers. Mine was such a complete all-rounder that he spent his youth and early manhood playing a variety of sports, which left no time to watch others do it. So he brought no football scarf when the family moved to Dundee from Glasgow with me but an infant. We arrived in Jute City in 1951, at a time when Dundee FC, a pre-eminent club in the First Division (then the top division) of the Scottish League, had just broken the British transfer record by signing Billy Steel from Derby County for £23,000 - thereby bucking the usual north-south trend, which had, of course, seen Steel leave Morton for Derby, three years earlier, as Kenneth Clarke recalls in his chapter, for a record English fee of £15,000.

The Dark Blues rarely played to crowds of less than 30,000 in the glory days of 1949-53, when they won two League Cups and finished runners-up in League and Scottish Cup. What little time Dad's job allowed him on Saturdays he spent at Dens Park, but his interest had waned (in favour of golf) by the time mine was awakening.

It was securing a place in Invergowrie Primary School's football team that prompted me to press him to take me to a league match. He claims it was simply the fact that United were the club at home on the first Saturday he had free from work which led to my introduction coming at Second Division Tannadice, rather than at First Division Dens. Dundee's prominence meant that all my school mates bar one (he favoured Hearts) supported them and I thought I did too until that momentous entry through the hallowed portals of Tannadice.

Dundee is unique in British (and probably world) football, the city's two League grounds being located just 200 yards apart, on opposite sides of Tannadice Street.

So allegiance to either club owes nothing to geography, nor indeed to religion, although the latter was not always the case. United were formed, as Dundee Hibernian in 1909, from within the city's Irish Catholic community and initially drew its support from that source. However, this had ceased to be the case by the time the club changed its name to Dundee United in 1923.

Paternal influence aside, footballing allegiance in Dundee seems to depend on the recent success, or otherwise, of either club. Hence, as I have mentioned, most of my generation affiliated to Dundee FC (honourable exceptions always prove the rule) while, since the mid-1970s, United have attracted the majority of young supporters.

What really cemented my bond with United was that first season's coinciding with the club's promotion run. Despite the arrival of a new manager, little was expected of a side that had finished the previous campaign third bottom. But Jerry Kerr was to transform the club's fortunes and his inaugural season culminated in a never-to-be-forgotten occasion. Only a point was required from the last match against Berwick Rangers at Tannadice, when I was one of 16,000 who saw the

'Dundee is unique, the city's two League grounds being located just 200 yards apart...'

Promoted! 30 April 1960. Mike Watson insists that he's among the invaders - somewhere.

Terrors (read on!) scrape home 1-0. I don't recall a thing about the game itself, not even the goal, but I do remember the pitch invasion at the end and seeing grown men all around me with tears in their eyes.

Could football really be that important? Is the Pope a Catholic?

The implications of United's return to the First Division, after an absence of 28 years, could hardly have been appreciated that April afternoon in 1960. Kerr revitalised the club and established it as a force. Most importantly, in the eyes of us United fans, he raised it for the first time above Dundee, shedding our 'poor relations' tag in the process. Just six years after winning promotion, Kerr led his troops to an astonishing European Fairs Cup victory over holders Barcelona, winning both legs. Tannadice housed its record attendance of 28,000 for the second leg, as we Arabs pinched ourselves to confirm we had not been beamed up from the real world to some sci-fi planet.

Terrors? Arabs? Yes, these terms do require some explanation. *The Terrors* is United's official nickname, dating back, as far as I can ascertain, only to 1949 when the club, languishing in the lower reaches of the old 'B' Division, had to suffer no fewer than three disallowed goals, yet showed tremendous battling qualities to emerge 4-3 victors over giants Celtic in a momentous Scottish Cup tie at Tannadice.

As for *the Arabs*, that's the rather esoteric collective noun applicable to United supporters. Some dispute surrounds its origin, but the most widely accepted version relates to 1963, a particularly harsh winter which denied United a home match for several weeks. In a desperate attempt to get the pitch fit for a Scottish Cup tie, the management at Tannadice hired a tarburner to melt the ice. That it did, though predictably it also left the grass in a rather threadbare state. 'No problem', thought the cash-starved directors, 'spread a few tons of sand around, paint some lines on it and away we go'. Referees 30 years ago were clearly more amenable than their modern counterparts, because the tie went ahead - and United won handsomely against my old friends, Albion Rovers. So much so, it was said they took to the new surface 'like Arabs' and that might have become the club's new nickname, had fans not turned up at the next few matches, while the sand remained, wearing crude approximations of Arab headgear. Thus the fans hijacked the name for themselves, and the headgear became *de rigeur* at

derby matches, as well as Cup semi-finals and finals. The club souvenir shops now sell authentic Arab *keffiyehs*, specially produced in
tangerine and black.

Despite Kerr's sterling work in establishing United as a member of
Scotland's top six, the club failed to challenge for honours. It required
the arrival of a little-known and largely untested young coach, midway
through the 1971-72 season, to lift United to the level where full-grown
Arabs would once again be forced to dry their eyes in the presence of
small boys. It took eight years, but, in 1979, Jim McLean's superb
young team did just that, beating Aberdeen in the League Cup Final to
capture the club's first major trophy. It was retained a year later to the
immense satisfaction of all Arabs, particularly as it involved a 3-0 drub-
bing of deadly rivals, Dundee, in the final - and at our opponents' Dens
Park no less. Two years on and supplies of paper hankies in the city
had to be rationed as the Premier League championship flag fluttered
over Tannadice, to the astonishment of Glasgow's ruling Old Firm and
just about everyone else besides.

The description of Dundee FC as 'deadly rivals' is nothing unusual in
local derby terms. What is unusual is that the rivalry between the
Dundee clubs has probably been most keenly felt at board level, with a
history of animosity and mutual intolerance characterising successive
generations, dating back to the 1930s at least. The current crop are no
different. In 1989, both the city and regional councils, plus the Scottish
Development Agency, offered the two clubs a multi-million pound pack-
age which would have produced a new 20,000-seat stadium on the city's
ring road. The clubs themselves would have been able to finance their
contribution through selling their current grounds. An ideal opportunity, you might have thought, for modern facilites to replace the outdated
Dens and Tannadice, with much of the finance coming from public
funds.

You might have, but interminable bickering between the two boards -
neither of which was happy at becoming tenants of a municipal stadium, but which relished even less the prospect of sharing facilities with
the other lot - ended with the plug being pulled on the whole project by
the potential backers. That amounted to a tragic loss for the city's fans,
whose interests were submerged and lost amidst waves of directorial
insults and allegations of bad faith.

Nor did the enmity rest there. As United embarked on the first phase of transforming cramped and hemmed-in Tannadice Park to all-seater status (in the face of opposition from many Arabs) Dundee FC's megalomaniac chairman launched an impudent bid to buy a majority of Dundee United's shares with a view to merging the two clubs. The outrage from both sets of fans made his continued presence in the city a security risk and eventually the ill-conceived plan was dropped, though not before both clubs sought legal redress through the courts.

In comparison to the traditional siege mentality of the wise men actually running the clubs, the relationship between the fans has been positively benign. Crowd trouble at city derbies is almost unheard of, though it is most improbable that more than a handful of (probably drunk) Arabs would be found at Dens, or Bluenoses at Tannadice, on any other occasions. The rivalry between them, though undoubtedly intense, lacks any form of hatred. Thankfully, the city clubs have been spared the cancerous sectarianism which has long afflicted both the big two in Glasgow and - to a much lesser extent, as George Foulkes explains - Edinburgh.

Indeed, the relationship between supporters of Dundee and Dundee United is much more akin to that between Everton and Liverpool, as was clearly demonstrated before, during and after the most famous city derby of all, the 1980 League Cup final, which, as I say, was transferred from Hampden Park - a rare triumph over the Glasgow-biased traditionalism of the Scottish Football League. The clubs were allowed to toss a coin for the right to stage it. Dundee won that; United won the match. Despite fears that violence might result from the triumphalism of the winning club's fans, or the demoralisation of the loser's, the occasion emerged as a victory for the city of Dundee.

By the early 1980s, Jim McLean had built a team capable of competing with the best in Europe. In 1987 came United's finest hour, the UEFA Cup final against Gothenburg. This final has, of course, remained a two-legged affair. Although the Swedes took the trophy on a 2-1 aggregate, the disappointment was to a significant extent tempered by the pride felt by all Arabs (and indeed by many Scots much wider afield than Dundee) at the achievement of a club of such modest resources in actually bringing a European final to Scotland.

While reaching finals became almost second nature to McLean's teams during the 1980s, the last step all too often proved one too far. For him, that final hurdle remained as far as the Scottish Cup was concerned - six finals between 1974 and 1991 and not once was the famous old trophy adorned with tangerine and black ribbons.

The Beautiful Game

But that was soon to change. The summer of 1993 saw the end of McLean's 21-year reign and his replacement by Scottish football's first managerial import, Serbian Ivan Golac, the Southampton full-back of the 1970s. To describe him as unorthodox scarcely does him justice; he is fully understood neither by his players nor the media. Not that he has language difficulties: his English syntax is the equal of anyone at Tannadice and indeed in advance of several.

What sets Ivan apart is his laid-back approach, as evidenced by his preparation for a EUFA Cup tie shortly after his arrival. 'Football is a beautiful game, something to be enjoyed by everyone', he opined to the open-mouthed amazement of his assembled players. 'Treat the ball as if it is an intimate lady friend. Caress it'. This brought the memorable rejoinder from an anonymous dressing-room voice: 'In that case, Dave Bowman (United's no-nonsense midfielder) is a wife-beater!' Thereafter, it was off for a stroll in the park and a discussion - embracing art, rock music and world travel - over cups of coffee and bacon rolls. Efficacious? Well, almost. Brondby were beaten, but returned to Copenhagen with the last laugh, qualifying for the next round on away goals.

On his appointment, Golac had announced, with what has since become familiar bravado, that he would lead United to a triumph during his first season. Given that the key to the Tannadice trophy room had not been removed from its hook for 10 years, this was to say the least greeted with some scepticism amongst the media in general and Arabs in particular.

That view seemed to be well-founded, with the club experiencing its worst League season for 18 years, ultimately escaping relegation by a mere two points. But all the while, and almost unnoticed, Golac's men were negotiating a rather laboured path through the various rounds of the Scottish Cup and by April had secured a semi-final meeting with Aberdeen. From the clubs' four League meetings during the season, United had emerged with but a single point, and when the men from the Granite City took an early lead at Hampden Park, the pundits' predictions that the Cup would produce more of the same appeared sound.

As it happened, recovering from the loss of an early goal, United went on to dominate the game and should have been on level terms long before central defender, Brian Welsh, headed the equaliser with less than two minutes remaining. Still the media believed that Aberdeen would exert their authority in the replay, but Golac would have none of it. He claimed his men had been denied their due place in the final and would secure justice at the second attempt. Which they duly did, even though midfielder Jim McInally's goal - the only one of the match - came against the run of play. No matter, Golac, by now a darling of the media, remained on course to deliver his promise of silverware.

If Scottish football had regarded a United victory in the semi-final as improbable, it viewed the task which faced the men in tangerine in the final as little more than making up the numbers. Their opponents were Rangers, whose multi-million pound squad had just won the League championship for the sixth consecutive year, had won all three Scottish trophies the previous season, and now needed merely to add the Scottish Cup to complete an unprecedented back-to-back treble.

Add to the vast gulf in both resources and achievement between the two clubs United's dismal Cup final record, plus the fact that - incredibly - they had never beaten Rangers in a Scottish Cup-tie throughout their 85-year history, and the task facing Golac and his team was comparable to scaling the north face of the Eiger in carpet slippers.

If that became the prevailing view, it was one whose utterance was prohibited within earshot of Tannadice Park. It had taken Golac the motivator to deliver his team to the final; now Golac the psychologist took over. Asked repeatedly about the club's so-called Hampden hoodoo following six Scottish Cup final failures, the Serb scoffed, ridiculing the idea with a 'that was then, this is now' philosophy. He did so knowing that he need convince the only people who mattered - his players.

SEVENTH TIME SUCCESSFUL
Dundee United win the Cup, 1994

ACCESS:
Mike Watson's
ticket

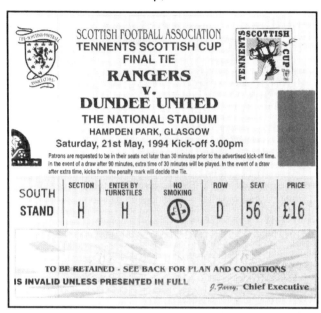

SUCCESS:
Mike Watson holds
the Cup aloft.
Craig Brewster,
scorer of the
winning goal
(wearing scarf),
seems
unimpressed.

That he achieved this in a thoroughly effective fashion was ably demon-strated in the days leading up to the final. The players were clearly relaxed, their preparation on the day prior to the final involving a day at the races, something unthinkable in the days of Jim McLean.

And so to the day of reckoning. For this Arab, it was, and largely remains, a blur. Yes, I was aware of the incredible noise generated by United's supporters, despite their being outnumbered 2:1 by those of Rangers; yes, I was aware of United being denied a clear first half penalty as well as being mightily relieved at a goal-line clearance which prevented Rangers taking the lead; yes, I was aware of, and satisfied with, the half-time score of 0-0, believing that the longer the game remained like that, the better United's chances of creating the one goal which could win it; yes, I was aware of Craig Brewster famously mak-ing that breakthrough in the 48th minute - and pronouncing to all around me that it was 'far too early!' After that, I recall virtually noth-ing. The 42 minutes which followed were by some distance the longest of my life.

The referee's final blast was sweet music indeed, the roar from Arab throats which rent the air containing exultation and relief in at least equal measure. For many, there was no holding back the tears, and I was certainly no exception. Ashamed? Not a bit of it.

Could football be that important? I believe the Pope is still a Catholic.

And I had waited 35 years for that moment; it would have taken a hard-hearted soul to suppress the resulting emotion. I promise to repeat the performance on the election of the next Labour Government - after a considerably shorter wait.

And did we celebrate! Initially, my own contribution was rather restrained, in the knowledge that I had to present myself in reasonably coherent form for a BBC radio phone-in programme the following morn-ing. I was able to turn that to some advantage, however. It began with a review of the Sunday papers; needless to say I did not progress beyond the sports pages.

That afternoon produced another memorable occasion, the triumphant return to Dundee with the cup. Only 12,000 privileged Dundonians had been able to get tickets for the final but Golac and his players paraded the trophy in an open-topped bus, enabling ten times that number to pay homage and share in the joyous and historic return of the Scottish Cup. It had not been seen in the city since Dundee FC captured it in 1910, a year after the founding of the club which was to become Dundee United.

The tour culminated in a civic reception given by the City Council, during which the cup was photographed in the company of as many Arabs as could get their hands on it. Mine was framed and hanging in my office at the House of Commons four days after the final.

A different world

For me, the 75-minute dash from Glasgow to Dundee at Saturday lunch-time, after a morning of constituency surgeries, is as essential a part of my week-ends back in Scotland as any of those duties. The need to switch off entirely from politics is adequately met and the escape it provides is effectively therapeutic, whatever the result of the match. For a few hours I enter a different world.

To football fans in Glasgow Central, for most of whom a Saturday afternoon involves either Celtic or Rangers, I tend to be viewed as enigmatic, but harmless. 'He's no wan ae us, but at least he's no wan ae them' is the verdict of both tribes, so at least I don't lose any friends - other than temporarily when United beat one of Glasgow's big two (and even that endears me, of course, to supporters of the other).

If I have one slight regret it is that United are now three divisions apart from my debut day opponents, Albion Rovers, denying me the opportunity to relive that habit-forming occasion of 35 years ago. The club has come a long way since then; and I have been privileged to march with them, through triumph as well as trauma.

I wouldn't have missed it for the world - or even a Labour Government!

The full reference to the history of Dundee United is given in the further reading at the end of this book.

BURY

VINCIT OMNIA INDUSTRIA

ALISTAIR BURT (Conservative, Bury North)

Despite lacking only the ability to head and shoot, he gave up the idea of being a professional footballer on leaving school and became a Conservative.

Having trained as a solicitor, he was elected a London Borough Councillor in Haringey in 1982 and a Member of Parliament for his native Bury in 1983. Served for five years as Parliamentary Private Secretary to Kenneth Baker before becoming Parliamentary Under-Secretary of State for Social Security in 1992. His responsibilities include benefit levels, lone parents and the Child Support Agency, but there has been no remission, so far, for his generally good conduct.

18

TRUE BLUE HEAVEN

Alistair Burt

I wouldn't say that I was fanatical about football, but I have been known, when challenged about the existence of God, to point to a football and say 'There you are'.

No mere mortal could have devised something so simple yet so sublime. The simplest game in the world and the best. Take my word for it, the Lord knew what he was doing when he gave mankind life, fire, *Warburtons* bread and football.

Of course, I'm biased. You cannot be brought up in Lancashire, with its array of old, distinguished and first-rate clubs without catching a love of the game as easily as you used to pick up your first girlfriend at Bury Palais. I had a further unfair advantage. My father, a family doctor for 41 years, is a Scot, a Fifer, with long memories of massive crowds at Hampden Park and rather smaller ones at Raith Rovers, where wee men in baggy shorts lit up the depression of the twenties and thirties.

Great Hands to shake and a Big Hand for the Shakers

The best is learned early and I imbibed football at my father's knee. When I was a small boy, the big match was, of course, the annual Scotland v England game. And it was *big*. Even if Stan Orme and his workmates found tickets easy to come by in Manchester - in the way he recalls in his chapter above - the chance of getting your hands on one in Fife were so slight that I can remember having a man pointed out to me in the main street of Cardenden, Dad's home village, as being such a man. You almost shook his hand.

There had been another man in that village whose hand I would have shaken if I could have. John Thomson, the Prince of Goalkeepers, had been employed as a miner in the pit where my grandfather was the manager, before his skill took him away from coal and off to Celtic, where he was in the first team at 18. For four all too brief years he set the standards both for club and country, until he died at the foot of a tragic Rangers forward at Ibrox in September 1931. He lies now in Cardenden cemetery, where still, to their eternal credit, supporters bring their flowers.

My father tells me it took many, many years before my grandmother would allow the ceiling in her front room to be repainted, as it bore John's fingerprints, playfully put there on one of his visits.

From such a father did I learn my football. And from such a footballing background he brought his love of the game to one of its cherished historical outposts ... Gigg Lane, Bury. Scoff not! The Shakers may be known today as one of the League's amazing survivors, but their history contains some great moments.

For starters, they have won as many FA Cups as Nottingham Forest (yes, Forest did win the Cup before Cloughie managed them) and more than Chelsea, Derby or Leeds Utd. Furthermore, in case you didn't know, Bury still hold the record for the biggest win in the Final, 6-0 *versus* Derby County in 1903. Eat your heart out Steve Bloomer, as they might have said.

Choosing my words with care, I have to admit that since that heady afternoon, fortune has not smiled as frequently upon us as it might have done. Fourth in Division One in 1926, Bury lost senior status in 1929 and never regained it. But football memories are long. There were still folk around in 1960, when I first went to the ground, who remembered the two FA Cup triumphs of 1900 and 1903.

To my great regret, however, I never met anyone who was present at the 1892 Lancashire Cup Final where the Shakers were given such a wonderful nickname. Club records tell us that the Chairman, Mr Ingham, undaunted by Bury's role as underdogs against Blackburn that afternoon, and clearly having been at the black puddings at half time, was moved to shout 'We'll give them a shaking, for we are the Shakers!' God bless him, for the name has stuck for ever.

190

BURY FC
FA Cup-Winners
1900
and
1903

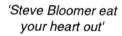

S. Bloomer, Derby County.

21
Bury, 1900.
Nearly 20 years had elapsed since a Southern Club had attained the dignity of appearing in the Final. A tricky wind upset all opportunities of combination and the Lancashire eleven quickly grasping the position abandoned their usual short passing game—tactics which soon resulted in McLuckie opening their score from a corner kick by Richards. Woods and McLuckie added to the score, half time arriving with the score standing at 3–0. The second half was a repetition of the first, and although only one further goal was scored—Plant from a corner kick—Bury ran out easy winners. Result : Bury 4 goals. Southampton Nil.

'Steve Bloomer eat
your heart out'

Derby's England star
could not prevent Bury's
record 6-0 win.

26
Bury, 1903.
Never in the history of the Football Association Cup has any club suffered such a sweeping defeat as did Derby County in front of 63,000 spectators at the Palace on this occasion. The victory was hardly what one would call a surprise, in view of the amazing record of the winners, who had gone clean through the Competition without having a single point scored against them. Ross scored the only goal for Bury in the first half, but on the change of ends Sagar scored within two minutes and then Bury simply ran their opponents off their feet. Four more goals followed in rapid succession. Result: Bury 6 goals. Derby County Nil.

Obsession and confessions

This, then, is my football heritage, and I'm proud of every bit of it. I suppose there must be more to life than football, but I cheerfully confess that, pushing 40, I'm still undecided. I cannot remember a time when I was not interested, but I'm lucky enough to remember dimly that first match.

Gigg Lane was a classic northern ground. On land given to the club by the Earl of Derby, Bury FC arose and became surrounded by terraced streets a short walk from the town centre. Dad had been a season ticket holder since 1949, but I remember him bringing me that first time very late in the game, as I was too young to have been able to stand it all. The gates, of course, were open with about quarter of an hour to go, to let the drifters away, so we went and stood on the Cemetery End, amongst a crowd of probably 12,000 or so. I recall neither the opponents nor the score, and alas cannot claim the romance of owning the programme, but I can still see the crowd and the players and hear the echo of their shouts. I was five, and I had my first identity. I was no longer a little boy. I was a Bury fan.

So that was it, hooked for ever - hooked forever on Bury FC. But - and here is the first of two big confessions - while my home-town team would always have my *ultimate* loyalty, I was hooked not just on Bury. There are some who claim that they cannot enjoy a game at all, unless 'their' team is playing, and, usually, winning. Now I go along with the zero enjoyment rating if you see your team lose. Nothing can make such an occasion happier than a wet kipper sandwich.

I was once privileged, I understand, to see England's finest display under Alf Ramsey since they won the World Cup in 1966. Unfortunately, this took place in May 1969 on a rainy Wembley evening where I sat in abject misery at my first England v Scotland international. Having worn my father's nationality with pride throughout my schooldays, though loyally supporting what I considered to be our adopted homeland against everyone else, I relished the chance of shouting for Scotland that night. I'd have failed the Tebbitt test. On a tube train packed with Scots whose language rapidly completed whatever education Bury Grammar School had not yet provided, we fancied the chance of a repeat of Scotland's glorious 3-2 victory of 1967, as celebrated by Gordon Brown, in his chapter. Fat chance! England won 4-1. I suppose England were good, but all I could think of was how to get through the abuse to come at school on the Monday.

But I must admit it is the *game* that I am in love with. I can watch and play it anywhere. I've been known to stop the car in a wet Huddersfield to watch a park match. And the most exotic goal I ever scored was under the ramparts of a Crusader castle in Acre, in a game between Manchester YMCA and local Arabs. That is the wonderful thing about football. I have never got over the joy of simply seeing anyone play the game well, whether or not a team I cared for was involved.

My second confession is darker still, though tangentially connected. Much as I love the loyal and faithful Shakers, as a dutiful woman always there, I have a mistress. Dressed in red, with dark stockings, she is bewitching. Although close in distance, she is a world away in class, and although I know it should not, my heart beats for her occasional touch. She is, of course, Manchester United.

My excuse for having this added passion is that of the two worlds. I love my football and I like to mix my visits to Gigg Lane, and my love of my home-town team, with something else. Until I was 31, the two never played each other competitively (though when they eventually did, I could not bring myself to desert the Shakers).

I have been lucky enough to see United quite a few times from the sixties onwards. Frankly, if your heart is not stirred by Best, Law, Charlton, Buchan, Coppell, Hill and their modern counterparts, then you are either dead or nursing a very large chip on the shoulder. And it cannot be surprising that I, living a bare 10 miles from Old Trafford, have made the pilgrimage there, when you think that people come from Tierra Del Fuego just to visit the souvenir shop.

So I am unrepentant. And when the two clubs are now as intertwined as they are - United play the odd Reserve game at Gigg Lane and we seem to share the great Wilf McGuinness, who is as often at Bury as at United - I think I can continue to combine the two.

As I say, there is only one team to which you can truly give your ultimate loyalty. Bury-born, Bury-bred, I have to be loyal to Bury FC.

Let's face it, if we locals were not, who would be? The clubs on Bury's doorstep - and the motorway has made that doorstep a circle with a radius of 50 miles or so - possess a core of local support augmented by those from many miles away, who may well have given up on their local club in the meantime. This is not a new phenomenon. Bury has always struggled for decent gates, sandwiched between the two Manchesters to the south and Blackburn and Burnley to the north. There is also Bolton to the west, but on account of their general inferiority and their habit of buying Shakers' stars for next to nothing when we are on our uppers, no self-respecting fan now mentions them.

Thus surrounded on all sides, Bury has seen its support dwindle in recent years. Yet that decline reflects not only the ever-easier access to neighbouring clubs but also a failure to appreciate how much football talent emerges at smaller clubs before heading off for the big time. For this to continue, the smaller clubs must survive, though they too must realise that there are few favours and that no-one has an automatic right to stay in the League - or, indeed, in existence at all.

Bury's history in the time I have been part of it has been against this backcloth. But what value they have given in that time - both to football and the town - in keeping afloat. The roll call of great and merely good players makes some reading and is packed with memories.

These We Have Loved

At the back, Neville Southall, Alec Lindsay, Colin Waldron, Bob Stokoe and Eddie Colquhoun. In midfield, Jimmy Kerr, Terry McDermott and Colin Bell. Up front, Bobby Owen, George Jones and Ray Pointer. Some names there. And I've seen them all play for Bury at Gigg.

Alec Lindsay was an excellent left midfield player who went to Liverpool and patiently waited for his first team chance. Although probably a better left half than Emlyn Hughes, Alec had to play at left back when he finally made the team, a position he kept for many years. His family were patients of my father, and Alec's father would proudly bring a medal or a cap to the surgery from time to time.

Jimmy Kerr's is the saddest story. He was brilliant, emerging just after Colin Bell in the late sixties. Like Bell, he had a terrific work rate and a stunning shot. He was destined for the brightest of futures but, after transferring to Blackburn, suffered a knee injury that could not be repaired. Had it happened now, who knows?

Ray Pointer was a sensation. A member of Burnley's championship-winning side of 1959-60, that Alex Carlile recalls in his chapter above, this great England forward - how could he have won only three caps? - signed for Bury in August 1965 and spearheaded a tremendous run by the Shakers, scoring 19 goals by Christmas. Unbelievably he was then sold. I was 10 years-old and I can still remember the wave of astonishment that went through the town. My Italian barber, Gerald, told me in his shop at the bottom of Walmersley Road and I burst into tears. There are many who date the club's decline as a serious contender from that very day and that is not as far-fetched as it sounds. In 1963, the club had finished eighth in Division Two. So, two years later, the dream of first division football was a real one, but many believe the club had lost its will to succeed when it sold Ray Pointer.

If Ray was a bright shooting star, my goalscoring hero was the longer-serving and dependable George Jones. An England youth international while at Gigg Lane, George had a short spell at Blackburn before returning to Bury. We loved him. Altogether now ...

> *'Oh Georgie Jones ... is wonderful ...*
> *Oh Georgie Jones is wonderful ...*
> *Full of life, full of health, full of vigour ...*
> *Georgie Jones is wonderful'*

If you sing it to *When the Saints go marching in*, you'll get the flavour.

The best of the lot was Colin Bell. I saw what my memory tells me was his first game at Gigg Lane, though it may not have been. Bury is not a big place, and back in 1963 it didn't take long for word to get round that a most unusual young lad had been picked up in the North-East. Dad took me to the Reserves one sunny evening and said to watch out for something special. Bury were playing Wolves Reserves in the old Central League. Bell shone out as if someone had clicked a switch. He hit the bar, but he could have done anything. In the years to come he grew into a magnificent player for clubs and country, until injury sadly struck him down with unfinished business awaiting him.

If those were the stars, then there were stalwarts too, perhaps hardly known to the uninitiated, but without whom the club would not have made it. Brian Turner was club captain in the early sixties, a gifted centre half, and a loyal one-club man. I was introduced to him when I was about six. I called him 'Turner', because that is how I had always heard him referred to. My Dad went beetroot and said I was to call him Mr Turner. It was the first time I realised that English footballers, unlike Brazilians, had more than one name. Pity! I'm sure it would lend something to the game.

There were others. Keith Kennedy, Craig Madden, Les Hart - 44 years as player, manager and physio. And if we are into the longevity stakes, there was groundsman, Tommy Marshall, who put 56 years into making Gigg Lane's turf renowned throughout the country. John Forrest, a local boy and a grand goalkeeper ... I could mention many more, for the fans reserve their greatest affection for those whose loyalty in a tough business matches theirs. They make the club.

On The Games

If those were the men, then what were the matches that live in the Bury memory?

I'm just too young to remember the early pioneering floodlit games in the fifties, but Bury were well up there with the best. The Bolton derby games of the sixties provided the biggest gates and the greatest surge of excitement; whilst our brief encounters with Don Revie's early Leeds side on the way up - as Second Division champions in 1964 - told me much of what I didn't want to know about football to come.

The Shakers themselves were on the way down. Relegated for a season in 1967, they went down again in 1969. They have never been back to the Second Division - although they made the play-offs of the old Third Division in 1990 and again in 1991. Instead, they have done a lot of sliding around between the two lower divisions. This has provided opportunities, however, for the odd promotion run in the league and for giant-killing in the Cups. Shall we forget the wave of emotion that greeted going up, in 1974, from Division IV? The fans' heroes of that year were surely Peter Swan - the great England centre-half of the early sixties, banned for many years for his part in a bribes scandal - and Derek Spence, a free-scoring Ulsterman who became the first player since the 1930s to be capped while with Bury. Both were larger-than-life stars and, to prove it, it's time for another song:

> *Swanee, how I love yer, how I love yer, my dear old Swanee.*
> *I'd give the world to see ...*
> *Bury F.C. ... Champions of Division Three.*

(sung to the tune of the National Anthem. No, just kidding, I'm sure you know it).

The match that lives in my memory as the greatest I ever watched for, well for just everything, was a Third Round FA Cup replay in 1976 between Bury and Middlesbrough. Bury were in the Third Division at

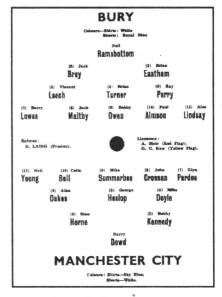

'The best of the lot was Colin Bell'.
In 1965-66, the cover of the Bury programme regularly showed Colin Bell (*right*), the club's young captain. It still did so in April, although he had signed for Manchester City the previous month.

197

the time and Middlesbrough lay third in the First. Managed by Jack Charlton, they had the tightest defence in the league. So, when the Shakers were drawn away to them, most folk saw the tie as a foregone conclusion. But no! A hard-fought-for 0-0 draw brought the clubs to Gigg Lane for the replay. I was at university by then, but the game was just into the New Year so all was well. As thousands were still making their way in, 'Boro struck twice in the first eight minutes. The match was as good as dead, against such uncompromising opponents.

From somewhere Bury dredged up the fight of the decade. Classically they scored 'on the stroke of half-time', as the sportswriters say, Jimmy McIlwraith popping up in the box. Big John Hulme equalised and, with enough minutes to go for the moment to be savoured and for every passing second to be heart-stopping thereafter, Andy Rowland hit the winner.

I went through every emotion in those 90 minutes that I believe I will ever need in my life. Black despair swamps the soul with the Boro's goals. Shakers' first lifts the spirits. You turn to your friends at half-time with a rueful smile and say things like 'Well, if only they weren't two down to start with' and 'Boro will never let them in again' whilst all the time you are just willing it to happen. The second goes in and this time all pretence is gone. You are yelling at the top of your voice with every attack, believing that just one more heave will do it and that with every roar from every throat, Big Jack's men will realise that it is not their night and pack up. The third goal. If there are three steps to heaven you have just reached the top. The noise is sensational and you bang your feet on the floorboards of the wooden stand for all you are worth. Your seat long abandoned, you whoop and punch the air with a clenched fist, determination battling with adrenalin for control of your senses.

But now the mood changes. Suddenly we have something to lose. The rhythm of the game is different. Every attack now has us as the vulnerable target. Time drags, you cannot bear to look. This is the moment that Nick Hornby captured so memorably in *Fever Pitch*, for this is the moment you bargain with God. You offer to do anything, if He will only let you win. More likely you offer not to do again that which is most uneasy on your conscience at that precise moment. But you offer.

The whistle blew. I roared with relief and, as the players left the field in a swarm of supporters, the tears fell in tune. I can still summon up tears with the memory of a perfect game, feel the emotional draining of an experience. Can it be shared with others - on a page? Maybe not that game, but a reader with soul will be there.

Fields of Dreams

At the end of the day, it is all about those tears for me. Few things stir the heart like a great game, though not always for the right reasons. When United lost at Wembley in 1979, I was still crying over Sammy McIlroy's dramatic equaliser when Alan Sunderland scored Arsenal's winner. I think I came to only during the laps of honour.

Silly? Perhaps, but very real. I always wonder how I would have got on as a player, weeping buckets over sensational 50-yard passes and great comebacks. Better then to have few, but very precious, playing memories. The privilege of being in Parliament has meant having the chance to play for, and occasionally captain, the Westminster Wobblers. This means two special things to me. Firstly, I can play with some fine blokes, even if their political views are really strange. Bliss is being in a room with ten other politicians and no-one talking shop!

Secondly, the Wobblers have given me the chance to play on my fields of dreams - Wembley and Old Trafford - though never, alas at Gigg Lane. I long to play at Hampden with the Wobblers, perhaps in a Scots v. English MPs clash for charity: the Child Poverty Action Group has first refusal. With no English blood at all, I would have to wear a blue Scots shirt. If I played in such a game, I could go to that final eternal match in the sky well pleased.

For now, my happiest playing memories are of two goals: collecting a pass from Bobby Charlton to score at Old Trafford and doing a Ricky Villa inside the penalty area at Wembley in a *Children in Need* charity special in 1991.

Did I shed a tear? You may think so. I could not possibly comment.

WEST HAM UNITED

MIKE GAPES (Labour, Ilford South)

An East Londoner (born Wanstead, 1952) who returned as MP (Labour and Co-operative Member, Ilford South, 1992) after VSO teaching in Swaziland (1971-72) and 15 years at Labour Party headquarters - National Student Organiser (1977-80); Research Officer (1980-88); and Senior International Officer (1988-92).

As a member of the Foreign Affairs Select Committee, he has so far visited only the world's major soccer-free zones: China and the USA.

19

FORTUNE'S ALWAYS HIDING

Mike Gapes

Would I prefer Labour to win the next election or West Ham to win the League?

That's a below-the-belt question to somebody who's been a member of the Labour Party for over 25 years and a West Ham supporter for more than 30 years. When this cruel choice was once put to me, I was able to rationalise my dilemma: 'Well, we've had Labour governments in the past ...'.

Hammers and Hammerings

I grew up in Hainault on the Essex borders of North East London. The nearest professional football was at Brisbane Road, home of unfashionable Leyton Orient. It was there that I saw my first League match, in 1961, with my dad, Frank, and my younger brother, Barry. A top-of-Division II clash with Liverpool ended 1-1, with Dave Dunmore scoring for the O's. A lot of the local kids were Spurs fans and, for a brief period, I supported both Spurs and West Ham. But by 1960, at the age of eight, my inclination towards the poor and the underdog had fully developed. Spurs, of course, went on to win the double in 1961.

Barry supported Arsenal. We shared a bedroom. His wall was completely covered in Red and White; mine in Claret and Sky Blue. Dad kept a careful neutrality between us. He was, for many years, Fixtures Secretary of the South Essex Football League and Secretary of Chigwell Football Club - which then had its own ground and pavilion. There was a time when Barry and I would accompany him to Chigwell's matches every Saturday afternoon. And when we asked whom he supported, Dad would always say 'Chigwell'.

It wasn't until I was 11 that I first saw the Hammers. On 9 November

1963, my dad, the Chigwell neutral, took my brother and me to see our teams in opposition at Highbury. An exhilarating see-saw contest in front of more than 50,000 fans ended in a 3-3 draw. I can remember little of the match but vividly recall the gigantic Ian Ure, the Arsenal centre-half, bundling little Johnny Byrne ('Budgie') into the crowd. Before Ure could get to his feet, big John Bond, the Hammers' right back, had run what seemed like the length of the pitch to sit on Ure.

A decade and a half later Billy Bonds, by then a regular in John Bond's No.2 shirt, would respond in a similar way to over-physical treatment of his team-mates. West Ham always had a reputation for being a pushover for physical teams of much lower ability. But Bond and Bonds - and several others, including the underrated Eddie Bovington in the 1964 Cup-winning side; David 'Psycho' Cross up front in the late seventies; and Julian 'Terminator' Dicks and 'Mad Dog' Martin Allen in the nineties - were not shrinking violets.

As a schoolboy in the 1960s, my Upton Park heroes included John Charles at left back. He was locally born and the first black player to get into the Hammers' side. But his career was sadly cut short by injury. I also liked the blond John Sissons on the left wing. Another favourite was the overweight Brian Dear. I can recall him rolling down the middle and scoring with a diving belly flop headed goal in a 3-1 win at Chelsea and his four goals in 20 minutes in a 5-1 home victory over West Brom.

Above all, there were the three stars when West Ham won the World Cup for England in 1966. The immaculate Bobby Moore, Martin - 'ten years ahead of his time' - Peters and, of course, Geoff Hurst.

We all agree, Standen is better than Yashin.
Hurst is better than Eusebio
And Tottenham [or whoever it was that week] are in for a thrashing.

Or so we sang on the North Bank terraces.

Jim Standen - a better keeper than Yashin and a Worcestershire bowler to boot - had his car serviced at the Jessups garage in Ilford (now part of my constituency). One day in 1965, my Uncle Len, who worked there as a mechanic, asked him to take my autograph book.

This proud possession contains the signatures of Moore, Hurst, Peters, Byrne and Bond; of Peter Brabrook and others.

From the age of 13, I earned money - most of it spent at Upton Park - from a newspaper round in Chigwell. Eventually, I was promoted to be a 'marker up' of the papers, at 5 a.m., who then went out as relief delivery boy, covering sometimes two or three rounds a morning. It was in this capacity that I delivered Bobby Moore's papers in Manor Road. My regular round included Geoff Hurst's house in Meadow Way. I saw Geoff Hurst just once, getting into his car. But I had to wait 25 years before I met Bobby Moore. I was working as a Labour Party official when I had the pleasure of being introduced to him at a fund-raising dinner, inevitably by Tom Pendry, acting in one of the football-promoting roles he describes in the final chapter of this book. Bobby was amused to be told that the young Hammers fan who had delivered his newspapers a quarter of a century before was now the Prospective Parliamentary Candidate for Ilford South.

When Bobby died, at the age of 51 in 1993, we Hammers fans felt we had lost part of our own lives. And in a sense we had. Our shock and disbelief has been recorded in the many books and articles sparked off by Bobby's death. Parliament's reaction may be less well-known. When I put down one of three Early Day Motions, I was pleased that over 30 MPs, of all parties and allegiances, added their names (see below).

No. 145   **Notices of Motions: 24th March 1993**   **6997**

1480   *BOBBY MOORE*   **25:2:93**

    Mr Mike Gapes
    Mr John Cummings
    Mr Tom Cox
    Mr Jeremy Corbyn
    Ms Janet Anderson
    Mr Elfyn Llwyd

                                                                  ★ 31

        Mr Frank Cook

        That this House expresses its profound shock and regret at the death of Bobby Moore; recognises his contribution as a truly great footballer at schoolboy, club, England youth, under-23 and full international level, as captain of England in 108 full internationals, as captain of the World Cup winners in 1966, and as captain of the West Ham United team which won the F.A. Cup in 1964 and the European Cup Winners Cup in 1965; and gives its deep condolences to his wife, family and friends and to West Ham United supporters everywhere.

As a teenager, as well as supporting West Ham, I kept up my interest in Leyton Orient. A group of friends from Buckhurst Hill County High School would go together to stand on the East Side and chant 'East London' in support of Dennis Rofe, Ray Goddard and the irrepressible Mark Lazarus, as the O's won Division III. The following week some of us would go to West Ham and the rest to White Hart Lane. Supporting the 'Os' was a bit of fun. Supporting the Hammers was serious.

Some schoolfriends followed Manchester United. On 6 May 1967, I went with one of those friends, Tommy Wise, to see the Hammers at home to United, who needed only a point to clinch the League Championship. Tommy and I stood together on the South Bank, the visitors' end. Best, Law and Charlton were rampant. At half-time, it was 4-0 to the Reds. When John Charles hit a 40-yard blinder consolation goal, it seemed I was the only one cheering on the South Bank. We eventually lost 6-1 at home.

Normally, I stood on the North Bank with my friend, Malcolm Horswell. He always saw more than I did as he was six inches taller. We went together on the bus and tube. Later on, a friend up the road, Robin Henderson, and his dad, Cliff, would take me in their car. I would stand on the old and rusting Chicken Run, long since knocked down and replaced by the East Stand.

Standing at the front of the Chicken Run, you were close enough to reach out and touch the players as they took a throw. The sight of Billy Bonds and Harry Redknapp is still vivid in my mind, with Billy shouting 'Run Harry, Run' - to which we would all shout 'give it to Harry', as the red-haired Redknapp sprinted up the line past some pedestrian full back, received the pass from Billy and hit a great cross in for Geoff Hurst or the late-arriving Martin Peters.

Preferring to stand on the North Bank or Chicken Run, I seldom had a seat. One exception was in October 1967, when West Ham were playing Stoke City and were three up at half-time - all past Gordon Banks. This was amazing and sure enough it did not last. In the second half, Stoke hit us on the break four times as Peter Dobing skinned poor John Cushley, the former Celtic reserve centre-half. This was in the period - after Ken Brown and before Alvin Martin - when our central defence was extremely weak. Another occasion when I for some reason got a seat was the 8-0 thrashing of Sunderland on 18 October 1968. Harry Boy did the business against Cecil Irwin, the bald Sunderland full-back, and Geoff Hurst scored six.

Working My Way

In 1971, after my 'A' levels, my regular attendance at Upton Park was interrupted for a year while I went to Swaziland as a Voluntary Service Overseas teacher at St. Philips Secondary School. I was not completely starved of football since I played in and watched school games. I recall a national club competition at the Somhlolo Stadium, where guest teams included Soweto's Kaizer Chiefs. And during the 1972 Easter vacation, I hitch-hiked to Lesotho where I watched the home nation draw 0-0 with Zambia in a World Cup qualifying game in the cold, windswept Maseru stadium.

When I first arrived in Swaziland, the only British team my pupils knew about was Manchester United. I was determined to change that. I got the Hammers' results from BBC World Service on Short Wave, but had to wait three or four weeks before reading Trevor Smith's match report in the *Ilford Recorder*. My mum sent it regularly, along with packages of books and materials collected from local schools for my poor, badly-equipped, rural mission school.

The football reports were cut out and pinned to the classroom wall as 'educational aids'. There was particular interest, among the boys, in the goal-scoring achievements of the young Bermudan international, Clyde Best. I tried to show how a black man could get to the very top in the English Football League - a positive example to my students, who were surrounded by apartheid South Africa. Clyde Best was a great prospect. But a combination of being played too often out of position on the wing and the disgusting racist abuse to which he was subjected - not only by visiting fans but by a large minority of our own crowd - led him to leave prematurely to play in America.

In August 1972, I flew back from Southern Africa overnight and arrived home on a Saturday morning. West Ham were at home that afternoon. So, jet lagged and suffering from 'reverse culture shock', I went with

205

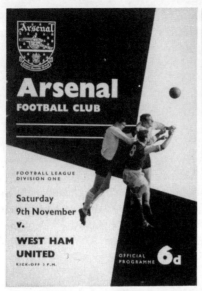

ARSENAL

Colours — Shirts: Red, White Sleeves and Collars.   Shorts: White.
Stockings: White with Red Tops.

(Goal)
R. Wilson
1

(Right-back)   (Left-back)
Magill   **McCullough**
2   3

(Right-half)   (Centre-half)   (Left-half)
Brown   **Ure**   **Barnwell**
4   5   6

(Outside-right) (Inside-right) (Centre-forward) (Inside-left) (Outside-left)
MacLeod **Strong** **Baker** **Eastham** **Anderson**
7   8   9   10   11

Linesmen:
Mr. A. P. OLIVER
(Leigh-on-Sea, Essex)
Red Flag

Referee:
Mr. A. JOBLING
(Morecambe, Lancs.)

Mr. F. D. BOOTH
(Sheffield 10, Yorks.)
Yellow Flag

11   10   9   8   7
Brabrook **Hurst** **Byrne** **Boyce** **Sealey**
(Outside-left) (Inside-left) (Centre-forward) (Inside-right) (Outside-right)

6   5   4
Moore   **Brown**   **Peters**
(Left-half)   (Centre-half)   (Right-half)

3   2
Burkett   **Bond**
(Left-back)   (Right-back)

1
Standen
(Goal)

WEST HAM UNITED

Colours—Shirts: Claret with Sky Blue Sleeves.   Shorts: White.
Stockings: White.

WEST HAM UNITED (0) 1	MANCHESTER UNITED (4) 6
1 ~~Jim Standen~~ *Colin Mackleworth*	1 Alex Stepney
2 Jack Burkett	2 Shay Brennan
3 John Charles 1	3 Tony Dunne
4 Martin Peters	4 Pat Crerand 1
5 Paul Heffer	5 Billy Foulkes 1
6 Bobby Moore *(Capt)*	6 Nobby Stiles
7 Harry Redknapp	7 George Best 1
8 ~~Ron Boyce~~ *Peter Bennett*	8 Dennis Law 2 *(1pen)*
9 ~~Trevor Hartley~~ *Ron Boyce*	9 David Sadler
10 Geoff Hurst	10 Bobby Charlton 1
11 John Sissons	11 John Aston
12 *Trevor Hartley*	12 RYAN

Mike Gapes's marked-up copies of the programmes for his first
Hammers game in November 1963 and for the game in which
Manchester United clinched the 1967 Championship.

Robin Henderson and his dad to see the Hammers beat Norwich 4-0. I had spent a year in an isolated rural mission and now I was standing on the terraces with 28,000 other people cheering Trevor Brooking.

As an undergraduate at Cambridge, I was very active in Labour Party and student politics - but I regularly went to Upton Park or convenient away games on my 50cc motorbike. I had no desire to go to any other club and certainly not to the Abbey Stadium. Then it was back to London - for a year studying at Middlesex Poly and then a job as Student Organiser at Labour Party headquarters in Transport House. With most weekends taken up by conferences and meetings, regular attendance at Upton Park became difficult. The job offered opportunities, though, to see games all over the country. For instance, in March 1980, I so organised my speaking tour of the North East that it finished at Newcastle Poly on a Friday evening. Later that evening, I saw Dexy's Midnight Runners singing *Geno*. Then, on the Saturday morning, I put my luggage in the locker at the Central Station and walked to St. James Park to watch the Hammers hang on for a lucky 0-0 draw. The only memorable event was a firebomb thrown into the Hammers fans on the terraces. I was fortunately in the seats but had a clear view of the flaming bottle going through the air over our heads. The train journey back became eventful, too, when a large number of Portsmouth fans got on at Darlington. Happily, they were friendly to the small West Ham contingent.

Violence at football matches can be exaggerated by the media and it is certainly less prevalent now than in the sixties and seventies. I was first threatened and chased as a 12 year-old by a drunken Blackburn Rovers fan on Upton Park's North Bank in 1964. Video cameras, better intelligence and segregation of supporters by police and clubs have improved the situation. Yet much still remains to be done to create a family atmosphere at British football matches and to stamp down firmly on racist and neo-Nazi abuse and violence.

Those of us who put out anti-racist leaflets, outside football grounds in the late 1970s and early 1980s, were not encouraged by the prevailing 'hands off' approach of most clubs. So I was very pleased, as an MP, to write to West Ham at the start of the 1993-94 season, congratulating the club for giving strong support to the campaign by the Commission for Racial Equality - backed by the PFA and more fully described by

Alan Simpson in his chapter of this book - to 'Kick Racism out of Football'. Better late than never.

In 1980, I changed jobs to become a Research Officer at Walworth Road. This brought me into touch with Dino Constantinou - an Upton Park regular, along with his friends, John Cruse and Paul Cockerell, whom he knew through the Newham Labour Party. I had known them when I was involved in student politics. Now we all started going together, meeting at about 1.30 in the White Hart in Green Street and then walking down to stand behind the goal on the North Bank. Several years later, we were joined by, Kevin Gillespie, whom John had known since he was five. Tragically, Dino was killed by a hit-and-run driver in January 1992 - a week after he had sat next to me watching a woeful 1-0 FA Cup replay victory over non-league Farnborough Town.

Wembley Way

In 1975, when the Hammers beat Fulham 2-0 in the FA Cup Final, I had been too busy getting my degree to follow them all the way to Wembley. So I was determined to get there the next time. It came in 1980. I saw them in every round, including the tight sixth round win against Villa at Upton Park. The only way I could get a ticket was from a tout outside the ground. Needless to say, it was for the South Bank. I stood wedged in among thousands of Brummies wearing claret and blue scarves and singing 'Come On You Lions' as I, wearing my own claret and blue, sang 'Come on You Irons'. No one noticed my true allegiance until the 89th minute. Then Alun Evans handled and the Hammers' penalty king, Ray Stewart, walked up to score from the spot. A minute to go and 1-0 to the Hammers. I leaped into the air, looked round and made a hasty move towards the exit.

Ironically, the semi-final was at Villa Park. This time, I was lucky to get a free ticket via a friend in Putney Labour Party. Ian McGarry is now the General Secretary of Equity, the actors' trade union. Seated among Everton fans, we saw Stuart Pearson equalise an early Bob Latchford goal.

The replay was set for Elland Road ten days later - in the middle of the National Union of Students Conference in Blackpool. Paul, John, Dino and I managed to scrape together enough vouchers to get four tickets. I drove up to Blackpool on my own, in my little blue Mini; organised the Labour students' stall, fringe meetings, leaflets and election material; and then left the conference early, giving a lift to another Hammers fan. We parked in the gloomy back streets, paid a teenage boy 50p to 'look after the car' and went our separate ways to meet our respective mates.

The atmosphere in the ground was electric. The noise deafening. The mutual abuse and aggression in the songs menacing. A very tight game went into extra time. With only a few minutes to go and the score 1-1, a Hammers attack broke down. Everton cleared. The ball was hit back into their area and there, amazingly, inside the box to score with a diving header, was the most unlikely hero, a man who seldom headed the ball at all and only ever scored from ferocious, long-range, speculative shots. But there he was - Frank Lampard, the great, underrated, long-serving left back. West Ham were at Wembley.

I said goodbye to my friends and made my way back to the car. I was singing.

> *Wemb-er-ley, Wemb-er-ley. We're all off to Wemb-er-ley.*
> *We will really shake them up when we win the FA Cup.*
> *West Ham are the greatest football team!*

We left Leeds on the M62, my scarf dangling triumphantly from the car window. It soon became clear that this was a mistake. Every other car going west was full of disgruntled Evertonians. The abuse and insults were no problem but being chased on and off the motorway and followed into a garage forecourt in Salford by a big van, containing seven drunken 'fans' who then threw oil over my windscreen, was no joke.

Fortunately, we suffered no more serious reprisals for our win and were soon back in Blackpool. Arriving at the Imperial Hotel around midnight, I was greeted by elated Labour students celebrating a great victory. 'We Won' they said, their thoughts on the NUS elections. 'Yes. We Won' I said, my thoughts on Wembley.

Dino, Paul, John and I all got tickets for the final. Trevor Brooking's header gave victory to the better side as the Second Division underdogs vanquished the hot favourites, Arsenal. It would have been outrageous if Willie Young's professional foul on the 17 year-old Paul Allen had affected the result. We drove back down Green Street to crowds of cheering fans and spent the evening celebrating in the White Hart.

Unlike me, my brother, Barry, had been to Wembley many times in the seventies, including the year Arsenal won the double. And he was there, that day in 1980, too - at the other end of the ground. I telephoned him, the next day, to talk about the match and Trevor Brooking's heading ability. This was not gloating - well, yes it was - but it was a pleasant change after what seemed like decades in which Arsenal had had the upper hand.

The following year, led by David Cross and Paul Goddard up front, we ran away with the Second Division championship and drew the League Cup Final at Wembley with Liverpool (losing the replay at Villa Park). Then John Lyall began to create the team which came so close, in 1985, to winning the League. The combination of the local Tony Cottee and the St. Mirren star, Frank McAvennie - originally bought, as we understood it, as an attacking mid-fielder - rattled in 46 goals. They were ably supplied by the aggressive Mark Ward and the magnificent Alan Devonshire - back after a long absence, following the terrible broken leg against Wigan in the FA Cup in January 1984. I can still hear that crack and the deathly hush which followed it. And for once the defence did not let them down. Alvin Martin and Tony Gale were magnificent and, after a bad injury the previous year, Phil Parkes was back at his peak.

A nasty business

The late eighties saw Margaret Thatcher's hostility to sport culminate in the attempt to introduce the compulsory ID cards - a foolish scheme, defended in this book by David Evans but attacked by more than one Conservative contributor. The idea was defeated by the unity of clubs and fans, ably led by the Football Supporters' Association. In a letter to *When Saturday Comes* and *The Guardian*, I pointed how my job might take me to Italy, where I could join my hosts in watching Lazio, or likewise to Spain and Real Madrid; but, under the ID scheme, I would not be able to reciprocate by taking foreign guests to see the Hammers. I also played my small part, collecting signatures against the plan on the North Bank before the home game against Charlton. It was the only time in all my years that I had ever had free admission to Upton Park.

Unfortunately, the club was then to ruin its rapport with the fans and create serious, long-term, financial problems for itself by its ill-fated 'Hammers Bond' scheme. By 1989, I had decided, along with John and Kevin, to get a season ticket in the West Stand seats. On those occasions when one of us could not go, we gave our seat to Dino or Paul instead. But the compulsory nature of the Bond scheme - launched at a time of recession and mass unemployment in the East End - angered most Hammers fans. Although I did not join in the pitch invasions, which I felt upset the players, I well understood the reasons for them. Our club had become a capitalist business.

Very large numbers of longstanding fans decided not to renew for the 1992-93 season and I was one of them. But my commitment to the club remains undiminished. I continue to reshuffle my team of the best West Ham players over my 30 years of watching them. It currently stands at

1	Ludek Miklosko	
2	Billy Bonds	
3	Frank Lampard	
4	Martin Peters	
5	Alvin Martin	Substitutes/Reserves:
6	Bobby Moore	
7	Liam Brady	Phil Parkes, Ray Stewart,
8	Frank McAvennie	Ken Brown, Paul Allen,
9	Geoff Hurst	Bryan 'Pop' Robson, Tony Cottee.
10	Trevor Brooking	
11	John Sissons	Manager: John Lyall.

And I was very pleased to be able to table an Early Day Motion, at the end of that 1992-93 season, in the following terms:

This House congratulates West Ham United Football Club, its players, its manager Billy Bonds, his deputy Harry Redknapp and all supporters of the Hammers everywhere, on their magnificent achievement in gaining their rightful place in the Premier Division of the Football League where their football skills and marvellous supporters will be greatly appreciated for many years to come.

August 1994

*'... yet another
example of Billy
passing to Harry'.*

Billy Bonds

Harry Redknapp

The Hammers did not let me down in 1993-94, a season that saw them in their natural position - in mid-table in the Premier League and doing well in the FA Cup, until going out to a team from a lower division. It was not so natural that Billy Bonds's 27-year association with the Hammers should come to such an unfortunate end in August 1994, when he was replaced as manager by his close friend and assistant, Harry Redknapp.

But, then again, it was yet another example of Billy passing to Harry.

John Lyall, chosen to manage Mike Gapes's Select XI

SUNDERLAND

HILARY ARMSTRONG (Labour, Durham North West)

Succeeded her father, Ernest Armstrong, as MP for Durham North West in 1987. A former Lecturer in Community and Youth Work, she has specialised, in parliament, in Education.

Has been a member of the Education Select Committee and of Labour's Front Bench Education team, until she became Parliamentary Private Secretary to the Leader of the Labour Party, John Smith, June 1992-May 1994.

20

WEAR BY FAR THE GREATEST TEAM ...

Hilary Armstrong

FOOTBALL. I am sure that it was at football matches that I first learned the art of heckling. The comments as I wandered around the ground, hearing what the great wits of the North East had to say, and not being able to resist chipping in with referees being unsure what to do about a cheeky young girl, were all very good training for the benches of the House of Commons.

My introduction to football was at the Northern League level in the days when it was an amateur league. Our team was Stanley United. Stanley is the small mining village that my father was born in, a mile up the road from Crook and about 25 miles from where we then lived in Sunderland. United were the side he had played for - the stories about his being a very tough centre half were legion - and their great rivals were Crook Town. The ground is on the top of the hill - so there was always a biting wind, with snow often threatening.

Keeping it in the family

There, I could be involved in everything. Dad picked up players from Sunderland to take them to the game. Cousins, aunts and uncles were making the tea, on the committee, on the gate. The team were part of the family - goodness, two of my cousins married players! I remember the wedding of one; I was bridesmaid and the groom was team captain. Stanley were playing Crook, so the majority of the guests disappeared half way through the reception, and came back later having won.

My loyalty was territorial and complete. Stanley were our team, and it seemed quite natural to turn out to watch them in the freezing cold and driving sleet of a northern winter afternoon. Swathed in layers of jumpers and long-johns, scarf tightly wrapped round my neck, hood up and gloved hands in pockets, I would stand at my father's side and discuss tactics with as much knowledge and gravitas as a 10 year-old can muster. Were they being creative enough in midfield? Were the defence lacking in pace? Did our centre forward have authority in the air? When not talking, I would run round the pitch and shout at the referee, ending up with toothache as the howling wind blew into my mouth. I loved those afternoons. Dark, cold and wet they may have been, but I remember them with enormous pleasure, both because of the time spent with the family, and because that is where my continuing passion for the game began. The enthusiasm has remained with me over the subsequent 30 years.

The qualities that so inspired me as a child are quite easy to pinpoint. I loved the involvement that the game generated. When Stanley took to the field I was out there with them. I lived every pass, ran for every ball and agonized over every missed opportunity. When they scored, I would scream and jump with excitement. When we lost, it was a personal tragedy. This identification was made easier by the family's involvement. Dad would chat with the scouts who were often sent down to check out talent for the major teams, and I listened avidly to discussions of the merits and demerits of various stars who played for the Northern clubs. After the game I would go upstairs in the clubhouse and help the tea-makers. Aged nine or ten, I was probably more of a hindrance than a help, but they were much too kind to say so. Going home we would indulge in a long *post mortem*.

This was the start of my love of the game and of my identification of football with the most important things in my life - home, family and the North East. When we returned to Sunderland it would be for Granda, my maternal grandfather, to argue about how Sunderland had done. We lived near Willie Watson and Granda would have amazing tales about those days. Although I mainly remember the stories of the crowds, with the terraces being so tightly packed that people had to be passed out over the heads of the crowd.

I have never been able to understand people who attach themselves to teams from a million miles away. Liverpool fans who hail from Southampton. Man Utd fanatics who live in Norfolk. Okay, those teams are big, successful and glamorous. They're always on the telly and they always feature in the match reports; but somehow, even if you are the most loyal of supporters, there's something about the team that is not really yours, and football, for me, is so much about a sense of belonging.

As I got older and I went to secondary school, I wanted, of course, to assert my independence. I graduated to supporting Sunderland and began going to matches every alternate Saturday, standing on the Roker End with a group of friends. Football is in essence a working class game and Sunderland is a strongly working class area. Standing on the terrace in the 1960s and 1970s, I was part of a continuum of feeling. Like our parents and grandparents who'd supported the team, we went along for very specific reasons. Sunderland FC gave us something to feel part of, a bigger whole into which we were absorbed and felt comfortable. Most importantly of all it gave us a chance at winning.

Roker Park is a very special ground. Near enough to the sea for you to be able to smell it, you can see the gulls wheeling overhead. When I first went to the games Charlie Hurley was my hero, later to be replaced by Dave Watson. True to my days at Stanley, I was still rather vocal, yelling and shouting at everybody, whether encouragement at our players or abuse and vilification at the opposing team and the ref. I must have been an incredible pain in the neck, but somehow I got away with it. Perhaps because the Roker End has always been famed for its noisiness. You can hear the Roker Roar in Sunderland town centre, and the feeling of being part of that, when the team are on song and the crowd is behind them, is simply magical.

Wear all going to Wembley

Of course, for Sunderland fans, 1973 is a date forever carved on our hearts. We went down to Wembley as rank underdogs. Our opponents, Don Revie's mighty Leeds - the 'Super Leeds' recalled by James Clappison in his chapter - were at the height of their power. They had won the previous year's FA Cup Final and looked odds-on to win this one. They had made a habit of being in the League Championship's top two and were thereabouts again - making Sunderland, languishing mid-table in Division II, seem pretty unimpressive. However, the team had had a great cup run and were in good form. They were also coming out onto the Wembley turf with nothing to lose and everything to fight for.

217

FA CUP-WINNERS 1973

'When Ian Porterfield scored...'

'Bob Stokoe ran out to embrace everybody...'
- including Tueart and Porterfield

'The whole town turned out for the team's homecoming...'

Great events in one's life always take on a cinematic quality in retrospect. For me it was a real family affair. I went down to London with Mam, Dad and my elder brother. Dad, by this time, was a Member of Parliament and clearly members of the family saw one great advantage of this: here was another way to press for tickets. It almost seemed as if his performance as an MP was to be measured in this way. Somehow, using all of our contacts, most of us managed to get a ticket. I was at that stage working in Newcastle, so had to put up with much scoff at the lads' prospects. For once, however, Sunderland fans were to have the last laugh.

When Ian Porterfield scored we all went crazy. The rest of the game was sheer agony. I hardly dared look for most of the second half. About halfway through that second half Jim Montgomery, Sunderland's goalkeeper, pulled off what was described as the best save ever seen at Wembley. He was afterwards named Man-of-the-Match for what was nothing short of an heroic performance. I know the quality of the save from the video. I'm not sure that I actually saw it on the day.

Finally, after what seemed more like 90 days than 90 minutes, the referee's whistle blew, time was called and we had done it. Sunderland manager, Bob Stokoe, ran out onto the pitch to embrace our goalie - and then everybody else - and the crowd went absolutely crazy.

When we did eventually leave the stadium, we met up with Mam and Dad, with me pressing for a sharp exit so that we could be home for the return to the town of the lads, with the FA Cup. I walked round for days afterwards with a grin on my face. The civic reception for the team's homecoming was another wonderful occasion. The whole town turned out, with people lining the streets as far back as the A1. Police figures from the period show that after the cup win, crime in the town dropped dramatically for a period of several weeks, something to do no doubt with the marvellous sense of community success we all felt. Productivity in the shipyards also rose at the time. Who says that the morale of a workforce is not a factor in competitive industry?

I was also present at Sunderland's next cup final appearance, in 1992; this time, it was me who was being pushed for tickets. My nephew, Jonathan, is now a Sunderland fanatic and I suspect he would never have forgiven me if he had not got a ticket to the final. Once again we were underdogs, facing Liverpool. Our route had been a nail-biting one. In the quarter-finals, we faced Chelsea at Stamford Bridge. I went along with Jonathan. Chelsea went ahead early on. It wasn't looking good. Jonathan tells a rather embarrassing story about me running round the directors' box shouting my head off when John Byrne scored the equaliser. I hope his tale is exaggerated but, to be truthful, I was so excited I can't remember that much about it. Anyway, having earned the draw, we beat Chelsea 2-1 at Roker Park and continued our march to Wembley.

This time we were on the losing side. The same John Byrne who had saved our bacon in the quarter-finals unbelievably missed a penalty in the 18th minute. Sick as a parrot wasn't in it. Once over the stomach-twisting disappointment, I remember feeling terribly, terribly sorry for him. It must be the worst and loneliest moment in the world when something like that happens. It says a lot about the importance of football in the town that almost as many people turned out to welcome the team back as in 1973.

Community Counts

Back in the seventies I was contemplating an even closer relationship with the team. At that time, I was a community worker in a district of Sunderland called Southwick. Previously dominated by coal and shipyards, it was seeing its jobs disappearing very quickly and was regarded as a problem area. Hence my appointment as community worker.

One of the strongest interests that bound everyone in Southwick together was a passion for football. One of my first actions was to set up a girls' football team, which was hugely popular, although I probably enjoyed it as much as, if not more than, the girls. In fact when Sunderland hit a real crisis period after 1973 and were looking for a new manager, a friend and I fantasised about applying for the post - as a job share. We did feel that the club somehow missed out on using the vast potential of the community that it was based in.

It always seems a pity to me that the people who really know about football, people who dedicate enormous amounts of time to the game and to working with young people and ensuring that it flourishes at a local level, never get to use that knowledge in the major league game. As in so many other areas of life, in football it's money that seems to talk loudest. The game's real selling point is surely the incredibly strong community base it has. A town's football team is the embodiment of local pride and feeling. Indeed, the team can function only because of that local support, and there needs to be more understanding of this amongst the people who run the game at the top end.

Sunderland, to be fair, have made enormous efforts to ensure that the club stays in touch with the community it springs from. The first team players are regular visitors at hospitals and charity events and the club has organised two very successful programmes with local schools: the Childlink Scheme, which provides free seat-tickets for schoolchildren; and the Soccer Classroom, which allows classes of children to come in and use the club as a vast learning resource for a day.

And Sunderland has always been a family club. They run a number of cheap entry schemes for pensioners and unemployed people, as well as encouraging women supporters to attend. All this is more than just pious mouthings. If football doesn't look after the people who make the whole thing possible, then the game will of necessity degenerate into a minority sideshow. Equally, the Stanley Uniteds of this world may not be glamorous, but they nurture the talents which will later shine at Anfield, Elland Road or Roker Park. One of the reasons I get very angry about the commercial deals which run football these days is that they do not seem to recognise that the talent in the top clubs will be nurtured only by a good structure at school and local village and town level.

Meanwhile, my loyalty to Stanley and to Sunderland is as firm as ever. My constituents are fairly evenly split between Sunderland and Newcastle fans. One of my constituency executive members is Chairman of Crook Town. I suppose it would be more politic to be neutral, but I couldn't manage it, so I don' t make the pretence.

In fact, the partisanship of my family is so strong that you could almost hear the intake of breath when my husband, Paul, turned up to our wedding wearing a tie in Newcastle United colours. A West Ham fan, he swears it was entirely accidental.

221

EVERTON

ALAN SIMPSON (Labour, Nottingham South)

Once had dreams of playing left midfield for Everton. Has now settled for playing on the left as secretary of the Socialist Campaign Group in parliament and as captain of the Commons football team.

Despite participation in running, football, tennis and squash, he has written books on housing, employment, racism and Europe. At the drop of a Parliamentary Question, he would still swap places with Roberto Baggio (Italian penalty coaches, please note).

21

PIGEONS AND PIPEDREAMS OVER GOODISON

Alan Simpson

The ball curved through the autumn air, dropping gracefully behind the line of the QPR defence. It traced the arc of a love affair that Everton supporters have kept alive for decades - a love affair with football played in a classical, elegant style; with skill, imagination, teamwork and clinical finishing. Young Barlow was onto the ball in a flash and drove it, first time, for goal.

The pigeon on the stand roof died quickly. It hadn't anticipated a ball driven so hard (and wide) from the pitch below. Some 19,000 hearts fell with the pigeon. Another season of disappointment for loyal Evertonians - amongst whom I still count myself. High hopes that the old magic would be remembered - and return - regularly give way to a realisation that the club's main contribution to today's Premier League has been to give new meaning to the word 'mediocrity'.

Yet, despite the miss and the 3-0 thrashing which followed, this occasion was still a rare treat: an all too infrequent pilgrimage to Goodison Park for an ex-patriot Evertonian who had left the city over 25 years ago and who has had to content himself, ever since, with a spiritual, rather than physical, presence on the terraces. This is the world of permanent away games.

Three's a crowd

It's a double-edged sword, being an emigré supporter. During the good times, Saturday afternoons, around five o'clock, would see me rising into the air with a triumphant 'Yes-s-s!'. Sometimes the crowd - which usually consisted of myself and my two small sons - went into ecstasies. But it's hard to sustain a Mexican wave with only three of you. Dizziness sets in quickly and it's fairly disconcerting when two-thirds of the crowd suddenly announces that it needs a wee or a cup of tea.

Away from your home ground, you're lucky to find anyone interested in a discussion of your match, let alone find a write-up of it. The best you can hope for is a few column inches tucked away somewhere - a sort of *Reader's Digest* summary: life in three column inches. There is no prospect of a Saturday evening with the full unexpurgated account in Liverpool's *Football Echo*, where the splendours of the game are re-worked for you to drool over and the extent of Everton's dominance - even down to neat, synchronised exchanges between the police and the toffee-lady in front of the terraces - oozes out of every paragraph and is talked about for days.

The other edge of the sword is the bad times. Then, at least, it's com-forting to know that, from a hundred miles away, people don't notice the tears so easily. There aren't so many who want to take the rise out of you. No intense local rivalry which is likely to make the next few days sheer hell. Just me and the kids, sitting on the settee like brass monkeys, while Desmond Lynam grinds the heel with a cheesy grin ...

> *'Well, Everton have been stuffed again. There's a turn up for the books. Still, the convent side did turn out their first team. And several of their squad had their own boots'.*

The sadist.

One of the most intriguing aspects of being a supporter-in-exile is that you become something between an oracle - filling in details of how games must have been won, the style of play and the tactics that the team would have drawn upon - and a confessional:

> *'Father, we have lost'.*
> *'Say after me, child, "We wuz robbed, we wuz robbed ..."'*

To cushion the blows, my father stopped sending me the *Football Echo* when the seasons began to turn sour. Like good wine, the *Echo* doesn't travel well on bad days; especially if they weren't also bad for Liverpool. So the oracle gets properly replenished only on the rare occasion of a return to the hallowed turf. That, and a charity game for SHELTER afterwards, was what had taken me back to Goodison Park for the QPR game in November 1993.

I don't want to be too hard on Barlow. He had the misfortune, during 1993-94, of being the only Everton player who wanted to get into the penalty area and have a crack at goal. His misses were the more memorable because they were often the majority of Everton's attempts at goal. At the merest hint of excitement, most of the team were prone to pull out - a quality which a whole succession of Cabinet Ministers must surely have looked upon with envy. But for a team looking to win matches, this is not good news.

Treble vision and time warps

My trouble, though, is that I now realise that I cannot watch an Everton game on television or listen to one on the radio without picturing at least two different sides on the park. The first is the team of my childhood - of Alex Young, Roy Vernon, Brian Labone and the legendary midfield of Ball-Kendall-Harvey - and the second is the team which ushered me into adult life: Lineker, Sharp, Reid, Sheedy, Steven, Ratcliffe and Mountjoy.

Everton's 1993-94 squad '... *gave new meaning to the word "mediocrity"'*.
Back row *(l-to-r)* Ebbrell, Moore, Hinchcliffe, Southall, Reeves, Kearton, Angell, Jackson.
Middle row *(l-to-r)*, players only: Rideout, Ablett, Stuart, Warzycha, Barlow, Unsworth,
Holmes, Grant. Front row *(l-to-r)*: Cottee, Radosavljevic (Preki), Horne, Beagrie,
Mike Walker (manager), Watson, Snodin, Kenny, Ward.

They both worked on patterns of play I could understand and adore.
Midfields would hum with ideas and imagination. Defences would be
solid, skilful and composed; attackers would be as bold as bus drivers
and sharper than greyhounds. It has left me ill-equipped to understand what the team of my heart is doing today. It also leaves you open
to a disconcerting sense of treble vision when listening to match commentaries on the radio.

How many times have I heard the commentator say '... and Everton
cross the ball in ...', only to find my mind cutting into the commentary
to send Lineker or Andy Gray plunging to meet it? Better still are the
moments when it is Alex Young who rises above the rest and hovers in
the air as all around him rise and fall in leaden ordinariness.

These are the football moments that you pass on to your children: the
wafers and wine of a communion with something special kept alive in
your dreams rather than in the day's results. For a time I might even
have convinced my children that Alex Young really could hover in the
air for hours; the only person in history who could get caught in the up-
currents of Goodison's undersoil heating. But nostalgia is no protection
from the remorselessness of the commentaries which usually continue
'... and the ball sails over the heads of Everton's diminutive front-line'.

At one time, rumour on Merseyside had it that Everton were not so
much selecting a team as casting for a re-make of *Snow White and the
Seven Dwarfs*. Even the music that the team ran out to was to begin

'Hi ho, hi ho, it's off ...'

The faithful who looked for a cunning plot concealed in this strategy
were then confounded by the succession of long balls sent ballooning
down the park, more in hope than expectation. Were the auditions not
for *Snow White*, but the next episode of *Casualty?* Had the club got a
really good deal on an insurance policy? Were they all drunk? Were
we?

Often I have found myself looking at the team sheet in the Sunday
papers, and trying to fathom out what the plan was. At one stage, the
club had signed enough wingers to have formed their own formation
dance team - and none displayed the desire to score. What do you call a

collection of such species - a woe of wingers? A wilt of wingers? The crowd used another word. These have been bleak times for those who have been brought up on a richer diet of triumphs and trophies.

Bleak times, black marks

There have been times when I've felt that Everton should just sell their whole team and start again. At one stage, I ventured to draw up a shopping list of my own, of signings Everton might consider if they believed that a completely fresh start were needed. The line-up looked something like this:

		David	
		JAMES	
Earl	Paul	Paul	Sol
BARRETT	PARKER	McGRATH	CAMPBELL
	Paul	Carlton	John
	INCE	PALMER	BARNES
	Ian	Les	Andy
	WRIGHT	FERDINAND	COLE

Oh my God! What have I said? I have strayed into the land of unutterable heresy. Something with even greater stigma than Everton signing a player from Liverpool. All of the players on my list are black. Perhaps I should have said '**BLACK'**, because it is a word whose absence has hung over Goodison Park like an accusation.

The argument about Everton's lamentable record on black players is whether it stemmed from the boardroom or the terraces. My own view, from a distance, is fairly straightforward. Many of the same people (and certainly members of the same families) go to watch both Everton and Liverpool. They have had few difficulties in judging the likes of Barnes, Walters and Thomas on the basis of their abilities; not their skin. Traditions of racism can be found in Liverpool as much as in any other city but there are also huge traditions of kindness, humour, generosity and acceptance. Everton draws its supporters from the same communities and cannot hide behind different prejudices.

Living in Nottingham has given me an extra angle from which to view this longstanding racial chasm in my own club's credibility. The angle was Brian Clough. I've never met a manager who was so up-front in his hostility to racism. He would challenge its right to be on the terraces, confront it in his work with schools and youngsters, denounce it in the club's programme and defy it in his selections and signings. If there were a lead to be given, a stand to be taken, it would come from the top. Everton, oh Everton, how I longed for you to follow suit.

When the Professional Footballers Association and the Commission for Racial Equality drafted the advert condemning racism that they asked clubs to put in their programmes at the start of the 1993-94 season, I was over the moon. Here was a chance Everton surely wouldn't miss. Even a 'safety in numbers' approach would bring the club back on side with the angels. But no ... Everton were not amongst the giants who gave a lead, nor the majority who followed suit. The club remained silent on the question of racism - an issue that plagues the football terraces in much the same way that it threatens the lives of families and whole communities in the places they still call 'home'. If Everton had a cunning plan to combat racism then it was as unfathomable as the ones they seem to take onto the pitch. The moment passed. Another pigeon dropped silently from the roof of the stand.

It isn't the fans who pick the team. Nor are they the ones who make the signings. It doesn't matter whose names my children and I have pencilled in on our 'shopping list' in Nottingham, nor the names favoured by my family still in Liverpool; at the end of the day it is the men with the chequebooks who make the decisions. And it all stems from there. At the time of writing, the smoke has yet to clear from the boardroom shoot-out at Goodison Park. When it does, the one thing you can bet on about the survivors is that not one of them will be black.

Fortunately, the arrival of Mike Walker might be Everton's salvation in more ways than one. During the 1994 close season, he unleashed a flurry of bids for black players. Martin Dahlin almost came ... but didn't. The bid for Chris Armstrong never got past the programme-sellers, but a long ball to Bruges brought Nigeria's Daniel Amokachi back on the end of it. Now he has only to find people who can pass to him - a question of competence rather than racism.

English football is not blessed with a surfeit of exhilarating talent at the moment. And a fair slice of the talent that is around lies in the feet and flair of emerging black players. A club cheats only itself and its fans when it cannot recognise such a rich seam of possibilities when the seam isn't white.

A distant optimism

Being away from the spotlight of laser intensity that shines over football on Merseyside does help you put your allegiance into perspective. Undying loyalty for an unsuccessful and utterly flawed club takes some explaining. It is a triumph of optimism over reason; a triumph to be found amongst tens (hundreds?) of thousands of people caught in the web of permanent away games that their chosen team seems embroiled in. It's not success that counts -

> *... You liar! You only say that when your team has been playing so badly they could barely organise an unconditional surrender! ...*

- it is the belief that something better (remarkable) is just round the corner, just about to happen for you.

And so it is with Everton. Whatever the distance, I still get caught in the epidemic of optimism that sweeps through Merseyside as kick-off time approaches ...

> ...A new manager ... the plan is going to change ...

> ...A new line up ... a fiendish and mesmerising plot to sweep aside all-comers ...

> ...Another day ... and the old magic from Everton's 'school of science' will be remembered and reclaimed ...

From a distance, you can bask in the possibilities. From a distance, your aim is clear and your judgment certain. From a distance, at least the pigeons sleep safely.

PORT VALE

JOAN WALLEY (Labour, Stoke-on-Trent North)

Having been to school in Biddulph, when the North Staffordshire coal-field, its pits, pots and Stan Matthews had made the area world famous, she became a local MP in 1987.

Is a staunch supporter of the Football in the Community, Lads-n-Dads and other local sports initiatives - for girls, too! An advocate of women and children, as well as men, watching football in safety, she condemns the way government policy is denying young people access to sport.

Is keen to encourage responsible away supporters visiting Vale Park or the Victoria Ground to stay and sample traditional oatcakes, the industrial heritage captured in Arnold Bennett's novels and the award-winning, Burslem-brewed Titanic Stout.

22

MEMORIES OF STOKE ... AND MEMBER FOR PORT VALE

Joan Walley

Stoke-on-Trent. The Potteries. North Staffordshire. This area has always been proud of its coal, pots and football.

The packed attendance at the Kings Hall, Stoke, in November 1992 - to hear Labour's John Prescott oppose the closure of the remaining pits at Trentham and Silverdale - couldn't have been much smaller than the one which had assembled there, back in 1938 before I was born, to oppose the possibility of Stanley Matthews's leaving Stoke City.

Football matters here - and I want it to carry on mattering

Apart from the annual dinner of the All-Party Parliamentary Football Committee (APPFC) - where I've enjoyed guest speeches by the likes of Bobby Charlton, Tom Finney and the late Billy Wright - there aren't too many highlights in the parliamentary year for opposition MPs. So, ever since I joined this committee and discovered that I'm the only woman who regularly attends its meetings, I've been determined to get to its annual dinner, even if it meant paying the most discriminatory price demanded: reduced-rate tickets are available upon purchase of a tie. When I objected that I had no use for a gents' tie - so how about a woman's scarf? - I was taken less than seriously. One member of the committee - from my own side of the House, alas! - suggested garters, instead. Yes, sexism is alive and kicking in the APPFC. I continue to fight it.

Meanwhile, I was not going to waste an APPFC invitation, in 1993, to a photographic exhibition, organised by the Football Trust, of all the football grounds that had been improved with the help of Trust money.

As soon as I arrived at the exhibition, Joe Ashton, Chair of the APPFC, summoned the official photographer to take my photo standing next to my chosen football ground. 'We'll send it to the local newspaper', he said. A quick overview confirmed my worst fears. No photograph of Vale Park. And none of the Victoria Ground, either. It seemed just about every other league football ground was there except ours.

I told him straight. The only photograph your photographer takes is one of me next to two empty frames. And the headline in *The Sentinel* will show how you have ignored North Staffordshire and its triumphant teams of 1992-93: Stoke City FC, Division II Champions, and Port Vale FC, Autoglass Trophy Winners, deserved better than that.

More anon of how the dream came true in 1993 - only to be relived in 1994. And yet, 30 years earlier, the dream had already come true. In 1962-63, it seemed as if the whole of Stoke-on-Trent was alive with football and bubbling over with success. Stanley Matthews - who had eventually left for Blackpool in 1947 - had come back and played a part in that season of seasons when loyal Stoke supporters finally had something to celebrate. It really was a dream come true. At the time it seemed to matter far more than most other things.

For me, it had all started when Norma Litchfield's family moved back to Stoke-on-Trent in 1961. I was 12. Until then, I had had no interest in football. Saturdays had been the day for doing my mum's shopping and then going to my grandma and grandad's, up the street, to help out with housework and errands. But now my priorities became the match. Saturdays would never be the same again. Some of our schoolfriends were beginning to spend the entire day preparing themselves for a Saturday night out - making new dresses, washing their hair and leaving it in rollers for the whole afternoon. Norma and I had from when we got home at about ten past six to 7.00 p.m to get ready to join them.

Alternative Saturdays were match days: we didn't really have the money to be away supporters. Sunday was the day for analysing the sports pages and - fancying myself as a football reporter - for writing up yesterday's game. My match reports and relevant newspaper cuttings and mementoes - like the *Best Wishes* postcards signed personally by Stanley Matthews - were gummed into my football album. I'd covered the album in red-and-grey upholstery fabric - scraps from Fraylings

We Demand No Transfer: 3000 protesters against the prospect of
Stanley Matthews's transfer from Stoke City, Kings Hall, Stoke, 1938.

Return of the Native: The 46 year-old Matthews re-signs
for Stoke City in October 1961

Bros., where my dad worked, and the nearest I could get to Stoke City's red-and-white stripes.

Football dominated my early teens. And it soon improved my familiarity with the geography of the British Isles. Not only the pools coupons but even the spinner at the wakes week annual fair now made geographical sense . The latter offered fabulous prizes for the holder of the lucky football team ticket and I could now place Bury and Cardiff on the map. Even the 'O' Level English exam invited an essay on 'a crowd'. Mine was, of course, a football crowd.

The crowd at the Victoria Ground was loyal and steadfast and had supported the Potters in large numbers. An attendance of 34,000 was not unusual. In that magical season of 1962-63, Stoke were once again heading for promotion. Tony Waddington's side gave us lots to shout and cheer about.

Masters of another era certain individual players may have been, but we didn't mind one bit that Dennis Viollet's heyday had been with Manchester United or Jackie Mudie's with Blackpool. Goalkeeper Jimmy O'Neill, with 17 Republic of Ireland caps, had just come from Everton, while Jimmy McIlroy (a hero of Alex Carlile's chapter, who had not finished collecting caps for Northern Ireland) joined us from Burnley in time for the game against Norwich - even if his car broke down and he had to hitch a lift to Carrow Road, where we lost 6-0.

And we again had Stanley Matthews wearing the No.7 red-and-white striped shirt. The sun came out to shine when he scored against Luton Town and we had clinched promotion. A glow to last a lifetime. And we roared so loud.

> *Stoke City won promotion in 1963*
> *And indeed my lads, it is true, my lads*
> *I've never been known to lie*
> *And if you go down Boothen End Stoke*
> *You'll see the same as I*

Those were the days!

By the time I left home, in 1967, for Hull University, I had three ambitions in life. Impressed by Sally Trench and her work among London's down-and-outs, I wanted to visit the Bowery in New York. Next, there was the one I didn't dare admit to anyone, because women didn't become MPs just as women weren't catered for as football supporters; and, in any case, that idea - although it had taken root - was still growing. The third ambition was to see Stoke play at Wembley.

They got there in 1972, by which time my support was less active. I'd followed the Potters from Hull. But, in my early postgraduate years in Swansea and London, I'd acquired new interests. *Charles Buchan's Football Monthly* of my early teens had long been succeeded, first by *Honey* and then by the *New Statesman*. So it was that I now got to the Boothen End only occasionally. But once they made it to Wembley, against Chelsea in the League Cup Final, I had one preoccupation. How to be there with them as I had always promised I would be?

By now, I was working in London for the Alcoholics Recovery Project, a voluntary organisation which encouraged homeless alcoholics - through a network of walk-in offices and residential short-stay and long-stay hostels - to dry out and build a new life. With the help of a DHSS loan, I had travelled to the United States to see how they dealt with homeless alcoholics and had visited the Bowery. So, having made it to the Bowery, I had to work out how to get to Wembley. Fortunately, I acquired a ticket and I was on my way.

The sight of all those loyal fans of all ages, streaming into Wembley in their red and white, was enough to make me weep. As we sang *Abide with Me*, it didn't matter that this was only the League Cup, a poor second to the glorious FA Cup. Merely to *be* there with Stoke City was, of course, to achieve my ambition; but, now, nothing would satisfy me short of seeing them play at Wembley *and win*. And win they did - 2-1.

She Who Must Valiant Be

So you can imagine my predicament, some 13 years or so later, when Stoke North Constituency Labour Party selected me to be their candidate and invited me to make my acceptance speech. Up until then, I don't think any of the constituency delegates knew of my red-and-white past. The Victoria Ground is in the neighbouring constituency of Stoke

Central. The geographical centre of the North constituency is Burslem, the Mother Town of the Potteries, and the location of Vale Park, home of Port Vale FC. What could I say? I told them how I had followed Stoke City and pledged that I would attend to the interests of football in Stoke North.

The interests of my constituents include, of course, the concerns of any of them who happen to support Stoke City. I have had occasion to make representations, on their behalf, when their welfare as followers of football was at stake. The Lottery Bill is a case in point. It needed amending, as it went through parliament, to ensure that money towards safety, improvements and innovations - coming from the pools, via the Football Trust - would not be endangered by a National Lottery.

It was an issue in which the APPFC had a significant lobbying role. And I was helped, in playing my part, by my love and knowledge of the game, acquired at the Boothen End - an invaluable induction which most women of my generation had not enjoyed. Otherwise, though, I leave the affairs of Stoke City FC to the MP for Stoke Central.

That explains the proper nature of my *professional* position in respect of the two clubs. But it doesn't begin to answer the bigger question: how would I cope *as a fan*? Would I switch my loyalties from Stoke City to Port Vale - from the traditionally more successful Potters to the Valiants, who have been perceived, despite their king-sized pitch, as the local underdogs?

The decision was made for me by our Tom. Once we had moved back to North Staffordshire, I doubt I would have made time to watch football if it had not been for him. Already participating in the Football in the Community scheme, Tom, like most of Smallthorne Primary School, supported Vale.

I wasn't going to let a seven year-old go to football matches on his own. So I went with him. Simple as that. Sometimes Jan, my husband, stays at home with Daniel, our older, non-footballing son; at other times, he joins Tom and me on the terraces of the Family Stand - sponsored by *The Sentinel*, 'Friend of the Family' - which I officially opened.

As the local MP, I have supported applications to the Football Trust for maximum grant aid for ground improvements - improvements for which Port Vale had previously lacked the resources. Under its present Chairman, Mr W.T (Billy) Bell, the club has been enthusiastically committed not only to meeting safety standards but to other improvements beyond the call of Taylor - from the family enclosure to an award-winning disabled stand (so oversubscribed that the club wants to extend it) and an away supporters' terrace which, covered as it is by the second-hand stand roof from Chester, might perhaps claim to be the first recycled terrace in the country.

None of these developments featured in the exhibition I mentioned at the outset. Quite simply, the Football Trust had overlooked this football-proud conurbation. I don't think they will do so again. Before I left the exhibition, I secured their agreement to photograph one of the new Vale Park stands for inclusion in their next annual report.

Port Vale has always been a community club and its early commitment to the family and disabled stands is evidence of this. Another is its Football in the Community scheme, run by Jim Cooper, which reaches out to all sections of the community, not least to children - boys *and* girls - in schools and through holiday programmes.

Dreams Come True

As if having lost the 1992 General Election, which should have been Labour's victory, was not bad enough, to top it all, Port Vale went down to the Third Division. The only saving grace was that the establishment of the Premier League meant that the Third Division was suddenly the Second, after all.

Stoke City were there waiting for them. After a dearth of derby matches, there were *five* that season - two in the league, a 'double' for Stoke; but two cup wins for Port Vale, in the FA Cup after a replay and in the Autoglass Trophy. I got to two of the games: one league; one cup; one at each ground. For good measure, I persuaded the club and the police to allow NUM members - whom I duly joined - to parade around the Victoria Ground pitch before the league game, with their banner opposing pit closures.

Stoke were clear leaders, all season long, and Vale a good second with an unbeaten home record. With both teams riding high, young and old, men and women, had something to look forward to and feel proud about. It was good for the Potteries and good for Burslem - overshadowed only by the threat of those pit closures. While Stoke were out of reach at the top, Port Vale - despite having sold leading players, Robbie Earl and Darren Beckford - looked capable of a 'double': promotion and the Autoglass Trophy. Now Vale fans would have *their* Away Day to Wembley. In fact, we were to have two trips to Wembley.

The day the dream came true was, as I intimated earlier, 22 May 1993. Port Vale supporters in their thousands, all dressed up in black, white and yellow, left the Potteries for Wembley. We went by coach - nearly every pub, school and Methodist Church, or so it seemed, had organised a coachload and decked out the vehicle for its journey down the M6/M1 to the Twin Towers. We went by car - hundreds of carloads on a congested motorway. So great was the exodus from Burslem and Tunstall that a huge hoarding went up:

Would the last to leave please turn out the light?

To my great anger and disappointment, very few of us went by rail. A club whose ground boasts both a Bycars Stand and a Railway Stand had no shortage of cars to Wembley, but no direct rail service. By discounting the Autoglass Final as a major fixture at Wembley, British Rail had organised engineering works at both Wembley Park and Stoke-on-Trent, ruling out any station-to-stadium chartered service. What a way to run a railway line - especially as the opposition was Stockport County, 25 miles further up the same West Coast main line!

The 160 miles to London might just as well have been a carnival parade, including the Lord Mayor's car and civic party. As when Stoke (and I) first went to Wembley 30 years before, this was the day every loyal Vale fan had waited for. Manager, John Rudge, and the Club had done us proud. Outside Wembley stadium, it seemed like home-from-home, as friends and neighbours caught up with each other and Radio Stoke set up their outside broadcasting team.

The outcome was never in doubt. A game that lasted a lifetime and passed by in the flick of an eyelid left Port Vale the winners of the

Autoglass Trophy, 2-1. Bernie Slaven and all the others were heroes. By the time they returned to Burslem Town Hall for a civic reception, the whole of Stoke-on-Trent, or so it seemed, was there to cheer them - atop a double decker bus, with the Autoglass Trophy they had received from Bobby Charlton only yesterday.

Only one thing marred the celebrations: the prospect of having to return to Wembley - this time to face West Bromwich Albion in the play-offs for promotion to the First Division. To wait so long to reach Wembley and then to have to go twice in eight days seemed grossly unfair especially when Port Vale's record had kept them second, behind Stoke City, until virtually the last match of the season. That match was at Blackpool. However many goals Vale scored, they could not prevent Bolton Wanderers overtaking them, in the finishing straight, to snatch that coveted second place.

We lost to West Brom at Wembley and had to do it all over again in 1993-94. This time, it was Vale's turn to come late, leaping over Plymouth and Stockport to go into the last game in second place. So now, with Vale again finishing the season at the seaside - Brighton on this occasion - Argyle and County knew that, even if they ran up a cricket score (Plymouth managed, you may recall, to win 8-1 at Hartlepool), Vale had only to win at the Goldstone Ground to clinch automatic promotion.

And win they did!

Unequal to the Task

Reliving all these football memories, old and new, reminds me just how important football is to me. As with politics, so with football; it is not always enough to see your team play; they have to play and *win*. It is not something you can be neutral about.

Football remains the main national spectator sport. Yet government cuts to education spending mean that fewer and fewer primary schools offer football training or even run school football teams. In Stoke North, if it were not for the work of Port Vale's Football in the Community Scheme, there would be no football in some schools. Yet this scheme is under threat because the Government has moved the goalposts, obliging the club to find sponsorship to match that from Pizza Hut.

Similarly, government cuts to local authority budgets have left councils unable to promote football as much as they would want. The Lads-n-Dads initiative in North Staffordshire transcends football club loyalties. Heavily dependent on voluntary effort, local business sponsorship and the total commitment of hundreds of lads and dads - and many a mum, too - this scheme organises junior soccer on a shoestring. There is football talent in abundance and a good many young hopefuls signed up for the local clubs' schools of excellence. Even the shortage of qualified referees for these matches is chronic. Desperately needed funds for referee training, equipment, hire for use of pitches, maintenance, strips, etc., simply aren't there at a time when footballers in the Premiership change clubs in million pound deals.

If only the minutest percentage of the transfer fee paid for a Stoke City or Port Vale player were to be donated to that club's Football in the Community scheme or to the local Lads-n-Dads organisation, this would represent a significant increase in their resources - not to mention the symbolic importance of the clubs' thus investing in the community which supports them.

On top of these resource problems, we face the changes arising out of the Lottery Act. I explained earlier how we lobbied - with some success - against the Bill, but any diversion from Football Pools to the Lottery must reduce the amount of money which clubs outside the Premiership, such as Port Vale, have relied upon. Grants could be cut back without any guarantee of alternative funding.

There is, however, some good news to report. Following representations from the Member of Parliament for Stoke North, British Rail came up trumps: not only will they avoid engineering works at Wembley Park on all major Cup Final dates; they have generously sponsored the Football in the Community Scheme by providing Jim Cooper with goal posts and the *InterCity* trophy for a knock-out tournament between Lads-n-Dads teams.

It is not just lads and dads who play and watch football. Girls increas-

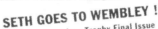

Football in the Community:
Trubshaw Cross skipper, Ben Allan,
scorer of the only goal, holds the
InterCity trophy by its
neck - watched by
Jim Cooper *(left)*, Joan Walley *(right)*
and what was, we're assured,
a much smaller-than-usual
Vale Park crowd, October 1993

*'Vale fans had their
Away Day to Wembley'.*

The Port Vale fanzine,
The Memoirs of Seth Bottomley,
celebrates both the trip to Wembley
and the ground improvements at
Vale Park.

241

ingly play the game; Port Vale's Football in the Community Programme caters for them and the Lads-n-Dads scheme is considering how to do so. Port Vale also sports its own women's team and women increasingly make up a significant part of the regular crowd of home and away supporters. All the more reason for clubs to reconsider the facilities they provide. I remember the look of horror on the groundsman's face at Port Vale when he saw me leading the Chairman of the Football Grounds Improvement Trust to view the Ladies toilet immediately prior to kick-off some years ago so that I could make the case for a refurbishment grant. I am pleased to say that those toilets have been done up.

But far more needs to be done to cater for women and girls. Improvements are needed from the terraces up and from the Board Room down. There remain many who have not understood that the greater involvement of women in football requires changes in the way we deal with all aspects of the game - from the facilities at the grounds to media coverage and the employment of women all across the football industry. The traditional tendencies that still exclude women from the Board Rooms of some of our league clubs, and the institutions in league with this discrimination, deserve to be challenged in the interests both of equality and of football.

I have drafted a Parliamentary Bill to allow women access to all parts of football grounds. But I don't expect there to be parliamentary time - let alone time in my own schedule - to push it at the expense of more pressing priorities: priorities such as winning the next General Election and improving the quality of life of the men and women, young and old, in my constituency who support Port Vale and/or Stoke City through thick and thin - support which only occasionally wavers - and who deserve better than 15 years of a Conservative Government.

The Wonder of Football

May 1994. For football in the Potteries, it was a month both for new hopes and for nostalgia of a very special kind.

It began, on May Day, in the King's Hall - again! This time, the hall is packed not with protesters but with table after table of young footballers - hundreds of them with their managers - a spectacle watched proudly from the balcony by their parents. Up on the stage, four trestle tables are loaded with what must be thousands of pounds worth of trophies - all made in Burslem. I join two Port Vale players on stage, goalkeeper Paul Musselwhite and Kevin Kent (ex-Mansfield and ex-Lads-n-Dads), who hand out the trophies.

Days later, we are celebrating the 80th birthday of the subject of that Kings Hall gathering of 1938 - Sir Stanley Matthews. The location this time is the New Victoria Theatre - for a memorable performance of *Come on Stan*, a celebration of his local and international triumphs.

And yet there *was* something to protest about in May 1994. Even as the strains of Port Vale's adopted team song, *The Wonder of You*, echoed triumphantly around Burslem, we had another mass protest, again to block a prospective departure. This time, though, the protesters were Vale fans; the venue was Vale Park; and the preservation order was being served on a manager: John Rudge, with 15 years of loyal service behind him, was being wooed by Bradford City.

Ever loyal, John Rudge rejected what was, by all accounts, a very substantial offer so as to remain with Port Vale. This is the acceptable face of football, but money counts for more than it should. Television contracts and footballers' wages bear no relation to the real world most supporters live in.

Port Vale and Stoke City will go on featuring strongly in those lives. I, for one, recognise and support the value that football adds to all our lives.

243

HEART OF MIDLOTHIAN

GEORGE FOULKES
(Labour, Carrick, Cumnock and Doon Valley)

Has represented his Ayrshire constituency since 1979, after an apprenticeship, in Edinburgh, in student and local politics.

President of the Student Council at Edinburgh University, he became Bailie on Edinburgh Corporation and Chairman of Lothian Region Education Committee. Has specialised, at Westminster, in Foreign Affairs, enabling him to follow Scotland to Sweden and Hearts to Madrid.

23

HEARTS OF MY HEART

George Foulkes

Tradition. Religion. Or perhaps a mere whim? Whatever its origins, support for a particular football team can be a powerful, binding loyalty.

So why Hearts? As a young child at the primary department of Keith Grammar School in NE Scotland, a brief fling with Aberdeen could have become a lifelong passion. Or the loyalties of my secondary schoolmates in North London for Arsenal or Tottenham could have rubbed off on me - a very slim chance.

Jelling into a Jam Tart

It was a slow maturing affair, this now fierce passion for the Jam Tarts. While I was a student in Edinburgh, the seed was sown. Given my Free Church childhood, it was unlikely to be planted in the Hibernian turf at Easter Road.

Then, in the seventies, came the gentle growth. Elected to the Edinburgh Corporation in 1970, I had the privilege to represent the people of Sighthill Ward until the reorganisation of local government in 1975. Although the hallowed ground of Tynecastle Park lay outside the boundaries in Gorgie, it was from Stenhouse and Whitson, from Saughton and Broomhouse, and from the Calders and Murrayburn - all of them neighbourhoods of my ward - that the crowds marched up the Gorgie Road every second Saturday.

Even so, it was still a somewhat vicarious passion for me until the 1980s - at which time my affection should have turned elsewhere. The sitting Labour Member for what was then the South Ayrshire constituency had formed the breakaway Scottish Labour Party. Selected, as the official Labour candidate, to oppose him in 1979, I won the seat.

So it was that the unpredictability that is politics suddenly transferred me, like a star striker, from Edinburgh to a west coast team in the Premier Division at Westminster. It is a transfer system in which there is at least an expectation you should change your colours to those of the local team. One or two of my colleagues claim, in this book, to have answered this call, while others advance ingenious excuses for not doing so.

I had a double alibi. In all the 800 square miles of the constituency, there is no senior football team. Up in the north, around Mauchline and Auchinleck, they support Kilmarnock with a fervour equal to their antipathy for Ayr United, who are widely supported around Coylton, Maybole and Girvan in the South. So either way I'd lose.

And to add the ultimate in excuses, the real passion is for junior football with more teams to the acre than in any other part of Scotland. How, then, could I choose between Cumnock Juniors and Auchinleck Talbot, whose rivalry makes the Old Firm duel look like a mere tiff? Not to mention Glenafton Athletic, Muirkirk, Craigmark Burntonians, Annbank, Maybole and Lugar Boswell.

Then there is the real reason for sticking with the true love. Football is a passion to be shared and politicians have too few opportunities to share things with their families.

Not that my family was uniformly willing to share my passion for Hearts. Liz, my wife, was a mite sceptical about football and Jenny, my daughter, horse-mad. But, when both sons - born in Edinburgh and, unlike their father, with true, unambiguous Scottish roots - took to Hearts in the mid-1980s, the three of us had an enjoyment that we have continued to share. Roderick, the elder, was to become a guts and thunder supporter and Alexander, with the Leslie Welsh memory of Hearts facts, a collector of every conceivable memento.

From now on, there would be no alternative. Saturday afternoons would be politics-free. Season tickets were bought for the home games. And the trek, on alternative Saturdays, around the Premier grounds of Scotland began.

Thus it was that we set off, into the second half of the 1980s, which

It's the way he tells 'em. Bill Shankly, one of the 'most famous sons' of junior football in George Foulkes's constituency, returns, in 1976 - doubtless to talk of life and death and matters of more importance.

'John Colquhoun, once Chairman of Stirling Labour Party and one of the most skilful and enthusiastic players ever on the books...'

were to provide the joy and the passion and - Hearts being Hearts - the cruellest of disappointments.

After a stuttering start to the 1985-86 season, Hearts had pulled themselves together and were powering towards a dramatic double - not just one trophy on the horizon but two almost in our grasp. The League and the Cup were there to be taken.

Then Hearts' bad luck struck. A virus which hit Tynecastle laid low some of the key players just before the final league match with Dundee at Dens Park. But even so, it should still have been a fairly easy task. We had only to draw to be certain of the title and, even if we lost, Celtic had to beat St Mirren by five clear goals to win on goal difference.

Midway through the second half the game was drifting towards a nil-nil draw 'nothing each', as we Scots say. Then disaster struck. Albert Kidd robbed Hearts of their finest hour with not just one, but two, late goals. And the news came through from Love Street that Celtic had beaten St Mirren by enough to win the championship on goal difference. Grown men burst into tears as the trophy which Hearts had worked so hard for, and which they deserved so much, slipped away.

Yet an opportunity to acquire the long overdue silverware remained. Hearts would meet Aberdeen, the following Saturday, in the Cup Final. Alas, the continuing presence of the virus and - even more virulent - the legacy of the shattering disappointment of the League hung around at Hampden. Not even the inspirational leadership of Sandy Jardine could lift Hearts enough to overcome this. They lost 3-0.

It still seems incredible that the team won nothing in that stirring season. Yet they should feel proud of their efforts. These thoughts were spoken by Sandy Jardine, when he deservedly received the accolade of Player of the Year, and were echoed by supporters all over the country. We live to fight another day and, one year soon, it *will* be Hearts' year.

Politics and Football at Tynecastle

Meanwhile, as a politician with a penchant for pontificating, I have managed to refrain from ever commenting publicly on the progress of

Hearts, either on or off the pitch. That has been an amazing exercise in self-restraint since, from 1981 to 1994, the club's Chairman was the arch-Conservative, Wallace Mercer.

From heroic beginnings, when he rescued Hearts from the despondency of the First Division, guiding us back to Premier League football and to the near-triumphs of 1985-86, his more recent path was less certain and more erratic. Chris Robinson's 1994 takeover came as a welcome relief.

The fans treated Wallace with a mixture of respect and suspicion. The respect derived from his original salvaging of the club and his willingness to listen. The suspicion was owed to his background as a property developer and to his misguided attempt to takeover Hibs. I must confess that he has always been polite to me. I hope I have been equally polite in return, even if I have occasionally been tempted to chant along with the sentiment, on the terraces, that 'he's a fat Tory bastard'.

But the real champion of the fans, the provider of continuity and strength on the Tynecastle board, was the Edinburgh bookmaker and long-time Labour member, Pilmar Smith. A friend and confidant of many Labour leaders in the city, Pilmar was to be seen, year after year, on the march at the annual Scottish Miners' Gala. Equally, he was the first person on the board players turned to in times of need. To me, he represents the spirit and essence of the club, the latest in the long line of people who have given their lives to football at Tynecastle, and his departure from the board is the one sad aspect of the 1994 take-over.

He was not the only Labour man around Gorgie Road. Back from his sojourn in the south is John Colquhoun, once Chairman of Stirling Labour Party and one of the most skilful and enthusiastic players ever on the books. And John Robertson had the dubious distinction of starring in a Scottish Labour election broadcast. It was as ill-fated as the quest for the League Championship in 1987 for John called on the people of Scotland to make it a double: Hearts for the championship and a Labour victory! Maybe that was when I learned to keep my comments on football private - although I did once suggest, behind the scenes, that Hearts might consider changing ownership. My idea for a club which was the property of the fans, players and local people, represented by the district and regional councils, never got off the ground.

So Tynecastle remains for me a welcome retreat from the rigours of politics, where I can complain or compliment, agree with or demur to the occupants of seats around us in the Centre Stand, without the worries of responsibility. Just like bar-room politicians on politics!

The Soul of the Club

Until two years ago the boys and I had season tickets in the family enclosure and became part of a wonderful fraternity. There was the teacher and his son; the publican's wife and her little boy; a Co-op chief executive and his daughter; and many more besides. The view was magnificent, with no pillars to block it, and we saw every move from just to the right of the halfway line, a few feet above the pitch and only a few yards from it.

When the sun shone we were warm and red and when it rained, as it sometimes does even in Edinburgh, the water torrented from the edge of the stand roof and we got very, very wet. But it was always wonderful and the camaraderie was great.

Eventually, when we could no longer pretend Alexander was under 16, as he towered over me with his long legs and his seven o'clock shadow, we took the plunge and moved to the Centre Stand. With a little help from Pilmar, we landed two beautifully located seats behind the directors' box.

Now the sun is almost always shielded but we are always dry. And although the pillars now intrude, both goals are still in fine view and the comradeship is as good as that in the family enclosure. Everyone is older, maybe wiser, but certainly more worldly-wise. Advice is often offered to the directors just in front but diplomatic deafness is the order of the day.

Around us now are mostly pensioner couples, but also Eric Milligan, Convenor of the Regional Council; the Local Government Ombudsman; a Judge and a Peer; and the teacher, who has migrated up with us although his son has opted for the terraces. Yet the 'Jambo' spirit is the same.

'Hearts has more
fanzines than
any other
club I know'.

Alexander sits next to a man who has been coming since 1945. During the 1992-93 campaign, he threatened not to renew his season ticket. We all knew it was an idle threat. Roderick, whose work means he can join us only occasionally, stands in the shed on the terrace. The stories he tells us make my hair curl, but they come from another corner of the same soul of this old club.

No Idle Talk

The old couple in front of us are aristocrats. They have shares in the club and keep us in touch with the shareholders' meeting and get-togethers. If only I had the time! Something for my retirement, perhaps?

The essence of any football club extends beyond the matches. Hearts has more fanzines than any other club I know. Each of their titles tells us something more about the spirit of Hearts. I've explained the local geography of *The Gorgie Wave*, while *Always the Bridesmaid* and *Trophy, Please?* hardly need an explanation. But *No Idle Talk* is a little more obscure.

Just before the teams emerge from the dressing rooms, Tynecastle reverberates to two entirely different versions of the Hearts Song. First it is sung by a chorus as a marching song and then as a ballad by an ancient crooner. But, unlike the pathetic efforts of most other teams, it is a real song, one verse of which has a resounding conclusion:

> *Our forwards can score and it's **no idle talk***
> *The defence is as strong as the old Castle rock*

What a wonderful rhyme! And what equally great sentiments! There is certainly still very little idle talk around Tynecastle at any time. That song has some other evocative lines. Take the chorus:

> *The talk of the toon are the boys in maroon*
> *And Auld Reekie supports them with pride*

The references to 'Auld Reekie' and the 'Castle rock' each identifies firmly with Edinburgh, its traditions, its solidity and its history.

Hearts are part of Edinburgh, as are Hibs. They represent equally proud and essential, but different, parts of the history of Scotland's capital. Wallace Mercer's ill-advised attempt at a merger was doomed from the very beginning.

But equally, the rivalry between the two clubs is different from that between Rangers and Celtic - less raw, less polarised but in some ways more profound.

Life and Death

So *now* do you understand why I still support this team of near-success - the almost champions, so often the bridesmaid?

In my constituency, there is what remains of Glenbuck, home of the Glenbuck Cherrypickers and of more professional footballers than any town a thousand times its size. Its most famous sons include the Shankly brothers, Bob and Bill.

> *Football is not a matter of life and death ... it's much more*
> *important than that.*

Certainly a hyperbole - but not far off the mark if you hail from Glenbuck. The eight junior, and many amateur, clubs continue today the footballing traditions of the Shanklys and their generation and are part of the complex warp and weft that is Scotland from Cape Wrath to Whithorn. The miners of Ayrshire put into football as much effort and dedication as they did to gouging the black gold from the ground. The loyalty of those miners propelled me into Parliament when they supported me against the breakaway Member. That loyalty gave me, in turn, the inspiration and the determination with which I now try to represent them - in their redundancies and retirement - and their sons and daughters, too.

These Ayrshire folk are understanding enough to excuse me one eccentricity - that seed that has blossomed, in a corner of my heart, for that wee fitba' team that aye makes it mark. Indeed, there are some of them who will concede, or even readily agree, that there's nae other team to compare wi' the Hearts.

SWINDON TOWN

NIGEL JONES (Liberal Democrat, Cheltenham)

Has represented his native Cheltenham since 1992 and has watched the England team lose in more countries than he cares to remember. A computer man, he nevertheless leans towards fantasy rather than reality in football, cricket and - some opponents would claim - politics.

Led the MPs' section of the *Daily Telegraph* Fantasy Cricket League. Claims to bowl slow left arm, which is not much use when playing sweeper. Once took a hat-trick in a game his side lost by seven wickets.

His membership of the Parliamentary Office of Science and Technology may explain why he is one of the Honorary Keepers of the Parliamentary Beer Club and has almost finished a spy thriller (publishers, please note).

24

BOBBING ALONG WITH THE ROBINS

Nigel Jones

I was there. Wembley. 15 March 1969. The League Cup Final. First Division high flyers Arsenal, the hottest favourites for years, against Swindon Town of the Third Division.

What was I doing there, a fortnight before my 21st birthday? What were my credentials to be at a Wembley final?

Since I was knee-high to a grasshopper, I had been interested, to differing degrees, in *two* teams of Robins: my home-town team, Cheltenham Town; and my nearest league club, Swindon Town. Having relatives in Swindon - and a cousin who had played for Bournemouth and given away a late penalty on the sacred turf of the County Ground - strengthened the interest at a distance, with which I followed, in the Sunday 'paper and the *Gloucestershire Echo,* the prowess of players I had never seen - until the FA Cup Fourth Round in 1967, when I watched Swindon beat Bury 2-1.

Regular visits followed. There might be two lots of Robins in my life but Swindon Town were now clearly my team. That 1968-69 season was the kind of season that doesn't come along very often. Promotion from Division III and that trip to Wembley: a double-helping of the success for which Swindon had waited so long.

What The Papers Say

So *that* is what I was doing at Wembley with the Division III minnows from Wiltshire. True, these 'minnows' were, as I've mentioned, on their way to promotion; but could they emulate Queens Park Rangers, who'd completed, two seasons before, the unlikely double of promotion from Division III *and* the League Cup?

The odds were, as I say, very much against Swindon. The Horse of the Year Show had recently been held on the hallowed turf. And it showed. The muddy conditions would surely favour the much fitter Arsenal team. Armstrong, Radford and Gould would leave the Swindon defenders standing. And Frank McLintock and big Ian Ure would keep out the Robins' lightweight attackers.

But it wasn't quite as predicted by the newspapers - with the notable exception of the *Swindon Advertiser,* whose football correspondent was an objective man of unbiased views.

The whistle went. Not much happened for half an hour, with most of the play in the centre of the park. Then Swindon's number ten, Peter Noble, a Burnley reject, chased a no-hope ball which big Ian would have no difficulty turning back to his goalkeeper, Bob Wilson. Goodness knows how the mix-up happened. Perhaps Ure slipped. Perplexed at gaining possession unexpectedly, Noble panicked and got rid of the ball as fast as he could. It shot across the goalmouth to collide with Roger Smart's knee, whence it ricocheted into the Arsenal net.

One-nil. Surely just a slip-up to be put right in the second half as Swindon tired? But no! The second half belonged to three men. For once, Don Rogers was not among them. Swindon's dashing, old-fashioned winger never really got the ball. Obviously, Arsenal had researched his scoring exploits and had worked out a plan to snuff him out of the game. The three Swindon heroes were their full-backs - John Trollope and Welsh international, Rod Thomas - and a little known, and not very tall, goalkeeper.

Peter Downsborough had been the scourge of Swindon Town fans for years. He was the sort of 'keeper whose judgment was so fine he would watch the ball onto the cross-bar - and sometimes just beneath it. And his technique of picking the ball out of the net was unmatched in any league. Yet in the second half at Wembley he played out of his skin. Shots rained in from inside the area, from outside the area, and from both wings. With one save he punched the ball away not for a corner but for a throw-in nearer the half-way line than the corner flag.

And then it happened. An optimistic long ball up the middle, a missed clearance by the Swindon defence and Bobby Gould lashed in the equaliser which even the inspired Downsborough could not reach. Five minutes later, the final whistle. Extra time. Another half-hour of this. I suppose we could get thrashed now. How embarrassing!

John Smith - Swindon's portly, but talented, number nine - was substituted early on in extra-time. Ex-Tottenham, Smithy was the kind of mid-field general whose first-touch control gave him plenty of time to carry on a conversation, usually a blunt one, with someone in the crowd at the County Ground while seeking out someone upfield who might be interested in receiving the ball. Willie Penman came on, his all-white strip glowing. Everyone else was covered in mud except Don Rogers, who liked to stay on his feet throughout the match.

Then, again at the far end of the ground, Swindon won a corner. In a goalmouth scramble, Rogers received the ball and managed to thread it through a mass of tangled legs and bodies into the net. The place erupted. They must have heard the cries of *Swin-don, Swin-don* at Paddington Station to where most of the Wiltshire fans had expected, by now, to be heading, dreaming of what might have been.

Half-time of extra-time came and went. Arsenal brought on George Graham as substitute to spark the Gunners into a last ditch, all-out attack. Another clean shirt to match that of Don Rogers. You could hardly recognise which side the other players were on, let alone who they were. But the Swindon fans knew the shape of their players. The trouble was all the action was up the far end of Wembley Stadium, in and around the Swindon goalmouth. Could we hang on to the slender, and - in the opinion of the football correspondent of the *Swindon Advertiser* - deserved lead?

Then, in the last minute, Wembley experienced the goal of the season, right in front of us, up our end - or, rather, the Arsenal end. Willie Penman gathered the ball deep in his own half and booted it upfield. Rogers, who didn't believe in getting involved in all this defending nonsense, was hovering on the half-way line, inside his own half. As he had hardly broken sweat in the match, he still had plenty of energy left. Sure-footed as ever, he sped off like a greyhound, the ball seemingly glued to his foot. Into the penalty area to meet the advancing Wilson. A quick shimmy of the Rogers thighs and the goalie was sprawling in the mud. A hefty boot and the ball made the net bulge.

I cannot tell a lie. I felt sorry for the Arsenal fans, but only for a moment. They came expecting to win. We came hoping to play well. The next hour is still a bit of a blur. Skipper Stan Harland held the cup aloft and the far end of the ground emptied of Arsenal fans. We caught the tube to central London and danced the night away in and around Leicester Square.

The Emotion of Promotion

Did I say Leicester? Yes, I was there. Wembley. 31 May 1993. The play-off final, between Leicester and Swindon for promotion to the Premiership.

While this was the first-ever play-off final in the new Division I, Swindon were no strangers to this end-of-season scrap. They had clinched promotion from the old Division III, in 1987, when they won the inaugural two-legged play-off final. Then, when the finals moved to Wembley in 1990, Swindon won the Division II play-off, beating Sunderland 1-0 - a triumph, in his first season as a manager, for Ossie Ardiles, who had transformed the Robins from a kick-and-rush side into a footballing outfit. Instead of being promoted, though, they were, of course, demoted by the Football League on some trumped-up charge of financial irregularities - soccer's equivalent of electoral malpractice.

Now, in 1993, they were back at Wembley, against Leicester City. Neither team should have been there really. Swindon - by now under player-manager Glenn Hoddle - had finished fifth in the division with Brian Little's talented Leicester City sixth, each of them 12 points behind third-placed Portsmouth. But Pompey had gone out in the home-and-away stage to Leicester while fourth-placed Tranmere had never recovered from the first five minutes of the first leg at the County Ground, in which the Robins had taken a two-goal lead.

Getting to Wembley was all a bit of a rush. The blessed Liberal Democrat hierarchy had decided to hold their Spring Conference in Nottingham, that Bank Holiday weekend, and I had to launch a new policy on Housing at noon. Bit tricky getting to Wembley for a three o'clock kick-off.

'I was there...'
15 March 1969

'I was there...'
31 May 1993

Possible to do it in a helicopter, perhaps. But did anyone in the party have access to a helicopter? Not a hope! Not even the dashing Ashdown, with his military and Westland contacts, could rustle one up at such short notice. The only way to get to Wembley was to start off the debate, leave the platform and the Conference Centre, ignore the rest of the debate (which I understand was a bit fiery) and drive down the M1 - keeping strictly to the 70 mph limit, your Honour.

Fortunately, there were no traffic hold-ups on the way. Just every motorway bridge in Leicestershire festooned with banners:

Good Luck Brian
Brian Little's Blue and White Army

Arrived at Wembley 10 minutes before the kick-off, against the advice, given on the ticket, to take one's seat an hour and a half before the game started. Met brother Roland and son Sam, who had followed this advice and were joining in the community singing with gusto.

Out came the teams. Usual formalities. And then a first half of little excitement and few chances. Until just before the break when Craig Maskell cleverly back-heeled the ball for Hoddle to place the ball in the Leicester net and give Swindon what people in our half of the ground described as a well-deserved lead. The football correspondent of the *Swindon Advertiser* is reported to have snapped his pencil in two, such had been the tension, but recovered to pen the immortal words 'Justice was starting to be done on Wembley's hallowed turf'.

Half-time and all's well with the world. What would Hoddle tell the players in the dressing-room?

One's enough. Play it steady lads.
And keep an extra two at the back

Well, that was the general advice from the Swindon fans around me. But defence was not on the agenda. Early in the second half, Craig Maskell hit a glorious cross-shot in off a post; and, shortly afterwards, central defender Shaun Taylor, who had come up for a corner, bravely headed the third.

Poor old Leicester! 'We are going up, we are going up' chanted the Swindon supporters, while the Leicester fans stayed silent. It was going to be as easy as the Newbury by-election had been earlier that month. We could relax for the final half hour while Swindon ran in five or six. Those pre-counted chickens failed, alas, to hatch. Fifteen minutes later, it was 3-3 and things were looking decidedly dicey.

Bloody defenders, never could defend.
What on earth was Bodin doing getting caught out of position?
Digby should have had at least two of them.

The Wiltshire moaners were having their say. There was only one thing for it. Bring on Chalkie!

An ageing and much travelled striker, Steve White had scored over 200 goals in a career spanning Bristol Rovers, Luton, Charlton and Swindon. A great servant of the club, he had ignominiously managed to hit both posts with the same shot in the 1990 play-off final. This time, Chalkie was only a substitute, with Craig Maskell and Australian, Dave Mitchell, the striking duo. The best Chalkie could hope for was a few minutes at the end.

On he came with 12 minutes left. Everyone on both sides looked worn out. Within five minutes, Steve had won the match. Turning in the area to latch onto a long pass from Hoddle, he was felled by the Leicester goalkeeper, who must have lost his presence of mind. Up stepped Welsh international, Paul Bodin, to take the penalty. The crowd was hushed. You could have heard a pin drop.

Six steps, thump, GOAL!

Jimmy Greaves, who was commentating, thought it the match of the season:

Get rid of the Cup Final and all that rubbish.
Get these play-offs on. They're brilliant.

Captain, Colin Calderwood, collected the magnificent trophy, with Hoddle bringing up the rear.

'...the goal of the season'.
Don Rogers relives his
1969 goal, and victory,
at Wembley.

'Bring on Chalkie!'
Steve White, in his
Swindon glory, but now
moved on to Hereford.

Motion on Promotion

The occasion called for an Early Day Motion (EDM) in the House of Commons. An EDM is the graffiti of parliament. Anyone who feels like it can put down a motion which is then carried on the order paper for the rest of the session. You can express views and seek support from other MPs on any issue under the sun - from, say, the situation in Kashmir or the lack of 'flu vaccine to the need for a cat in the Commons to catch an allegedly growing swarm of mice.

The end of the soccer season is a heaven-sent opportunity for MPs whose local clubs have done well to put down a motion and get some good local press. Manchester United (for winning the league), Oldham (for avoiding relegation) and Raith Rovers (for getting promoted) all featured in May 1993, along with West Ham (see Chapter 19).

I must admit to having put down a motion earlier in the season, congratulating Cheltenham Town on reaching the second round proper of the FA Cup for the first time in my life. As the MP for Cheltenham - having won the seat in 1992 with a swing against the Conservative John Taylor, an ardent Villa fan - I was the only signatory. My colleague Don Foster, MP for Bath, wanted to do a joint Cheltenham/Bath/Yeovil EDM, because these three Liberal Democrat-held constituencies had non-league football teams who drew with league opposition in that round. Sadly, only Yeovil won their replay, but when Don asked the Right Honourable Member for Yeovil (our boss, Paddy Ashdown) to sign the motion, the gallant one enquired 'What's the FA Cup?' Enough said.

Anyway, back to the Swindon victory. It is polite not to put down motions congratulating your favourite football team when you are not actually the MP for the area concerned. You expect the appropriate Member to do the business; and then you can sign it, too.

Could I get Simon Coombs to do the decent thing? I know the man is a Tory, but he's a rather decent kind of Tory who's into high technology and cricket. As a Parliamentary Private Secretary, he ought not, traditionally, to put down motions at all. But fair's fair! Some of us had waited a lifetime to see Swindon Town reach this pinnacle of success. And Leicester MP, Keith Vaz, had already tabled a motion wishing Leicester well in the final. In the end, I had to threaten to break with parliamentary protocol and table the 'Congratulations to Swindon Town FC' myself before Simon acted. The headline 'Town MP snubs Swindon super-heroes' would surely have haunted him into the next election.

Up Where We Belong

A rather different caption was soon available on car-stickers:

Up Where We Belong

That's not how Portsmouth fans felt about the team that had finished 12 points below them, but this acclamation expressed the views of Robins fans who felt we had already won promotion, fair and square in 1990.

But did Glenn Hoddle and the Swindon superstars have the depth and quality to survive in the Premiership? The question was very soon redundant. Within a few weeks the manager, captain and other key players had left the club *en route* for London.

Manager Hoddle went to take over troubled Chelsea and captain Calderwood to shore up a leaky Spurs defence, teaming up again with Ossie Ardiles. Dave Mitchell went off, for some inexplicable reason, to play in Turkey, but ended up in Millwall. And the season was not very old before Micky Hazard, who had come on as a second substitute for the final minute at Wembley, had joined Calderwood and another ex-Swindon player, David Kerslake, at White Hart Lane. By December, even Wembley man-of-the-match Martin Ling wanted to go, after being dropped, but he was persuaded to stay.

A bit tough at the top, wasn't it? Not easy to score. Not easy to win any points at all. A 5-0 thrashing by Liverpool, in our second home game, was perhaps to be expected. A 5-1 defeat at Southampton, three days later, was a lot more serious. If you can't get a few points off the Saints then you are going to struggle.

THE OFFICIAL FOOTBALL COVER SERIES
No.18 15TH No.18

The Winning Goal at Wembley - May 1993

SWINDON TOWN
FIRST HOME MATCH IN THE
FA CARLING PREMIERSHIP

SWINDON TOWN'S FIRST HOME MATCH IN
THE FA CARLING PREMIERSHIP
VERSUS
OLDHAM ATHLETIC
18 AUG 93 SWINDON WILTS

MATCH RESULT
SWINDON TOWN   0   OLDHAM A 1
                                      Bernard

Evening Advertiser

Swindon Town FC
County Ground
Swindon SN1 2ED

Winning goal - losing start.
From the first-day cover
series of the
Swindon Advertiser -
proof that philately will get
you nowhere.

*'John Gorman ... kept to
the footballing philosophy'.*

265

Undaunted, new manager, John Gorman, gradually welded together a side that was looking capable, by Christmas, of earning another season in the top flight. But, then a string of injuries and several near misses, including draws against Manchester United and Norwich, meant that they were never going to manage enough three-pointers to catch up. A win at home over Spurs and the double over QPR were insufficient. The big problem was a leaky defence - perhaps a sign that the loss of Calderwood and Hoddle had left a gaping hole that could not be repaired easily. Even drafting in Brian Kilcline, veteran of many a relegation battle with Coventry, couldn't stem the flow.

Frankly, they deserved to stay up. They didn't resort to strong-arm tactics but kept to the footballing philosophy which had brought them success under Ardiles and Hoddle, in turn. It was good to watch, too. You knew they were going to go forward with overlapping full-backs. You also knew that they were vulnerable to quick breaks, as Matt Le Tissier showed in both matches against Southampton.

Sam and I went to the home match against Southampton - as one of the editors of this magnificent book can testify. David Bull is a long-suffering Southampton supporter who claims to have been at Wembley when Bobby Stokes won the cup back in the mists of time. As David made his way, from our pre-match conference at the County Ground, to the Stratton end where I had stood as a teenager, Sam and I were shepherded into the executive box at the invitation of the Swindon President, Cecil Green. Cecil is a gentleman of the old order and had a lifelong friendship with my late uncle, Keith Rushworth.

Uncle Keith was a player, director, chairman of directors, vice-president and president of Cheltenham Town FC. He once had the awful task of firing a none-too-successful manager by the name of George Summerbee - the father of Swindon (later Man. City and England) favourite, Mike; and grandfather of Nicky Summerbee, who has now followed, in dad's footsteps, from the County Ground to Maine Road.

My Cheltenham Robins once graced the Southern League and, more recently, the GM Vauxhall Conference. Former Forest goalkeeper, Jim Barron, was manager for a while and brought the ageing Scottish international, Andy Gray, to play for a few months. The Whaddon Road ground erupted when he eventually scored his first goal for the club. Sadly, Cheltenham were relegated to the Beazer Homes League in 1992 and have twice missed out on promotion, finishing runners-up in 1994.

One of newly-promoted Swindon's pre-season friendlies, in 1993, brought most of the Wembley squad, tanned from well-earned holidays in the Caribbean, to Whaddon Road. Needless to say, the local MP attended. Over the years, the two clubs had played plenty of neighbourly friendlies, but this was the first encounter between my constituents' team and *my* team. Until then, I had been able to satisfy those local supporters who, knowing of my life-long Swindon affliction, felt that I ought now to support Cheltenham Town. I do. As I indicated at the outset, I find no conflict in having two teams of Robins. I like to think that, on this occasion, the real week-in, week-out Cheltenham fans understood that you cannot forget your real team. It's a bit like asking someone to change his or her religion.

The result was a satisfactory one-all. Chalkie White hammered one in just under the bar from three yards. Swindon substituted everyone during the second half. At one time, they had three No 11s on the pitch - to the envy of a Cheltenham director:

'They've got more than one set of kit!'

The problem with being a Swindon Town supporter is that you have to wait for so long between the high spots.

League Cup Winners 1969.
Division One Play-Off Winners 1993.

At that rate, by the time they win something else I'll be retired. The good news is that I'll be able to have a season ticket and attend every match.Meanwhile, there's that one automatic promotion place to aim for in 1994-95. Yet I suppose we'd settle for another visit to Wembley for the play-offs.

After all, we're unbeaten at Wembley!

BLACKPOOL and LIVERPOOL

NICK HAWKINS (Conservative, Blackpool South)

Member, since April 1992, for Blackpool South, a constituency that includes Blackpool FC's Bloomfield Road ground, where he gets to as many home games as he can. His footballing career has been enthusiastic but almost totally devoid of talent, apart from the ability to turn up. Secretary of the Tory Backbench Sports Committee and passionately committed to sport of all kinds in schools, having written a paper on this for the Bow Group, of which he was Chairman in 1992-93. Has many other political interests, but sport remains an abiding love.

Three caps so far for Westminster Wobblers, including Wembley in 1994. His team, *Blackpool and Bedford United*, finished a disappointing 27th in the Politicians Division of the *Daily Telegraph* Fantasy League - the fifth highest Tory side in a Labour-dominated contest, won by his Conservative colleague, David Sumberg.

25

MY TWIN TOWERS - BLACKPOOL TO WEMBLEY

Nick Hawkins

I am a passionate believer in equality of opportunity. All kids should have the chance to play sport, regardless of their ability. I say that as one who played, as a small lad, every kind of sport he could, but who was never that good at anything.

With superior coaching, I did become a reasonable competitive swimmer. And, with practice, I improved at both rugby union (at school) and cricket (throughout) and have had my moments.

But football! My only real assets have ever been keenness and the ability to turn up as and when required and as promised. I was once praised for being good at 'running into space' - I could see where the gaps and opportunities were - but that compliment kindly glossed over my inability to use the ball when it came my way. In the context of a match, I certainly couldn't shoot - whatever I might achieve in practice, I can recall having put the ball in the net, in a competitive game, only once. That may appear to equal the goal-scoring record boasted by my colleague, John Greenway, in his chapter - except that my 'goal', for a 'political' team in a student match at Oxford, was ruled out for offside. As I remember it, I was even accused of *preventing* a goal: a guest-player from Ruskin College reckoned that what I had treated as a pass would have gone in if I hadn't touched it and my being offside would then have been overlooked.

Growing up with football

I grew up in Bedford. The local, Southern League, team, Bedford Town, seemed always to be bust or very nearly so - staggering through the 1960s and 1970s, from crisis to crisis, until they went out of existence in 1982 (to be reborn, in a minor way, in 1989). They had had their moments - notably that FA Cup Third Round win at Second

Division Newcastle in 1964. But that was before my time: I was only six. By the time I was old enough to take an interest, the giant-killing days of the *Eagles* (after the bird in the coats of arms of the town and of my school) were over - although they did get to the Fourth Round again in 1966 (losing to Everton) and to the Third Round the next season.

That 1967 tie - a home defeat, 6-2, by Third Division Peterborough - marks my only recall of seeing Bedford Town's name on BBC's *Grandstand*. Television was, of course, my only hope of seeing football played at any decent level. My father was (and is) very keen on just about every other sport, but wasn't interested in taking me to football matches. I could, however, envy some of my schoolfriends, who were allowed to take the train, down the line to Kenilworth Road. Luton were on the up during my teens - from Division IV in 1968 to Division I (for a season) by 1974. These were not, however, the days of fame and glory under the benevolent and inspired chairmanship of my now parliamentary colleague, David Evans, who recounts below his role in the successes of the 1980s.

In the early 1970s, the Kenilworth Road terraces could be fairly rough by the standard of that fairly non-violent county. I can still hear and recall the words from the chorus sung by the fans:

'*We are - the Oak Road - boot boys*'

All in all, then, it should be clear why my formative football years, from the late 1960s through the 1970s, were mainly about seeing games on TV, decorating my bedroom walls and reading football books and magazines.

Watching the televised game and reading, in *Shoot!*, about the stars invariably meant adopting a distant - successful - team as one's favourites. Thus, when I was about 11 or 12 and at Bedford Modern School (which played mainly rugby), my mate, Tim Kelsey, was an ardent Leeds United fan. These were the days of the great Don Revie sides, with the likes of Allan Clarke, Eddie Gray, Billy Bremner and Peter Lorimer - the 'Super Leeds' that James Clappison fondly recalls in his chapter.

Whenever I see archive film of that side, on TV, I think of the discussions Tim and I used to have. If you ever read this, Tim, I will now agree with you that that was a great side. My own first choice was Liverpool - with Ron Yeats and Tommy Smith and Ian St. John - and my second, Spurs (although, for some long forgotten reason, I deserted them a bit after they sold Dave Mackay).

In 1969-70, one of the football magazines issued pennants of the then First Division teams. I had the full collection - all round a large peg-board on my bedroom wall. I am able to say, with perfect honesty, that it included the colours of what is now my constituency team: Bloomfield Road is in my Blackpool South seat.

That was, of course, sadly, the last time that the 'Seasiders' were in the top flight. They were relegated the following season and have never returned ... Yet!

My favourite story, in my football annuals, was a wonderful article called 'The Great Escape'. Not the war story, but the tale of how Sheffield Wednesday managed to avoid relegation by a titanic effort over the last few games after seeming doomed as the season (in the late 1920s) neared its end.

It was a useful preparation for me, as Blackpool lingered in the Division II danger zone in the final weeks of 1993-94. I was at Bloomfield Road for the penultimate home game, a 4-0 thumping by Reading. The problem was that our wonderful striker, Dave Bamber, was injured. Without him the team isn't the same. He was back, though, for the last Saturday of the season and scored in the crucial 4-1 win against Leyton Orient. Together with Fulham's defeat at Swansea, this kept us up by a single point.

Grown-up football

I have touched upon my recent experience as an MP watching his constituency team. Between leaving school - and Bedford - in 1975 and being elected for Blackpool South in 1992, my football 'career' was that of a Liverpool supporter and a 'scratch' player.

I managed to be both during my first job, as a Barrister in chambers in

Birmingham, where both of our Clerks were soccer mad. The senior clerk, one Berry Knowles - no, that's not a printing error: I think his father must have been a Dornford Yates *aficionado* - had a regular seat in the directors' box at Molineux, whilst Steve, the junior clerk, was a Villa fan. I hardly knew anyone (except a few masochistic local solicitors) who went to St. Andrew's; but, living myself in Coventry, I used to enjoy keeping an eye on how the Sky Blues were doing.

They could certainly have done with Peter Ndlovu in those days; but, again, they had their moments. I was certainly on their side, not Spurs', when they got to the Cup Final in 1987, although by then we'd moved away and I was listening to the game on the radio driving through Brighouse, as the Huddersfield candidate in the 1987 Election.

During that 1986-87 season, I had become a corporate lawyer and entered the world of occasional invitations to see some decent football. I started right at the top - with an invitation from friends of a colleague to go to Anfield. To sit in the directors' box. To visit the Trophy Room. The lot! A boyhood dream fulfilled. It was the second leg of the League Cup semi-final against Southampton. Liverpool won 3-0. The style of one of the greatest teams ever assembled, playing in the evening under the lights, was unforgettable.

Election to parliament has brought even more football treats. I straightaway joined the splendid All-Party Parliamentary Football Committee, whose work is described in several other chapters of this book, and have played occasionally (despite the record confessed at the outset) for the 'Westminster Wobblers', the House of Commons football team so well-organised by Bryan Davies.

The North-West MPs went to Old Trafford during 1993-94, as guests of British Gas. We had a wonderful day and I thoroughly enjoyed listening to Wilf McGuinness's comic speech and meeting another boyhood hero, Bobby Charlton, with his wife and daughter, Suzanne. The only disappointment was the game - probably the worst that the great current United side played all season. A boring 0-0 draw with Wimbledon, to which the visitors' tactics, of course, contributed. There was some sparkle from Ryan Giggs. The rest was so bad that, when Alex Ferguson brought Mark Hughes up to meet us afterwards, they were apologising, in effect, for United's performance.

Finally, Wembley. I had been the local MP for all of six weeks when Blackpool won the old Fourth Division play-offs to clinch promotion to the new Second Division. I succeeded in getting through to the Club Chairman direct, immediately after the match, to send my congratulations - a tribute to the Wembley telephone system.

Within two years, I was back at Wembley - *as a player!* As the Westminster Wobblers came up the tunnel, they were greeted by the recorded sound of the crowd roar and by a Welsh camera crew. A quite extraordinary experience. And *lots* of space for me to run into.

I shall never again watch the teams come out for the Cup Final on TV, without saying

'Been there! Done that!'

Wobblers at Wembley.
The line-up includes Nick Hawkins (striped shirt) and a front-row, containing several contributors to chapters above.
l-to-r: Mike Watson (ch. 17); Alan Simpson (ch. 21); Bryan Davies (acknowledged opposite); Alistair Burt (ch. 18); Clive Betts; and Anthony Coombs.
(Inset) Dave Bamber, a 'wonderful striker' for Blackpool -
but would he make the Wobblers' team?

LEEDS UNITED

JAMES CLAPPISON (Conservative, Hertsmere)

Yorkshire born, he became a barrister and a candidate in two Yorkshire elections (1987 and 1989).

Two Bootle by-elections in 1990 were followed by election to Parliament in 1992. He is Joint Secretary of the Conservative Parliamentary Committee on Education and a member of the Select Committee on Health.

26

MARCHING ALTOGETHER - LEEDS, LEEDS, LEEDS!

James Clappison

I could not lay claim to be a fanatical Leeds United supporter on the basis of my current level of active support - other commitments, not least politics, have put paid to that.

There was a time, however, when I could do so. And, since for most of the time I followed Leeds they did badly, I could lay claim to be a 'loyal' supporter and not a fair-weather fan.

Life after Revie

When I was growing up in Yorkshire in the late 1960s and early 1970s, there was only one team to follow. Sorry, Sheffield! But the 'Super Leeds' of the Revie era were the only Yorkshire side in the big league and they drew supporters from all over the county - Hull, in my case. By the time I began actively to follow *my team* in the late 1970s, however, that great side had faded away.

Nonetheless, the side built by Jimmy Armfield was still a good one and was underrated - not least by the Elland Road directors. Tony Currie, Arthur Graham, Brian Flynn and Co. may not have filled the trophy cupboard but they certainly gave the fans plenty to cheer about. Some of Revie's players remained in this period; in the eventide of his career, Paul Madeley was still a class or two above everyone else on the pitch.

I have always felt that what happened to Jimmy Armfield was the classic case of a good manager who managed a good team; who was not given a chance by an over-ambitious board; and with disastrous results. The evidence of his soundness lay in the fact that the team played well for a season or two after his departure during the short tenure of Jock Stein and the controversial tenure of Jimmy Adamson.

'... two terrific matches against West Brom, both away, because of a ground ban.'

'the violence that left a Birmingham City fan dead in 1985'

During the 1978-79 season, I did not miss a match, home or away, until the 6-2 win at Hartlepool in the FA Cup Third Round. The team had a long unbeaten run and deserved to win something - sadly they went out in the Fourth Round of the Cup, after two terrific matches against West Brom, both away because of a ground ban.

The following seasons saw a gradual decline in the team and were probably some of the unhappiest in the history of the club. The fans turned against the manager, the unfortunate Jimmy Adamson, and the board later turned to players - Allan Clarke, Eddie Gray and Billy Bremner - from the Revie days in an attempt to revive the club. Leeds began to battle against relegation and the inevitable happened at the end of the 1981-82 season when they lost a night match at West Brom, sadly - but not entirely surprisingly - the occasion of some crowd disorder. I remember a silent, miserable motorway journey home to Leeds.

That was not, however, the lowest point in Leeds United's fortunes. That came, for me, in a 4-2 cup defeat at Scunthorpe in 1984 - although my memory of this may be coloured by the association with another, even worse, motorway journey home: my friend's car broke down on the M62 in the middle of a thunderstorm.

Through all of their struggles in the 1980s, Leeds retained a hard core of loyal support with a particularly big away following. This faithful band was not always welcomed with open arms. Problems with Leeds fans go back a long way. But before 1980, these tended to be isolated events - like the pitch invasion at home to West Brom in 1971 and the rioting during and after the 1975 European Cup Final in Paris, bad though these incidents were in themselves.

I subscribe to the theory that behaviour off the pitch is aggravated by lack of success on the pitch and this was certainly the case with Leeds in the 1980s. I intensely dislike hooliganism and churlishness and most Leeds fans have never been like this; however, in this period, the number of Leeds supporters who were of that ilk became worrying.

I think, for instance, of a very nasty riot at the Baseball Ground, which I remember as the only occasion I ever left a match well before the end. And incidents such as those at St Andrew's - the violence that left a Birmingham City fan dead in 1985 - and at Bradford, where they overturned a fish-and-chip van in 1986, sickened genuine Leeds supporters and the wider Leeds public. Fortunately, a mixture of belated action by the club and a revival on the pitch have recently done much to address the problem of crowd behaviour.

It has also been very pleasing to see both the club and its genuine supporters tackling the problem of infiltration by extremists - the Nazi salute brigade who tried to hijack the club. There was something very sinister about this contingent who abused visiting players and seemed to take over parts of the ground, especially the South Stand.

Most supporters found them embarrassing and sickening but it's all too easy for such extremists to take over. Fortunately, there were Leeds fans who were prepared to stand up to them, both inside and outside the ground - and the Leeds fanzines, the management and the club itself surely deserve praise for the part they played in driving away the racists and fascists.

In recent seasons, large and increasing numbers of fans have followed Leeds in a generally improving pattern, both on and off the pitch - witness the 1987 Cup Semi-Final, when 20,000 or so Leeds fans gave the team magnificent, well-behaved support, and the 1991-92 championship season, when big crowds, both home and away, were not marred by trouble. I felt that the defeat by Coventry in that 1987 semi-final was a bit of a turning point. Notwithstanding the heroics of Andy Ritchie and Co., that Leeds team just did not seem likely to be the winners of a major trophy - although they stood an infinitely better chance of winning something than I did, as the Conservative candidate in Barnsley, in the General Election a few weeks later.

Howard's Mend and Norman Conquest

Not long after, Howard Wilkinson arrived at Elland Road. My experience of Leeds United's earlier struggles has helped me to see the true measurement of his achievements. Surely, no club has a pre-ordained right to success, however big it is, and if it is fortunate enough to have a good manager, it should treasure him.

I still watch Leeds occasionally. I have one minor connection with my team of the old days in that Norman Hunter now coaches my daughter, Charlotte, an enthusiastic footballer who receives every encouragement from her parents: sexual equality is alive and kicking in the Clappison household.

Her genuine skill and prowess bear witness to Norman's ability as a coach. But there remains, alas, a crucial weakness in her game: she does not relish tackling and has no idea how to bite your legs.

'Now, Charlotte, you've got to
make your tackle *bite*'.
Norman Hunter coaches Charlotte Clappison

279

CHAMPIONS of FOOTBALL

*Four chapters on the politics
of football*

PHILIP GOODHART (Conservative, Beckenham, 1957-92)

Having spent the first part of the war at school in the USA, where he acquired a lasting interest in baseball, he spent the second part as a lieutenant in the Parachute Regiment, where he was a featherweight boxer.

Postwar, he served on the editorial staff of the *Daily Telegraph* and *Sunday Times*, in turn, before being elected to parliament in 1957. Held junior posts in Northern Ireland and Defence in the first Thatcher Government. Knighted 1981.

A former Chairman of the Lords and Commons Ski Club, his publications include *War Without Weapons* (with Christopher Chataway, 1968), a study of the relationship between sport and politics.

27

THE GOLDEN STRIKE

Philip Goodhart

Outside the Arsenal dressing room a crowd of several hundred Russians stood and rhythmically chanted: 'Law-ton, Law-ton, Law-ton'. It was a remarkable scene. In 1954, the Cold War was still particularly chilly and the Arsenal football team was the first English side to play against a leading Russian side for seven years.

Despite the magical presence of that great centre-forward, Tommy Lawton, the home team, Moscow Dynamo, had just thrashed Arsenal. The 'friendly' game had been comparatively even until half-time, when the score was 0-0. Then the superior fitness of the Russians was the deciding factor and Arsenal fell apart. The final score of 5-0 did not flatter their hosts.

Moscow Dynamo was a team that had strong links with the KGB (then the MVD) and the Soviet Union's secret service may have had a hand in the choice of Arsenal to receive an invitation to play in Russia.

We now know that Soviet agents were asked to check on teams that had a high international reputation but which were going through a bad patch.

From Your Foreign Correspondent

Arsenal in 1954 fitted that description perfectly. Twenty years after the successful sides of the 1930s, when they had been led by such great players as Eddie Hapgood and Ted Drake, the Arsenal side of the early 1950s still had, as John Greenway recalls in his chapter, more than its share of 'giants'. By 1954, though, their form was hardly inspiring.

The Arsenal team's reception in Russia was unlikely to enhance the confidence of the team. We had flown from London to Minsk, where low cloud prevented our flight from continuing to Moscow. The vodka had flowed in hospitable quantities and Tommy Lawton had been particularly entertaining with a vivid impersonation of a Soviet convict in a Siberian salt mine staggering under the weight of an enormous sack of salt.

After a few hours in a Minsk transit lounge, however, even Tommy Lawton's engaging presence began to pall and the news that we would have to spend the night in Minsk was not well-received.

Our party was soon divided by the hierarchical-minded Russians into three groups. The first, and most important, group consisted of the Club's owners; Tom Whittaker, the Manager; and the international stars of the team, such as Alex Forbes, Jimmy Logie and, of course, Tommy Lawton. They were whisked away in a small fleet of large, black saloons. A few minutes later a large bus conveyed the rest of the players off to the equivalent of the Minsk Hilton. That left the Arsenal trainer and myself.

I was there because there had been problems getting a visa to enter the Soviet Union. A couple of days before our flight to Minsk, the first British Parliamentary delegation to visit the Soviet Union since 1945 had arrived in Moscow. *The Daily Telegraph* had hoped to send its Soviet expert, David Floyd, with the delegation. When he decided that he couldn't go, I was chosen by the Foreign Editor instead. I had never visited a Communist country but I had sometimes reported for the *Telegraph* from America and Africa. At first the Soviet authorities had been reluctant to give me a visa, but eventually it had come through in time for me to get on the same plane as the Arsenal party. Once we reached Moscow, I would link up with the Parliamentary delegation, but I persuaded the newspaper's sporting staff that I knew enough about football to do a report on the Dynamo match.

Eventually a small van arrived at Minsk airport to carry the trainer and myself to the hotel. The long wait was worth it. Once we arrived at the hotel, we were whisked up to two penthouse suites. I had a double bed and a sitting room with a grand piano - and a television set that didn't work. My bathroom had a plentiful supply of marble; but no water of any sort.

It was a case of the first shall be last and the last shall be first, for the group of VIPs that had been driven away in the best cars spent the night in a collective dormitory which they shared with a number of Russian peasants, sleeping with their boots on - if Alex Forbes could be believed. It had not been a restful night.

After I left the Arsenal football team and accompanied the parliamentary delegation to Stalingrad and the Urals, my direct connection with football atrophied. I would occasionally go to Stamford Bridge or Highbury, or even White Hart Lane; but in March 1957, I became the Conservative Member of Parliament for Beckenham, a constituency

Secret Service Selection: The Arsenal team, selected by Soviet agents as fodder - five-nil fodder - for Moscow Dynamo, board for Minsk.
The party includes *(top right)* Tommy Lawton, not anticipating an evening performance in the Minsk transit lounge and *(front, second left)* Alex Forbes, clearly anticipating a sleepless night.
Players on the steps between them include Kelsey, Barnes and Tapscott, stars of Chapter 10.

where sporting interests centred on hockey (we had one of the best clubs in the country) and tennis (we had one of the leading pre-Wimbledon tournaments).

A Matter for Debate

In my early years as an MP, however, I became increasingly interested in the problems caused for our footballers by the Maximum Wage rule. Previous efforts by the Players Union to win parliamentary support against these 'last relics of feudalism', as William Mallalieu put it, are described in his chapter of this book. But, by 1960, the rule still limited to £20 per week the amount of money that a club could pay any player on its books. The Football League argued that without this cap on players' salaries the smaller clubs would be bankrupted and that league football would disappear in wide areas of the country. What did happen, of course, was that many of our best players began to go overseas to play and were lost to our national team. For me, the final straw was the departure for Italy, in 1960, of that great goal-scorer, Jimmy Greaves.

My dislike of the Maximum Wage rule was enhanced by my knowledge of the American sporting scene. I had been at school for a time in the United States and I still followed American football and baseball in the newspapers. In the late 1950s, American sporting finance had not yet been distorted by the vast sums that flowed in from television sponsorship, but I was well aware that Pete Rose or Johnny Branch, the baseball stars of the Cincinnati Reds (my paternal grandfather's home town), were earning a hundred times as much as Tommy Lawton in his prime. Why should our top athletes be rewarded so badly just because they had decided to devote their talents to our national game?

By the autumn of 1960, the Players Union was threatening, under the invigorating leadership of Jimmy Hill, to strike. I decided to try and raise the issue in Parliament. I was lucky enough to get an adjournment debate in the House of Commons on Monday, 21 November.

If press reports of adjournment debates are hardly commonplace, a press preview of one is rare indeed. Yet a young sports writer called Ian Wooldridge set the scene for his Sunday readers:

'Sometime near the moment Big Ben booms ten tomorrow night, a small, immaculately tailored man will rise from the Tory back benches and begin to harangue the House of Commons in the kind of upper-crust accent that only money can buy. In the case of Philip Carter Goodhart, it was purchased at Hotchkiss (a more English-than-English private school in Connecticut, USA) and polished at Trinity College (an educational establishment of some repute in East Anglia).

Mr Goodhart, indeed, might well have walked out of one of those cosy, mid-thirties novels about top people who always seem to be changing for dinner or tennis. He is a paid up member of the Athenaeum, Savile and Carlton Clubs. He sits in Parliament because of the confidence of 29,621 Conservative souls from the London dormitory district of Beckenham.

During brief moments of relaxation in this dying year of 1960, he has played tennis for the House of Commons, careered down the Cresta Run on a bobsleigh, graced the ski-slopes of Davos, and swept into the golden beaches of Honolulu on a surf board.

Philip Carter Goodhart, you might say, is socially OK.

That is why, by midnight tomorrow, he will have become the most dangerous and powerful opponent of those Football League Chairmen whose Victorian obstinacy is daily driving 2,000 professional footballers nearer the precipice of a disastrous strike.

For Philip Goodhart is to lead the rebels' cause in Parliament. In a fifteen minute speech in an adjournment debate, he will talk his way into history ... by demanding a new deal for the muddy-kneed heroes of half a million football fans whose status symbol, whether they like it or not, is still the cloth cap and tight-knotted neckscarf.

He seems such an improbable protagonist for the freedom fight led by the Castro-like figure of Union Chairman, Jimmy Hill, that I must confess to sordid suspicions. Was this, I wondered, ... another political careerist clambering onto a popular platform?

Twenty seven minutes over tea and talk in the House of Commons put my working class conscience at rest ... Mr Goodhart's credentials as a genuine tumult and shouting soccer enthusiast stretch from the boyhood seasons when he was a light-weight left winger until eight days ago when he yelled his favourite Chelsea team to victory over Arsenal at Highbury.

His fascination with other down-to-earth sports is no vote-catching phase in a political career. He is still a close fan of the legalised homicide that masquerades under the name of American football and, as a paratrooper lieutenant in the Army, he boxed his way to some prominence as a feather-weight ...

Did he meet Jimmy Hill before drafting his speech for tomorrow night's debate? "Yes", he said. "I did". Does he think the players have a strong case for action? "Of course", he said. "Over both the question of their contracts and the principle of the maximum wage".

Apart from that, the aces remained up Philip Goodhart's sleeve. He will play them tomorrow night in the biggest sports debate of the decade as the notes of Big Ben rumble across the darkened Parliament Square.

They are notes that sound the death-knell for diehard soccer bosses if the top people's MP plays his cards right in the cause of the working man's game'.

A Debate that Mattered

The debate went well. I argued that 'the most important section of our national sporting industry' was

'inefficiently organised, semi-bankrupt and only too often a thoroughly bad employer ... football players are bound to their employers by contractual conditions that would have been rejected with a snort of contempt by any intelligent young apprentice in the Middle Ages'.

I cited the transfer of George Eastham:

'The wage differential between medium talent and great talent is ludicrously small. There has been much talk recently about the transfer of Mr Eastham, ... for whose talent Arsenal paid £47,500 to Newcastle

'... the Castro-like figure of the Union Chairman'

Jimmy Hill (the one with the beard) and the PFA Management Committee celebrate the abolition of maximum wage in 1961.

George Eastham - disenslaved to lead out Arsenal. Jack Kelsey, 'probably the greatest goalkeeper' John Greenway ever saw (see Chapter 10), follows.

United. [He] is 24 years old and, as an inside forward, his first-class career will certainly be finished within ten years ... Even assuming [the] transfer fee can be written off over ten years, the figures prove conclusively that Arsenal puts Mr Eastham's value at between three and four times the maximum salary that Arsenal can pay [him] during his playing career'.

It was wrong that a player should be prevented from earning more than a pitiful fraction of the openly admitted value of his talent. It had been said that three-quarters of the Football League clubs were 'in the red'. That did not seem to be an overwhelming argument in favour of sticking to the *status quo*.

In the absence of a settlement, I reasoned that the Government had

'a right and duty to intervene ... Wages boards have been set up in [some] industries ... If that proves to be the easiest way, ... we should let it happen'.

I then went on to suggest that, if the dispute was not settled and if the Maximum Wage rule survived, there should be a 'Golden Strike': as it was the game's stars who would do best from the abolition of the Maximum Wage rule, they should be the ones who went on strike. All full internationals, all B internationals and all Under-23 internationals should withdraw their labour every other Saturday. It was, I believe, the first and the last time that a Conservative Member of Parliament had called, on the floor of the House of Commons, for a strike. I was followed by two Labour MPs. William Wilkins, the Member for Bristol South and an honorary trustee of the Professional Footballers Association, said that players 'should be treated in precisely the same way as any other employee in industry or commerce' with a contract of service which does 'not have all the disadvantages weighted against the player'. William Mallalieu intervened with a question:

'Who would stand for a contract which ties him after that contract has expired? ... A professional footballer signs a contract for one year. It finishes ... His club is free from it, but he is tied to it.'

I did have one ace up my sleeve. The Ministry of Labour had been holding conciliation meetings between the League and the Union and I

290

had talked at some length to Peter Thomas, the Parliamentary Under-Secretary of State at the Ministry (now Lord Thomas of Gwydir). I had persuaded him, without difficulty, that the Maximum Wage rule was incompatible with our Conservative philosophy and government policy. We had privately agreed that there would be an inquiry into the Maximum Wage rule, which would almost certainly call for its abolition. Peter did not go as far as this on the floor of the House:

'... *in the industry of professional football there are no effective arrangements for airing grievances and discussing outstanding problems ... Neither the players nor the clubs had an opportunity of an exhaustive examination, face to face, of the points of difference between them until they met under the auspices of the Ministry ... [where] we ... identified 22 points of difference ... I hope that the parties will see the advantages of establishing within the industry appropriate and permanent machinery for negotiation and consultation'.*

In private, of course, Peter was going further than that.

The debate was greeted with a roar of protest from the Football League. Yet, shortly afterwards, the Maximum Wage rule was abandoned. In the subsequent 33 years, very few League Clubs have gone bankrupt and the players who had flooded abroad returned to play in this country.

And, just five years after the abolition of the rule, England won the World Cup. Perhaps there was some connection.

DENIS HOWELL
(Labour, Birmingham All Saints, 1955-59; Birmingham Small Heath, 1961-92)

A Football League referee, 1956-70, he was Chairman of the Sports Council, 1965-70, and of the Central Council for Physical Recreation, 1973-74.

Continuously on the Front Bench, from 1964 to 1992, speaking on sport, twice as Minister (1964-70 and 1974-79), he was created a peer in 1992, as Lord Howell of Aston Manor in the City of Birmingham.

28

THE FIRST MINISTER

Denis Howell

The General Election of 1964 brought not only a Labour Government but also, to my great surprise, my appointment as the first Minister for Sport. Summoned to Downing Street, I found the Prime Minister in a remarkably enthusiastic frame of mind considering the disastrous financial crisis he had inherited. Together with other colleagues, likewise about to be offered appointments, I waited a long, long time in the outer office of the Cabinet Room. We later discovered that Harold Wilson had been closeted, with George Brown, the Economic Secretary, and Jim Callaghan, the Chancellor of the Exchequer, deliberating whether or not to devalue the pound. Such was the gravity of the situation in week one of the new Government.

When at last I was called in, Harold came directly to the matter. 'I would like you to go to Education and take on sport. If you agree I shall announce that you will become the first ever Minister for Sport'. He also appointed Jenny Lee to be the first Minister for the Arts. So, in spite of all its economic problems, the country at last had a government which took the quality of life available to its people to be a matter of proper government concern and leadership.

And yet I had advised Harold, in opposition, against making such an appointment for sport. He had established a working group which produced the most imaginative policy document on the subject which I have ever seen: *Leisure for Living*. It recommended the creation of a Sports Council under the direction of a Minister. I had told Harold that I supported the concept of a Sports Council; but, given the conservative nature of sports administration in our country, a Minister might not be a wise move. There were other ways of achieving the objective.

So I was now able to tell the Prime Minister that I was honoured but surprised that he had, after all, opted for a Minister for Sport. Harold explained that this was exactly why he wished to appoint me. 'You are well aware of all the pitfalls and all the nuances; you are the man for the job. Any questions?' Yes, there were. 'Have I got any money for this new Ministry?' 'No', said Harold, 'but always remember that when you have got no money it is a good time to do your thinking!'

Creating a Partnership for the World Cup

I was about to leave the room when I remembered a conversation I had had, months earlier, with Denis Follows, Secretary of the Football Association. He had tried to get the Conservative government interested in the World Cup of 1966, but had extracted only one promise: police escorts to take the teams around the country. So I turned back and reminded the PM that we would be staging this event. What would be the use of a Minister for Sport with a World Cup on his hands and no money? The response was immediate: 'How much do you want?' I hadn't the faintest idea. I had not yet met a single advisor or civil servant but I knew that if I missed this chance I would have blown it. 'Half a million pounds', I said. 'Right', Harold told me, 'but not a penny more'.

And so we started down the long road of government support for football, which today runs to the order of some £36 million per year, administered by the Football Trust - in ways appreciated above, by Michael Carttiss, John Greenway, Ann Taylor and Joan Walley.

When, later that afternoon, I reported to my Ministry I found an elderly gentleman sitting in my armchair, awaiting my arrival. He obviously knew I was coming before I did. He introduced himself as Sir John Lang, the government's principal advisor on sport. When I told him that I had just arrived from Downing Street with half a million pounds for the World Cup, his face was a picture: 'the Treasury will never wear it'. I told him he had better get round to discuss it with them because it would be my first priority: I intended to set up a high-ranking committee, which I would preside over myself, to work out a policy to ensure that the World Cup of 1966 was a success story. In a moment of inspiration, I told him that he would be my Vice-Chairman, so that the Treasury could be content that all their procedures would be observed. We made a great partnership.

In no time at all, I had assembled the most impressive group of advisors: Stanley Rous, Chairman of FIFA; Denis Follows of the FA; Alan Hardaker of the Football League; Walter Winterbottom - whom I had just appointed to be the Director of the new Sports Council which I established in 1965 - Cliff Lloyd of the PFA; Ron Greenwood, to represent the Managers; and Alan Everiss, to represent the Secretaries. If ever an idea took off this one did. We toured all the grounds where matches would be played, followed by TV and newspaper journalists by the hundred. No one in the country was left in any doubt about the importance of the forthcoming World Cup, some 18 months away.

We told the clubs - Everton, Manchester United, Aston Villa, Sheffield Wednesday, Sunderland, Middlesbrough - plus, of course, Wembley and the White City that their grounds had to be modernised so as to be suitable to play host to the world. But we also wanted to leave behind, at every ground, some permanent improvements for the benefit of English football. We asked each club for two sets of proposals, one for permanent improvements and one for temporary measures. Of course, they wanted to know how much we could give them but that was the one thing I could not tell them. The half million pounds was a secret locked away in my Ministry. We would tell them when all the bids were in and accepted and I left John Lang to work that out. He proposed 90 per cent grant for any temporary work which we had authorised and 50 per cent for more substantial improvements, such as new stands. It proved a realistic formula.

We had some fun on our tour. At Goodison Park we wanted a row of delapidated houses demolished. Sir John Moores, the Everton Chairman, told me that the Liverpool Council would not re-house the residents. I went over and spoke to them. They all wanted to move. I talked to the Council. If Sir John would buy the houses off them at knock-down prices and then demolish them, the Council would re-house the tenants. And so Everton got a new entrance to their ground suitable to welcome one of the semi-finals.

At my own club - Aston Villa - we met the board which consisted of three bachelors and two widowers. They were astonished when I told them that our first place of inspection would be the ladies' rooms. I explained that some very important people indeed would be their guests; and, unlike our country, the rest of the world did not leave their ladies waiting outside the Boardroom. The impression of England which most of these ladies would take home would be in part gained by the state of the facilities provided for their comfort.

Sheffield Wednesday were anxious to get a new stand and an indoor training area which we provided as an international hospitality centre. Hillsborough was to be a quarter-final venue, so I urged further developments - including the possibility of a new stand at the Leppings Lane end of the ground - upon two men so admired by Roy Hattersley in his chapter. The remarkable and enlightened Eric Taylor, who had long served Wednesday as Secretary and/or Manager, told me that there was no way the club could go any further: he had already over-committed it to its share of the costs. Dr Andrew Stephens who had been called upon, when Wednesday's doctor, to treat the young Hattersley's bronchitis, was by now the club's Chairman and soon to be the FA Chairman. He reluctantly agreed with Eric's assessment. So no new stand went up behind the Leppings Lane goal. Twenty-odd years on, the disaster of Hillsborough took place on that very terrace.

How all this work was done in the time I shall never know but it was - just. The first match to be played at Middlesbrough was the Soviet Union *versus* North Korea. On my way to my hotel I decided to look in at Ayresome Park. It was about four hours before the kick-off. To my astonishment, I found a large lorry backing up to where the Directors' Lounge was situated on the first floor. Waiting to receive it was Charles Hamer, the club Chairman, with a large roll of carpet and a hammer in his hand. The staircase to the new Directors' Room was taken off the lorry and put into place, whereupon Charles rolled the carpet down the stairs and followed with his hammer and tacks. 'That was a near one Minister; but we did it'.

Winning the World Cup was a cause of a great national rejoicing. The Government had been right to identify this international festival as our first priority in sport. In partnership with the game, we had succeeded in hosting the event in a manner which brought us all great credit. And, on the field, Alf Ramsey and his team had more than justified all our faith and planning.

The World Cup programme included a message from the
president of FIFA, Sir Stanley Rous, acknowledging - albeit
in ambiguous terms - the role of the Government:
'With the acceptable financial assistance from the Government...
visitors will be sure of seeing the matches in comfort...'

297

Football Enquiry

Football has been the great passion of my life for as long as I can remember. In our family, we were all born to be supporters of Aston Villa. When I damaged a knee in a school game, I started to referee. The annual match between the staff and the school was the first game that I can remember refereeing. After nine years in junior football and five years as a Football League linesman, I was appointed to the referees list in 1956, one year after I became a Member of Parliament. My concern for the good of the game could not be deeper. I knew all the problems, shortage of money for most clubs whilst the pools made a fortune from the game. The concentration of talent towards the top clubs. Inadequate grounds and poor facilities for the fans. The difficulty in getting the clubs to see further than their own self-interest. During my nine years in Parliament before I became a Minister, I had often talked over these problems with Stanley Rous, Denis Follows and Alan Hardaker. It was clear to me that only an outside influence was likely to break football's log-jam of negative thinking.

The close partnership which I had built up with the football authorities during our campaign to stage the World Cup enabled me to propose a new initiative. A committee of enquiry would take a fundamental look at football and all its problems. The FA and the League cooperated, realising that the Government sought not to run sport but to help sport organise itself more effectively.

Harold Wilson could not have been more supportive. He was concerned about the stature of the chairman of the committee. He rejected my first choice but was extremely positive about Sir Norman Chester, a lifelong football fan and Warden of Nuffield College, Oxford. Chester had a fine reputation for creating and building the college and his academic reputation, especially in the field of local government, was first class.

I soon received Sir Norman's enthusiastic acceptance and we put together a first-rate team which included Bernard (now Lord) Donoughue, a Fellow of Nuffield and a fan of Northampton Town, and David Bacon, a youngish accountant who followed Chelsea. Both played football regularly and were members of the Sports Council. So, too, was David Munrow. Mervyn Griffiths, the Welsh representative, will be remembered as the brilliant referee who took charge of the 'Matthews Final' of 1953, childhood memories of which are relived by Ann Taylor and John Greenway in their chapters above. Then there were Bill Slater, the former Wolves and England centre-half, and Brian Walden, then a Labour MP and forever a West Brom supporter.

In order to probe the case for financial assistance to football from pools income, I needed tax experts and a barrister capable of examining the representatives of the Pools organisation and delving into their finances. Economists Nicholas Davenport and Clifford Barclay joined David Bacon as the committee's inspectors of taxes and Lewis Hawser QC did a tremendous job as our legal investigator.

The committee reported to me in 1968, with the most thorough review that football had ever experienced. Among their most important recommendations were those dealing with school football and the right of every pupil to be able to choose between rugby or soccer. The need to reduce the size of the first division - now the Premier League. The status within the game of managers, players, secretaries and referees. Probably their best work was done on taxation and football finance. They proposed radical changes to limit the amount of tax being paid and their most important proposal was to establish a Levy Board deducting 10 per cent of all Pools money for the purpose of football improvements. The Government did not legislate for this levy, but it was to come about, as I shall explain, during the next Labour administration of 1974-79.

The Football Trust

By the time Labour went out of office in 1970, the 'Minister for Sport' had been transferred from Education to Housing and Local Government. Ted Heath kept it that way, except that Local Government was submerged, in 1972, in the new Department of the Environment. I was the Shadow Minister to Eldon Griffiths. He made little impression in the job and sought to undo the machinery I had set up - especially in respect of the Sports Council. He not only destroyed the Royal Charter on which it was created, but removed himself from the chairmanship, which I had occupied as a way of giving it the political clout it needed.

When I returned to office in 1974, my duties at Environment extended beyond sport. The media took a particular interest in my responsibility for 'water resources': I had become the 'Minister for Drought'. But there was serious business to be done on the football front, in the wake of the Ibrox disaster of January 1971. The death of 66 people when an embankment collapsed demanded action not only by Glasgow Rangers but by government. Yet, if legislating for ground safety was essential, it did not follow that government had to put up the money. Apart from the economic situation in the country an important principle had to be maintained: companies attracting the public to events in the course of their business had a legal duty to provide for their safety.

The pools companies were now paying the Football League for the use of their fixtures which the Courts had held to be copyright. I had always believed that the tax levy on football pools was far too high at about 37½ per cent, when compared to a tax of 8 per cent on betting and even less on bingo. By great good fortune it was at this time that Alan Hardaker brought Mr. Cecil Moores of Littlewoods to see me in order to discuss the tax burden on the pools and the considerable cost to football of the Safety of Football Grounds legislation. Hardaker and Moores told me that the new *Spot the Ball* competition, run by the pools, was doing rather well but Moores was fearful that this would result in its being taxed. If spotting the ball could be tax-exempt, the pools were willing to contribute towards the cost of the new safety measures.

I went off to ask Denis Healey, the Chancellor of the Exchequer, if he could find any money to assist the clubs in all this new expenditure. It did not take more than a few seconds for him to confirm what I already knew: there was no money. I then asked him if he had any plans to tax *Spot the Ball*. My impression was that neither he nor his officials had ever heard of it. I told him that, if I could inform the pools that he would not be taxing their new competition, then they would pay a voluntary levy of some 7½ per cent - the amount Hardaker and Moores had suggested. Healey agreed that I could do so. Cecil Moores was so overjoyed that he promptly upped the levy to 10 per cent. We were in business . We decided upon the creation of a trust - The Football Trust - to control the new funds now available to football.

In fact, the pools companies increased their contribution. By the time I left office in 1979, it had reached 14 per cent. It is now 21 per cent. The voluntary levy has been an amazing success story. In its first 20 years, it has provided some £200 million for the improvement and safety of football grounds, as well as making a great contribution towards football in the community: for examples, see, as I say, those recorded in the chapters, above, on Bolton, Norwich, Port Vale and York.

It is 30 years since Harold Wilson persuaded me that there *should* be a Minister for Sport. In my 11 years in the job, my association with football gave me great satisfaction. We built a new partnership between government and football in order to stage the 1966 World Cup. We established the Chester Committee of Enquiry which led to many new initiatives and a new spirit of cooperation. And between us we created the Football Trust, which has been a Godsend to football and its supporters. It has been a fascinating experience.

Football wins the Pools every Saturday

Every time you enter Littlewoods, Vernons or Zetters Pools you are helping the game prosper, in particular, paying the bill for necessary ground redevelopment work in line with the Taylor Report.

The Football Trust was formed to administer the Pools' contributions and help clubs at all levels to improve safety and comfort.

The Trust receives over £36 million every year, all of it coming directly or indirectly from Littlewoods, Vernons, Zetters Pools and Spot the Ball.

Up and down the country, clubs are building new grounds, stands, seating and roofing. All depend on the support of the FOOTBALL TRUST and on the success of the football pools.

 LITTLEWOODS VERNONS ZETTERS
Making sure football wins the Pools each week

 THE FOOTBALL TRUST
Helping the game

THE FOOTBALL TRUST, WALKDEN HOUSE, 10 MELTON STREET, LONDON NW1 2EJ

'... a Godsend to football and its supporters.'

DAVID EVANS (Conservative, Welwyn Hatfield)

An England Youth international, who was a professional footballer with Aston Villa, he was a director of Luton Town, 1977-90, and Chairman, 1984-89. A professional cricketer with Gloucestershire and Warwickshire, he toured Australia with the Club Cricket Conference, as captain in 1971 and manager in 1975.

Entered local politics, in St Albans, in 1980 and became an MP in 1987. A former Master of the Guild of Master Cleaners, his company secured the first local authority contract for the privatisation of refuse collection and street cleaning.

29

LUTON TOWN..........................2
ESTABLISHMENT UNITED 3

David Evans

I write as a former player, a life-long supporter of Arsenal and - latterly (1977-90) - a director of Luton Town.

These experiences should have taught me that the chance of any Chairman of a modest First Division club (in pre-1992 terms) exerting any worthwhile influence on the game was zero. And so it proved to be during my five years as Chairman of Luton, ending in June 1989.

Professional experience v. amateur rule

The one-club loyalist will be wary of anyone who claims to be a lasting supporter of one team, while serving on the board of another. Although an Arsenal fan, I lived - and still live - within a 15-minute drive of Kenilworth Road. In 1977, Luton needed money. I bought 10 per cent of the club and was invited to become a Director. It is not difficult to love more than one person, more than one sport, more than one child or more than one animal. And so it is with football - especially if you already love the game. I do, however, accept that most fans have time to love only one club.

Expectations that ex-players might put something back into the game should satisfy even my harshest critics that I had something to offer the board at Kenilworth Road. I had won six Young England caps and spent four years as a professional at Aston Villa.

My ability to contribute any of the lessons I'd learned as a pro' was limited, however, by the extent to which power lay firmly with the amateurs at the Football Association - volunteers who had served their time, first on their county committees and then as members of the FA

Council, until they assumed positions of power within the Council. Through that process they administered the game of football - *amateurs controlling a professional sport.*

Compounding this anachronism, there was the Football League Management Committee, superficially a democratically-elected body but within which the real power lay with those representing the large clubs, the smaller clubs bowing to their wishes out of fear. As we have since learned, the power now is substantially with the sponsors either through television or through club sponsorship. They, together with half a dozen major clubs, claim to have the interests of the game at heart; but, as true football fans know, this is laughable. If I am wrong, why is England forced to play important games when the clubs providing the players are playing twice a week? Answer? ... Money!

Time for Change

So it was clear to me, when I became Chairman of Luton Town in 1984, that, if the club which had not won a major trophy in a history spanning over 100 years was to make progress, then major changes had to be introduced.

The odds weighed heavily against the smaller clubs in many, many respects. The operation of the transfer market was a prime example. On the field itself the smaller clubs rarely received a fair crack of the whip. For example, the number of penalties per season awarded to the six major clubs often equalled those awarded to the other 16 put together. The big six received most of their penalties at home, where their large and vocal support sought to intimidate the referee. How was this to be overcome?

I was able to carry through several changes that helped Luton's cause - principally a ban on away fans and an artificial surface. The opportunity I had been seeking to keep away fans out of Kenilworth Road arose when Millwall fans ran riot there in March 1985. This incident brought me the full backing of the police and public at large. I had several reasons for wanting this change:

■   On average, the club needed 186 policemen per game to look
      after around 800 away fans. The normal turnstile receipts from
      those visiting fans amounted to £2,400 a game - set against a
      policing bill in the order of £10,000. The restriction to home
      fans meant that eventually just 17 policemen were needed - a
      remarkable saving of 10 officers in every 11.

■   The club was able to rebuild the stadium in such a way that
      10,000 home fans sounded like 40,000. So referees could be
      subjected to the vocal pressure which they would experience at
      the likes of Anfield and White Hart Lane. And I insisted that
      our team came out onto the pitch after our visitors so that the
      opposition would see and hear the welcome which Luton
      received from the home fans. I always reckoned that all of this
      was worth a goal a game. We also introduced boxes along one
      side of the ground with a facility for spectators to sit outside if
      they wished. This has since been copied by many other clubs,
      in particular Arsenal.

■   Admitting home fans only enabled us to introduce a member-
      ship scheme utilising a computerised entrance card and com-
      puterised turnstiles. The initial target of 30,000 members at £5
      each was quickly exceeded. Following the change, local busi-
      nesses and local people were increasingly prepared to support
      the football club - not only on match days but also with more
      general sponsorship. It is worth remembering that financial
      support is not just about how many people you can get into the
      ground but about how much backing is forthcoming from each
      of the supporters.

Small club ... big ideas

We, at Luton, were small but innovative. We acquired the best team
bus that money could buy and flew to more distant away games. Other
clubs have followed suit.

The most radical innovation was our artificial surface. It benefited us
financially - in use almost 365 days a year, it produced an income of

more than £16,000 a week - and it was a fillip, on match days, to our young fans who could take a football onto the pitch, half an hour prior to the kick-off. This facility was enthusiastically over-subscribed, with sometimes as many as 250 kicking a ball about.

But, most of all, it helped the team. Indeed, the decision to change the playing surface especially reflected my longstanding belief in Luton's passing game. Unfortunately, Kenilworth Road is sited so that, from Christmas to Spring, only one third of the ground is exposed to the sun and wind. Consequently - and the statistics underline this over the years - the club played well in the first half of the season and disastrously in the second: good football cannot be played on a mud patch. No amount of draining and re-seeding produced satisfactory results. The answer was an artificial surface which, I calculated, would also be worth a goal a game. Again, I was proved right.

There were drawbacks in that the team, having mastered the skills of the artificial surface, found it more difficult to play away from home on natural grass. I believe, to this day, that the Luton Town experiment enhanced the determination of the grass seed manufacturers to improve their product to a point where, now, many pitches are as good at the end of the season as at the beginning. Under threat of increasing numbers of artificial pitches, they were forced to look at new growing techniques.

We encouraged the myth that other teams could not play on plastic. Yet all of the great players who came to the club during that era enjoyed showing off their skills on a true surface - as against the many sub-standard grass pitches that reduced players to the same level. Luton, in those years, had some very good players with considerable skills; and even those who at first found it difficult soon learned and improved dramatically. I am sure that some of those who went on to gain international honours would not have done so without the opportunity to hone their skills on our pitch. One wonders, had artificial surfaces been given the backing of the big clubs, how much improvement we might have seen, not only in artificial surfaces but in all the skills that are sadly lacking in the present England team.

The above innovations - and there are many more I could mention - helped to redress the balance which had been so heavily tilted in favour

*'I was able to carry through
several changes that
helped Luton's cause'.*

The catalyst: Millwall fans riot at
Kenilworth Road, March 1985.

The outcome: a major trophy
won in April 1988 - two-goal
hero, Brian Stein, holds
aloft the Littlewoods Cup.

of the big clubs. Luton Town came seventh, in what was the First Division, in 1987; were FA Cup semi-finalists in 1985 and again in 1988; and finalists in the Simod Cup (1988) and Littlewoods Cup (1988 and 1989).

In 1987-88, we achieved our long-held ambition of winning a major trophy. It came about in dramatic fashion, on Sunday 24 April 1988, when we beat Arsenal 3-2, in the Littlewoods Cup Final - despite having been a goal adrift with seven minutes left to play.

Not Yet Far Enough

We would have liked the changes to have gone much further. Our plea that back passes be banned was heeded in 1992. Our idea of having two referees and four linesmen has yet to be adopted.

As it was, the management of the Football Association, the Football League and, in particular, the bigger clubs fought Luton's radical thinking every step of the way. Many of our opponents were keen to establish a breakaway league, a European league or whatever you wished to call it, and sod the rest. The success of clubs like Luton and, latterly, Norwich upset their grand scheme.

As I said at the time, key parts of the Taylor Report were misconceived. They gave the big clubs the chance they needed to distance themselves even further from the smaller clubs. It is interesting to note that the Taylor recommendations have been watered down to such an extent that they are hardly recognisable. The Football Spectators Bill was ridiculed by those representing the big clubs, in their efforts to convince the average football fan that the aims of the bill were contrary to his or her best interests.

Sadly, they managed to convince the Government as well. They were wrong. In the not-too-distant future this will be readily apparent when hooliganism re-emerges, necessitating the heavy police presence (which can be afforded only by the big clubs) to contain the hooligan element inside and outside the grounds. The only real solution is for fans to be members of a club and have identity cards which must pass through a computerised turnstile. The hooligan would then know that once he had misbehaved and had been identified, his pass would be taken away and he would be barred from games.

The average fan still finds it obscene to read of players demanding and receiving as much as £10,000 per week and of the clubs spending media money and fans' money on inflated transfer deals. It is not unknown to pay £3-4 million for players without full international honours. The big clubs, which believe they have been so clever, will eventually realise that their grand scheme of European football in one league may be thwarted in that, perhaps apart from Glasgow Rangers and Manchester United, other British clubs may not measure up to the modern-day requirements of a European League. For example, proper parking facilities are virtually non-existent at many grounds - as visitors to Highbury and White Hart Lane will be aware. Despite their facade, the facilities within some grounds are disgraceful. And, now, even the quality of football is poor compared with dozens of teams in Europe.

Certain of our major clubs may yet reap their own rewards should they pursue objectives of a European, or World, League. Having devalued our own domestic game to the detriment - even to the point of extinction - of some of the smaller clubs they will be seen as minnows in world terms and, relatively, little or no better than the clubs currently playing in the Diadora League.

It is a great game - the greatest apart from cricket - but it retains too many unsuitable chairmen (once described by me, when I chaired a club myself, as 'thick from the neck upwards, entrepreneurial, self-opinionated twits'); poor managers, seldom possessing decent management or communication skills; and greedy - very greedy - players. The consequence of this is a dying game with 400 ex-professional footballers on the dole this year.

If the decline is to be halted, then some of the forward-thinking ideas introduced or adopted by Luton Town from 1984 to 1989 will need to be embraced. Otherwise, I fear that football as we know it will be lost forever. I hope that I am totally wrong on this score. Alas, I doubt it.

TOM PENDRY (Labour, Stalybridge and Hyde)

Elected to parliament in 1970, he held junior posts in the Wilson/Callaghan administrations of 1974-79. In opposition since 1979, he has shadowed for Northern Ireland, Overseas Development and for Devolution and the Regions. Is now Labour's shadow Minister for Sport and Tourism.

Represented his county at soccer and Oxford University at boxing and won a Colonial boxing title. A founder member, 1983, and Chairman until 1992, of the All-Party Parliamentary Football Committee, he is also a keen cricketer who still turns out, in his sixties, for the Lords and Commons XI.

A long-suffering, yet ardent, supporter of Derby County and a member of Kent CCC.

30

FOOTBALL CHAMPIONS AT WESTMINSTER

Tom Pendry

Where were you, on that November evening four seasons ago, when you heard the result of the first Conservative leadership ballot between Margaret Thatcher and Michael Heseltine? It's a question to which most people can still give an exact answer, despite the passage of time. But a teasing addition to the sports section of pub quizzes, up and down the country, might be

'Where was Gary Lineker when he heard the result?'

Hard at work at Tottenham Hotspur's training ground? In discussion with Graham Taylor about England's prospects? Making a charity appearance? No, Gary was actually in Parliament itself, addressing a meeting of the All-Party Parliamentary Football Committee (APPFC) on the subject of 'Football's return to Europe: the players' view'.

Indeed, it was Gary who first read aloud the ballot result to the numerous MPs assembled in the Commons committee room to hear his entertaining talk. 'Well, it looks like it's gone to extra time', he quipped. 'If it's level after the next round, don't ask me to take the penalty shoot-out!'

Consensus and Concern

Gary is one of the many football personalities and administrators to have addressed the All-Party Committee, which was formed, in 1983, by the Conservative Jim Lester and myself, as a way of improving the lot of football within the corridors of power in Whitehall and Westminster. Since then, it has grown to be one of Parliament's largest and most influential backbench committees, uniting both sides of the Commons and the Lords, as club and party loyalties are put aside to argue the case for football.

Throughout the battles and the sadness that have touched our game in the last few years, the Committee has been able to act for the benefit of football and to achieve a considerable amount for the future of the game so many of us within Parliament love just as much as the rest of the country. The tragedies of Bradford, Heysel and Hillsborough meant that football was forced to the forefront of the political agenda. The APPFC has thus been able to move with it, and for football, as it has faced up to a new future.

So it is entirely appropriate that APPFC members have illustrated, on the pages above, what this committee can do for football - from some of the lobbying activities described by its current Vice-Chairman, John Greenway, to the work with the Football Trust that Joan Walley recounts. Yet the achievements, both within and outside Parliament, of this all-party group, seldom make the headlines. We prefer to achieve results through behind-the-scenes, consensual methods, rather than the confrontational approach that all too often provides the sole fodder for newspaper journalists and editors.

Nevertheless, the outcome of our efforts through, for example, sending delegations to Government Ministers; submitting evidence to official inquiries; marshalling arguments in Parliamentary debates; applying a little, gentle arm-twisting here and there; and gathering together information from our wide-ranging sources of contacts and friends within the game, is there for all to see.

In the most recent example of a deputation to a minister, I was wearing my Shadow Minister's hat: when I was asked by the late John Smith, following his election as leader in 1992, to shadow sport for Labour, I stepped down from the APPFC Chair, to be succeeded by Joe Ashton. The recipient of this deputation was Douglas Hurd, the Foreign Secretary. Few readers will need reminding of its subject: the treatment of Manchester United supporters in Istanbul to watch their team in the European Cup tie against Galatasary. I was joined by two other Committee Members, both local MPs, Tony Lloyd and Stan Orme.

This was one of those behind-the-scenes discussions that invariably go, as I say, unreported: few football fans would have known of our audience with the Foreign Secretary had it not been mentioned by David

The *Sunday Times* cartoonist (28 January 1990) is in no doubt as to who gave the ID cards the red card. Tom Pendry reasons that there were other contributions to the climb-down.

Mellor, another APPFC member, on his *Six-o-Six* programme.

Concessions sought at that meeting included the issuing of new passports so that they do not contain the word 'deported' and the payment, for these new passports, by the Turkish Government. It was also argued that compensation should be awarded to those ill-treated by the Turkish authorities.

As the Foreign Secretary's efforts were not successful, a subsequent meeting, of colleagues and myself, was arranged with the Turkish Ambassador. Although he insisted that those aggrieved should go through the Turkish legal system, the ambassador did see force in our arguments for new, 'clean' passports, paid for by the Turkish Government. He also promised to look at the case for the six fans who were detained for a considerable time to have clean records, so that they might travel with their team in the future. At the time of writing, it is not clear whether these arguments have been accepted by the Turkish Government.

Mistaken Identity Cards

Although our success in the Galatasary case may have been limited, the APPFC has had several high-profile victories - none more so than the defeat of the proposal for compulsory football identity cards. John Greenway explains, in his chapter, how the APPFC officers visited the Secretary of State on this matter. We also met with Lord Justice Taylor for more than two hours during the course of his inquiry and submitted evidence to him of the strong case against the ID card scheme.

And, although some might think that it was solely the contents of the Taylor Report that convinced the Government to abandon its scheme, the truth is that a major factor in its defeat was the reports reaching the Prime Minister from the Government whips - who attended our meetings throughout the passage of the Football Spectators Bill - that they could not deliver the votes of our committee's Conservative members for identity cards.

Nevertheless, the ID card campaign, coming on top of events at Heysel and Hillsborough, can now be seen as having played a very positive role in acting as a catalyst for good in football - not least, of course, in the rise of the Football Supporters' Association and the continuing expansion of the fanzine scene.

That positive role was never more conclusively demonstrated than in the coherent and impressive manner with which supporters' representatives gave evidence, in 1990, to the Home Affairs Select Committee inquiry into *Policing Football Hooliganism*. As John Greenway reports, no fewer than three officers of the APPFC were involved in writing the Select Committee's welcome report.

This book's use of football to provide support for the Child Poverty Action Group is another way of showing clearly the potential benefits that can flow to both the game and the community when politicians and football fans - and, of course, politicians *as* fans - work in harmony.

Fuller details of the Home Affairs Committee report are given in the bibliography that follows.

READ MORE ABOUT IT

The various publications - the collections, recollections, records and reports - referred to in this book are:

David Batters, *York City - A Complete Record 1922-1990*, Breedon, 1990.

Tony Benn, *Against the Tide: Diaries 1973-76*, Hutchinson, 1989.

David Bull (ed.), *We'll Support You Evermore*, Duckworth, 1992.

Susan Crosland, *Tony Crosland*, Jonathan Cape, 1982 (Coronet paperback edition, 1983).

Richard Crossman, *The Diaries of a Cabinet Minister,* vols 1 and 3, Hamish Hamilton and Jonathan Cape, 1975 and 1977.

Peter Cullen (ed.), *Bury FC - 1885-1985*, Bury FC, 1985.

Jimmy Guthrie with Dave Caldwell, *Soccer Rebel*, Readers Union, 1976.

John Harding, *For the Good of the Game: the official history of the Professional Footballers' Association*, Robson, 1991.

Roy Hattersley, *Goodbye to Yorkshire,* Victor Gollancz, 1976 (paperback edition, Pan Books, 1991).

Roy Hattersley, *A Yorkshire Boyhood*, Chatto & Windus, 1983 (paperback edition, Oxford University Press, 1984).

Jimmy Hill, *Striking for Soccer*, Peter Davies, 1961.

Quintin Hogg, *The Case for Conservatism*, Penguin, 1947.

Home Affairs Committee, Session 1990-91, Second Report, *Policing Football Hooliganism*, HMSO, 1991.

Home Affairs Committee, Session 1993-94, Third Report, *Racial Attacks and Harassment*, HMSO, 1994.

Home Office, *The Hillsborough Stadium Disaster 15 April 1989: Inquiry by the Rt Hon Lord Justice Taylor*, HMSO, 1990.

Nick Hornby, *Fever Pitch*, Victor Gollancz, 1992 (paperback edition, 1993).

Nick Hornby (ed.), *My Favourite Year*, H.F & G Witherby, 1993.

Stephen F. Kelly, *The Kingswood Book of Football*, Kingswood, 1992 (republished in paperback as *A Game of Two Halves*, Mandarin, 1993).

Jimmy McIlroy, *Right Inside Soccer*, Nicholas Kaye, 1960 (Sportsman's Book Club edition, 1961).

J.P.W Mallalieu, *Sporting Days*, Sportsmans Book Club, 1947.

Tony Matthews and others (eds.), *It's Twelve Inches High ... and it's made of solid gold,* Football Supporters Association, 1991.

John Motson (ed.), *Match of the Day: the complete record since 1964,* BBC Books, 1992.

Jeremy Paxman, *Friends in High Places*, Michael Joseph, 1990 (Penguin paperback edition, 1991).

Sir Stanley Rous, *Football Worlds*, Faber and Faber, 1978.

Alan Tomlinson, 'FIFA and the World Cup', in John Sugden and Alan Tomlinson (eds.), *Hosts and Champions*, Arena, 1994.

Richard Turner, *In Your Blood: football culture in the late 1980s and early 1990s*, Working Press, 1990.

Mike Watson, *Rags to Riches: the official history of Dundee United*, David Winter, 1985 (updated edition, 1992).

Brian Wilson, *Celtic: A Century With Honour - the official centenary history*, Collins Willow, 1988.